They Could've Been Contenders

They Could've Been Contenders

Jim McNeill

 Robson Books

First published in Great Britain in 2001 by Robson Books
10 Blenheim Court, Brewery Road, London N7 9NY

A member of the Chrysalis Group plc

British Library Cataloguing in Publication Data
A catalogue record for this title is available from the British Library.

ISBN 1 86105 444 0

Typeset by SX Composing DTP, Rayleigh, Essex
Printed by Butler & Tanner Ltd, Frome and London

For Jaqueline and Frank

Ex-fighter Terry Malloy Exorcises His Demons to Brother
Charley the Gent

'I could've had class. I could've been a contender. I could've been
somebody. Instead of a bum, which is what I am. Oh, yes, I am. It
was you, Charley.'

On the Waterfront
by Budd Schulberg

Contents

Introduction

Boxing has been described by some as The Noble Art and The Sweet Science; by others, as a barbaric pastime, a sorry excuse for blood-letting, vicarious machismo and cynical exploitation. And certainly, at times the fight game can be all of these, but there is also a great deal more. Indeed, much, much more.

We must keep remembering that this business isn't just about the mega-millions that big Lennox and little Naz can claim as their right; or the hyperglitz that has the sport teetering on the highwire above the sawdust ring that is wrestling. And it has only a tenuous connection to the inane rantings of the Ali wannabes and their posses of minders who persist in taking liberties with the intelligence of the fan base.

Boxing has also been described as showbiz with blood, but never forget that the blood is real and the dangers all too obvious. Nothing luvvie about this game.

But getting right down to the nitty, boxing is all about men who possess a special talent, or who at least believe they have that magic something; it is about their ambitions and their dreams and how they set about pursuing them. Of course, we musn't forget that these days there are also serious women practitioners and sincere good luck to them. But here, we will be concentrating on the guys.

Wonderfully gifted guys and genuinely tough guys and really funny guys and truly nasty guys and incredibly brave guys and hopelessly silly guys; a smattering of Walter Mitty guys and a smidgen of Don Juan guys, and just one or two undeniably weirdo guys who would have been at their ease dealing a gin rummy hand to Hannibal Lecter.

Guys like the marvellously eccentric welter Kirkland Laing, who went walkabout when a fortune beckoned, and heavyweight bruiser Joe Baksi, who took the wrong turn-off at London when a fading Joe Louis awaited him in New York. Guys like film actor Mickey Rourke, forever fantasising about ring glory, and Mitch 'Blood' Green, whose most famous battle took place on a Harlem street at four in the morning.

Fighters all, and along with the rest of our subjects, bonded by two common factors. Aside from the obvious that they all performed inside the ropes and under the hot lights with varying degrees of success, there is also the sobering fact that not one of them ever managed to earn even the opportunity to box for a world championship.

Never even challenged for the title? How could that possibly be, unless we're embarking on a guided tour of Schulberg's Palookaville? Never even got a crack? We've got to be talking broken-nosed bums and cauliflowered canvasbacks here.

But not necessarily. Times change, and in boxing at least, not always for the better.

As you are reading this, somewhere in some dark backroom, a new boxing sanctioning body might well be on the brink of birth. It is all quite simple really. Some of the chaps gather around a table, dream up a name for their organisation and knock out a piously worded charter; they hopefully dig up some financial clout from a soft mark to cover initial expenses, then dash off some rankings lists; and then they get busy on the fax.

Most likely the principal brainteaser will come when dreaming up a credible name, for boxing is awash with sanctioning bodies, all greedily intent on getting a slice of the action, and good names are getting increasingly hard to find. We have the World Boxing Council (W.B.C.) and the World Boxing Association (W.B.A.) and the International Boxing Federation (I.B.F.) and the World Boxing Organisation (W.B.O.) and . . . there are more, but why bother?

In the trade they are called the Alphabet Boys and they have been encouraged to spawn, thanks to the philistines in television who demand a 'world' title label on practically every fight screened – any old 'world' title tag will suffice, just as long as it can be plugged as being 'world'.

And so, when once there was just one champion per weight division, today there could be three, four, most likely more, although on very rare occasions an exceptional boxer might unify the major championship belts. He is unlikely, however, to hold them for any length of time because of the hungry politicking of the Alphabets.

A handful of world champions at every weight? The situation becomes brain-curdling for even the most devoted aficionado to keep track, particularly as nowadays there are a whopping seventeen weight classes instead of what were once the traditional eight. Seventeen multiplied by three, four, five, or more? Forget about it!

The new divisions were introduced, ostensibly, to minimise the health risks to boxers draining themselves to make a prescribed weight, which is laudable at face value. But is it too cynical to suggest an ulterior motive: the more divisions, the more champions, the more likelihood of television interest, the more dosh for the sanctioning boys?

And so now there are jumbo-packages of so-called world champions orbiting the globe, and make no mistake, some of them are really outstanding performers. The likes of Roy Jones and Shane Mosley, Felix Trinidad and Oscar De La Hoya could have looked after themselves during any era.

Likewise the super featherweights Floyd Mayweather and Joel Casamayor, and the Mexican light fly Ricardo Lopez, who has compiled an extraordinary record yet remains something of a secret outside his native land because he boxes in an unfashionable division.

That still leaves us with seventy, eighty-odd boxers who believe they have a legitimate right to call themselves world champions. Fair enough, if their belts can boost their earning-power and spread gaiety amid their circle of acquaintances. But bifocals aren't required to see that the situation has terminally devalued what once were proud and elusive prizes.

Consider this. Between 1945 and 1955, when the United States had a virtual stranglehold on the sport, there was a grand total of ten world title fights staged in Britain, by far the most memorable being the Turpin–Robinson stunner at London's Earl's Court in 1951. These days, a livewire promoter like Frank Warren can easily double that tally in a year.

Which means? Which means it must have been far, far harder to negotiate a title challenge in the old days; even to manoeuvre a prominent position in the ratings was a considerable accomplishment.

Consider again. In the nineties, Scotland's Paul Weir won the W.B.O. mini-flyweight championship in his sixth fight; he went on to become a double world champion in his ninth contest when landing the W.B.O. light-fly belt; in his twelfth bout he became an ex-champion.

Highlighting Weir is not aimed to denigrate his achievements, but is intended to underline just how speedily a boxer can now write his name into the record books: how quickly they can come and how quickly they can go again.

Now consider one last time. Cleveland's Jimmy Bivins started out as a professional in 1940 and boxed for fifteen years. He beat fighters like Ezzard Charles and Archie Moore, Melio Bettina and Joey Maxim and Anton Christoforidis – all sometime world champions – and he retired after outpointing Mike DeJohn in bout 112. Yet he never had a sniff at the world championship as either a light-heavy or a heavyweight. Crazy, isn't it? And Bivins was by no means a one-off.

Yes, it was a totally different glove game back then, and not much fun if you happened to be black. It seems incredible now that a talented boxer could be denied his rights because of colour, but for almost fifty years, right from the time when the last of the bare-knuckle heroes John L. Sullivan drew the line at facing West Indian Peter Jackson, black fighters, especially large black fighters, were doomed to the back of the bus.

The injustice was diabolical, but down through the years, many black fighters have been portrayed with a pathos that does their memory few favours – well intentioned, perhaps, but the often saccharine descriptions conjure up a troupe of shufflin' minstrels. The mighty Sam Langford and scar-faced Jack Blackburn, and Sam McVey and Joe Jeannette, and later Harry Wills and Larry Gains, and later again, Charley Burley and Holman Williams and Lloyd Marshall, all merit better than that. As well as being skilled practitioners, these men were all stone realists and not short of the smarts.

They were aware that the game was rigged against them, but it was still their preferred way of earning a living – sometimes a very lucrative living – and they took great pride in their considerable abilities. They knew what they could do, and they also knew that most of the champions knew what they could do. They had a status and a presence that almost rendered the word 'champion' irrelevant.

Given the chance, not all of them would have wound up with titles, but each deserved his opportunity. Today, they must surely have divvied up a handful of belts apiece.

Like the colour bar, the organised crime element, which for so long was a major influence, has disappeared from the business, most likely because there are greater profits to be had in dealing dope and organising stock swindles.

Not that the waters are much less murky now than in the days when mobsters such as Owney Madden and Bill Duffy and later, Frankie Carbo and Blinky Palermo were calling the shots; only now the 'trickeration', as Don King might say, is all to do with contractual small print, option clauses, and playing financial footsie with the sanctioning bodies. Up-market mugging.

That night in the Garden when Charley The Gent informed brother Terry: 'Kid, this ain't your night' is a scenario now hopefully rerun only in the grainy old movie, but as we shall see, back in 1950, the dialogue was all too familiar for a fine Californian lightweight named Tommy Campbell. Much later, serious skullduggery cost a highly promising light-middle Billy Collins his career, and some say his life, and it is an incontrovertible fact that the good old days were often shockingly bad old days.

Do not imagine, however, that this offering is intended to be a chronicle of the victimised, a sob story about boxing's persecuted.

It is no surprise to learn that boxers can be headstrong and there are many who have squandered their talents in cavalier fashion, ignoring the disciplines that are supposed to channel their energies into being better citizens. For example, Tony Ayala, once a phenomenal prospect, is again active after a hiatus of sixteen years spent in the pokey, and if he is seeking sympathy, then he can find it in the dictionary.

And nobody should shed tears for a dedicated Lothario such as welter Tony Janiro, a huge Madison Square Garden attraction in the forties, and still cited by ancient trainers when warning of the dangers of enjoying the bright lights that lead to steamy sessions in the boudoir.

Tony kissed away his chances with a laugh and a shrug of the shoulders, while others like Dave Sands and Les Darcy found the fates ganging up on them when glory was within their reach. We shall touch on men like Muhammad Ali's brother and Marcel Cerdan's son and the compulsion that inspired them to try their hand; and there will be countless other fighters who won't be touched upon at all, for this is but a random selection of the nearly men.

And the point of the exercise?

Hopefully, to reach out to the new enthusiast who has just forked out a hefty wedge to treat his partner to a night at the fights. As they tingle when Michael Buffer gets ready to rumble and the gaudy belts are paraded in the ring and the champ somersaults over the ropes, it will do them no harm to learn that once upon a time, there was a different fight game when only a choice few got to call themselves champion, and a world title fight was an extra-special occasion.

But more importantly, this is a sincere tribute to all the guys who, for whatever reason, never completed the journey to a championship fight; who, like Terry Malloy, could've been contenders, but never were.

PART ONE

Blackballed (1)

John L. Sullivan, a ring legend, would never face his outstanding challenger, Peter Jackson, because he was a black.

Jack Blackburn fought the best and knew the score, but he almost turned down training Joe Louis because he was the wrong colour.

Sugar Ray Robinson, regarded as one of the finest ever, blanked Charley Burley although they were both blacks.

When investigating boxing and colour,
nothing is simply black and white

1

Peter Jackson:
'A Real White Man'

JOHN LAWRENCE SULLIVAN fought under three different codes: the London Prize Ring Rules (brutally basic, bare-knuckle, but sometimes with kid gloves); the Marquis of Queensberry Rules (three-minute rounds, no wrestling, gloves up to eight ounces); and his own very special rule that he would never do battle with a black.

The great John L. introduced prejudice to pugilism.

By modern standards, Sullivan wasn't a particularly big heavyweight, and although he packed a fearsome wallop and possessed raw courage in abundance, to compete successfully today, he would have required at the very least a six-month seminar under an Emanuel Steward before being let loose in the ring. Saying that, the odds would have been high against the boozy Boston Strong Boy ever surviving such a stretch of self-discipline.

Sullivan, however, engaged in the last of the spectacular heavy-weight bare-knuckle classics when beating Jake Kilrain in 75 bloody rounds at Richburg, Mississippi, in 1889, and three years later lost the right to be called world champion when, with the gloves on, he was knocked out in 21 rounds by Jim Corbett at the Olympic Club in New Orleans. If only for these two epics, he has earned his place in ring history.

He must also be acknowledged as sport's first international superstar. His barnstorming tours throughout the United States, as either a boxer or with his troupe of actors, attracted sell-out crowds; well-heeled devotees showered him with expensive gifts, most memorably a diamond-encrusted championship belt valued at $10,000; on a British trip, he was fêted like the royalty he performed before and met; and in Dublin, an estimated crowd of 15,000 turned out just to welcome him at the quayside.

From his exploits in the ring and his theatrical ventures, Sullivan earned over one million dollars during a period when some families were scraping by on about ten bucks a week. The champ was an extremely serious money-maker.

There was, however, a dark downside to Sullivan. He was a wife-beating womaniser, a trigger-tempered bully, a bigot, and, for most of his career, an alcoholic, whose renowned pub boast was that he could lick any sonofabitch in the house. Empty words, a beery blast of hot air, for the sonsofbitches John L. was challenging had to be white sonsofbitches.

Peter Jackson was certainly no sonofabitch, nor was he white, and so, when he disembarked at San Francisco in the spring of 1888 after the long voyage from Australia, there were already two major strikes against this 26-year-old who made Sullivan his prime target.

Jackson was a striking individual, standing an inch over 6ft and, in his prime, weighing around 200lb. The son of a fisherman, he was born on 3 July 1861 at Christiansted on the Caribbean island of St Croix. When he was six, the family gambled on finding a better life in Australia, both parents having to work their passages across, and they settled in Sydney; but after not too many years, the parents, disillusioned and homesick, returned to St Croix. The young Jackson, however, remained in Australia.

He was a powerful youngster and a natural athlete, and he was soon something of a local celebrity, excelling at rowing and especially swimming. Many years later, he was still performing swimming exhibitions in San Francisco, and there is an unconfirmed tale that he it was who introduced the Australian crawl stroke into America. But there were no sponsorship deals or scholarship grants back then, and before he was eighteen, and following in the family tradition, Peter went to sea, working as a deckhand.

A stint on one schooner was dramatically to alter the direction of his life because the ship was owned by an American called Clay Callahan, who also happened to be an avid boxing enthusiast. Immediately impressed by Jackson's physique, his interest heightened when he witnessed the young man flatten a burly longshoreman with a single punch, a right-hander that helped settle a dockside dispute in favour of the shipowner.

Awestruck, like so many who for the first time have glimpsed close up something extraordinary, Callahan immediately suggested setting up a meeting with Larry Foley, who taught boxing and was just about the sport's most influential figure in Australia. However, the notoriety of the punch-up on the docks had preceded them and Foley already knew all about the right hand. A quick once-over in his gym persuaded the trainer that this was a lad with distinct possibilities.

Jackson learned fast, soon developing a style of his own, more subtle and refined than that of his bruiser contemporaries, but allied to a tremendous natural strength and hitting power. He was not, however, the only star in Foley's firmament: many sound judges considered Frank Slavin to be equally talented, if not superior. A few months younger than Jackson, in height and weight they were almost identical, but Slavin was white and had no time for blacks.

This couldn't have been the first time that the West Indian had experienced prejudice, but it certainly was the first time that he had encountered the colour bar in what was by now his chosen profession. Far less face than Jackson in the ring, Slavin wouldn't even entertain engaging in mild sparring. Their animosity festered over many months, worsened after a quarrel over a girl, and developed into hatred, finally boiling over one evening in a Sydney saloon.

Already a flamboyant high-roller, the then teetotal Jackson sauntered up to the bar, and within Slavin's earshot, ordered drinks for the house. If, as likely, the gambit was intended to incense his fellow boxer, who had already lowered a few, then it was an instant success. Frank declined less than gracefully.

'I don't drink with niggers,' he snarled and all hell erupted. For twenty minutes the two men, who were to become among the best heavyweights in the world, forgot everything that Larry Foley had drummed into them, as they punched, kicked, butted, elbowed and gouged one another, their supporters wading in, until the saloon was a shambles when the constabulary eventually arrived on the scene.

Both sides claimed a victory but it had to be a no-decision, and it would be nine long years before the principals engaged in the return, this time properly supervised and for money, under the promotion of the august National Sporting Club, then housed in London's Covent Garden. Much was to happen to Peter Jackson in the interim.

In the five years following the saloon brawl, he cleaned up the locals – those who would fight him – and with opportunities drying up, he accepted the advice of the *San Francisco Chronicle* sports editor Bill Naughton, who had seen him box, and set sail for the States. The ultimate target was John L. Sullivan, but Jackson was under no illusions about the immense task before him.

When he docked in San Francisco, the American Civil War was still being replayed in the dark corners of many memories; almost a quarter of a century had passed since the last roar of the guns, and blacks were no longer slaves but, with precious few exceptions, they were no further up the social and economic pecking order. Thanks to his skill with his fists, George Godfrey was one of those exceptions.

Godfrey hailed from Sullivan's state of Massachusets, and in pugilistic circles was known as Old Chocolate. He was a highly regarded heavyweight, a worthy challenger for the championship, but John L. wasn't having any. While professing a willingness to face Godfrey, his financial demands were always far too steep for Old Chocolate's backers, who lacked monetary muscle. And so Godfrey had to content himself with his self-proclaimed title of coloured heavyweight champion of America.

This was, of course, a crown of cardboard, but the new boy-on-the-block Jackson saw a showdown with Godfrey as a short cut to the bigtime and terms were speedily agreed for a bout at the California Athletic Club in San Francisco on 24 August 1888. The contest was to be to a finish for a purse of $1,500 ($1,200 to the winner, $300 to the loser) – a paltry sum compared to the estimated $26,000 Sullivan would pocket for beating Kilrain the following year, but attractive enough to Jackson at the time as a launching pad for his American campaign.

Godfrey was massacred. Never before had he faced anyone with Jackson's speed and skill, and only his tremendous courage kept him going, but badly cut up and outclassed, he finally succumbed in round nineteen. Jackson couldn't have made a more sensational American début and the victory was to pave the way for an important match with the 6ft 4in San Franciscan Joe McAuliffe, whose press releases lacked something in political correctness.

'I always said I'd never fight a nigger, but I'll fight this one just to put him in his place. I'll teach that black bastard a lesson.'

The purse was $3,000, winner take all, the date was 27 December 1888, and the venue again the California A.C. The local hero went into the ring a 2/1 on favourite and actually succeeded in flooring Jackson for a four-count in the tenth, but for the remainder of the fight, he soaked up a tremendous beating until he was knocked out in round 24. When, four months later, the West Indian dismantled another prominent white called Patsy Cardiff in ten rounds, nobody could dispute his championship aspirations.

It was summertime, and for Jackson the living was cosy, if not exactly easy. The California A.C., hosts to his three fights, had appointed him boxing instructor at their gymnasium; a cross-country exhibition tour raked in more dollars; and in a jaunt over to London, he collected an easy $4,000 when he beat Jem Smith on a second-round foul. The dough was rolling in and rolling out. He splashed out on a horse and buggy, a silk topper, fancy duds and a cane, and it became a common sight in San Francisco to see him, usually accompanied by one of the city's beauties, driving at full gallop through the streets. The locals were less than impressed.

Peter Jackson was flying high, and for a fleeting period in 1890 it seemed as if he had at last cornered Sullivan. The Strong Boy called for a purse of $20,000 and insisted that there must be a side bet of $10,000 in a fight to a finish. John L. was obviously banking that the harsh terms would silence the black upstart, but unlike George Godfrey, Jackson didn't lack for wealthy backers and the match was tentatively – very tentatively – arranged for that summer at the California A.C. Fate, however, was to get Sullivan out of the fix. A boxer was killed in San Francisco's Olympic Club and all boxing clubs in the state were closed down for the rest of the year. Jackson would never again come so close to the championship.

John L. Sullivan was a racist from the cradle. First-generation Boston-Irish, he was raised in a neighbourhood into which few blacks ever strayed, and his attitudes were no different from the majority of his peers. That was a time when such calumnies as 'nigger' and 'coon' were in common use; when blacks considered themselves fortunate to fill the most menial of jobs; and when an English boxing authority, Fred Dartnell, in a muddle-mouthed attempt to praise Jackson, described him as 'a real white man'.

Most likely Sullivan didn't avoid fighting Jackson or Godfrey or any other black because he was physically afraid of them; he was much too macho for that. John L. didn't want to compete against blacks because he considered them inferior; they were beneath him and he took that belief to the grave. Only eight years before his death, he was still promoting white supremacy when reporting for the *New York Times* on Jim Jeffries's ill-advised comeback in a bid to wrest the title from its first black holder, Jack Johnson, in Reno in 1910. As far as Sullivan was concerned, the championship belonged to the whites by right.

It is worth noting that at the same time as Sullivan was enforcing his prejudice, in other weight divisions, black boxers were, on occasion, being afforded equal opportunities. In fact, the 1892 Sullivan–Corbett bout was the third leg of a boxing extravaganza staged by the New Orleans Olympic Club, and featuring championship fights on three consecutive days, including a featherweight encounter between Jack Skelly and George Dixon. Little Chocolate Dixon from Nova Scotia, as opposed to Old Chocolate Godfrey from Massachusetts, would knock out Skelly in eight rounds in the first defence of a title that he would hold with one small interruption, for eight years. Clearly, while Sullivan's bigotry was widely accepted in the sport, the blackout was less than total.

As we have seen, Jackson did not believe in touching the forelock. Back in Sydney, he had belted out the longshoreman and probably deliberately provoked Slavin in the saloon; he was especially vicious against McAuliffe following Joe's 'nigger' tirade; and when he tore through the San Francisco streets in his horse and buggy, a good-looking girl at his side, he was acting as a precursor to Jack Johnson, who was later to scandalise white society. On occasions, however,

Jackson revealed a gentle humour and even a bewilderment about his situation.

Asked once about the colour bar and Sullivan's refusal to fight him, he replied straight-faced that he would have no objection to the champion's colour if a match could be arranged. But the fact that black fighters were often regarded as somehow anatomically different really did bug him. That frustration was evident when he told boxing guru Fred Dartnell – the same Fred who had praised him as being 'a real white man': 'They [white boxers] are all after my body. Hit a nigger in the stomach and you'll settle him, they say, but it never seems to occur to them that a white man might just as quickly be beaten by a wallop in the same region.'

But back in 1891, the resentment had yet to eat into Jackson. He had narrowly missed one crack at Sullivan and still held out hopes of getting his deserved chance. With that aim still uppermost in his mind, he agreed terms to box James J. Corbett on 21 May on his home turf, the California A.C., where he still tutored in the gym. Corbett, a native San Franciscan, held a similar position at the Olympic Club, and with both of them pursuing John L., the pairing was a natural.

James John Corbett was born on 1 September 1866, son of an Irish livery stables owner. He worked in the Nevada Bank but spent as much time at the Olympic Club, where his boxing skills soon brought him to the attention of several wealthy backers. He became known as Gentleman Jim, but this was no clown, and in 1889, he confirmed himself as championship material following three brutal encounters with a fellow townie Joe Choynski. Like Jackson, he was doing everything possible to ensnare Sullivan, and also like Jackson, this was a fight he couldn't afford to lose.

The contest was to be fought to a finish, using five-ounce gloves and for a purse of $10,000 ($8,500 to the winner, $1,500 to the loser), and with Hiram Cook in charge as referee, the action got underway promptly at nine o'clock in the evening.

Like Jackson, Corbett relied a lot on fancy footwork and skilful boxing rather than brute force, but the contest quickly developed into a war, with the considerably lighter Corbett more than holding his own. The exchanges were fierce, with both fighters enjoying their spells of ascendancy in the first 35 rounds, but both suffered severe punishment, Jackson having the additional handicap of a badly sprained ankle. From round 36 onwards, the fight degenerated into a slow-motion slog, both men hurt and thoroughly exhausted, each hoping the other would topple over. Finally, just after one o'clock in the morning and the completion of round 61, good sense prevailed and referee Cook called a finish and declared the match no contest.

Having fought for just over four hours, the battered boxers took themselves off to the Hamman Turkish Baths, where they exchanged muted pleasantries, unaware that they were only a few hours away from another serious mugging, this time from the promoters, the lofty Board of Directors of the California A.C.

The boxers were looking forward to an even split of the $10,000, but the Board decided that in view of the announced no decision, they should pay the fighters only $2,500 apiece, and offer them another match at some future time agreeable to themselves and the Board for $7,500. This was larceny on a scale that would have had Bob Arum and Don King gasping with admiration, and despite the huge outcry raised by both Corbett and Jackson, the sharpies of the California A.C. got away with it. Having staged one of the most memorable fights of all time, they were concerned only in saving a miserly five grand.

Jackson was now just short of his thirtieth birthday and at his peak, but meaningful fights were becoming increasingly hard to find. He earned well from exhibitions – sometimes as much as $1,000 a night – and, like Sullivan and Corbett, he took to the stage, touring with his own troupe in a version of *Uncle Tom's Cabin*. A match with Sullivan* was no nearer, but incredibly, a bout against his old enemy Frank Slavin began to appear a possibility.

Slavin, now claiming the championship of the British Empire, had arrived in America in 1891 and had severely beaten Jake Kilrain in nine rounds in Hoboken, New Jersey, before shipping out to England with Jackson in pursuit. Before very long, the match was made for 30 May 1892 at London's National Sporting Club – exactly one year after the Corbett epic.

Why did Slavin finally relent and lower the colour bar? There have been all sorts of theories about settling old scores, but the most plausible answer is that the money was too good to refuse, a purse of $12,500 being on offer.

Jackson reached his peak that night at Covent Garden. As could be expected because of their history, the exchanges were ferocious and the West Indian produced miracles of endurance to survive a huge sixth round for Slavin. From then on, however, the fight was all Jackson's and in round ten he administered an awful beating, pleading with the referee to intervene, before finally putting Slavin down for the full count. All the bad blood that had existed between them was now spattered on the canvas.

A jubilant Jackson could not be aware that from that night, life was going to be all downhill for him. His electrifying performance convinced the white hierarchy that he was extremely bad news: Sullivan steadfastly didn't want to know; Corbett, who was to become champion in September, was understandably reluctant to consider a return; and Bob Fitzsimmons, the latest import from Australia and the reigning middleweight champion, deemed Jackson an unacceptable risk as he pressed his own claims.

The demons were finally sinking their fangs into Peter Jackson. After a lifetime of abstinence, he had started drinking very heavily, almost recklessly; his health, always so robust, began to fail and he contracted tuberculosis; his whole life was in freefall, and a boxing club that he opened in London in 1897 proved an overnight financial disaster. Everything was falling apart at the same time.

Very sick and short of funds, he returned to the States, where he managed to negotiate a fight against Jim Jeffries in San Francisco. Jackson shouldn't have been allowed in the ring, but he desperately needed the money and Jeffries, who was to win the championship the following year, disposed of him in three embarrassingly sad rounds.

There seemed to be no let-up in the downward spiral, and he was knocked out again, this time in four rounds by the moderate Jim Jeffords in Vancouver. For a spell he was hospitalised there, before an anonymous Vancouver benefactor paid his passage back to Australia, where in 1899 in Melbourne, he somehow contrived to stay on his feet for 25 rounds to earn a draw against a nobody called Billy Warren. At least he didn't bow out on a losing note.

But there was to be no happy ending to the story. Peter Jackson died on 13 July 1901, just ten days after his fortieth birthday. In the ten years from when he first landed in America, he had earned an estimated $200,000 from the ring and the stage, but like so many fighters before and after him, he wound up broke.

Lord Lonsdale, provider of the first of the British championship belts that still bear his name, was in no doubt that the West Indian was the finest prizefighter who ever lived, and in his later years, Jackson's old adversary Jim Corbett concurred, calling him the greatest fighter he had ever seen. Sadly, glowing testimonials are not enough to guarantee a boxer his rightful place in the record books, and for sure, no man had ever deserved a chance at the championship more than the elegant Peter.

That he was never granted the opportunity leaves an indelible black mark against not only John L. Sullivan, but also the race-blinkered America of his time.

2

Jack Blackburn:
'As Mean As He Looked'

JACK BLACKBURN rarely smiled when he was sober and never when he was on the booze. Jack glowered at the world, and the long razor scar that stretched from his left ear to the corner of his mouth only served to enhance an extremely intimidating countenance. One June day in 1934, however, when two black businessmen approached him with a proposition, he laughed outright, although the laugh was more bitter than hearty.

The scene was Trafton's gymnasium in Chicago, and the men, John Roxborough and Julian Black, were there to hire Blackburn to tutor a young heavyweight whom they planned to turn professional. The former lightweight had just celebrated – if that's the proper word – his 51st birthday the month before, his health was poor, and he was barely scuffling along, training a few fighters, earning his drinking money. He was certainly in no financial shape to knock back any proposal, but still he laughed when Roxborough and Black informed him that their heavyweight was coloured.

Blackburn had been around the block many times and was all too familiar with the realities of the fight business. With the memory of the despised Jack Johnson still too fresh in the minds of the white promoters who controlled boxing, he maintained that a black heavyweight prospect was just a waste of time, effort and expense. Lighter weights perhaps, but no way heavies. To make any worthwhile money with him, the kid would have to be exceptional, almost a world beater, and he wasn't swayed when the managers assured him that that was exactly what they had unearthed. Blackburn was immune to fairy stories.

But in his pressing circumstances, the initial offer of 34 dollars a week for a guaranteed four weeks sounded very sweet, even if the idea of working with the heavyweight was not. And so, grudgingly, he agreed to take a look at the young Joe Louis – the future Brown Bomber, who was to warm the cold heart and bring even the occasional smile to the face of Jack Blackburn for the remaining nine years of his life.

Jack was a hard man and he had lived a hard life, and until he teamed up with Louis, perhaps he never had any good cause to smile. His years with Joe brought him financial security, respect, and a fame that he had never found as a fighter. Of course, there were many who knew about Blackburn – fellow boxers and trainers and managers. Fight folk. Why else would Black and Roxborough first approach him? But he had never earned big bucks, and the headlines he made were for all the wrong reasons. And yet, he really deserved to have been a contender.

He was born on 20 May 1883 in Versailles, Kentucky, the son of a preacher. When he was ten, the family moved to Indianapolis and then on to Terre Haute, Indiana, where in 1899 he started to box. At that time, the sport operated underground in many states and was widely considered a disreputable means of earning a living, and it is possible that the preacher father did not approve of a fighter in the family. Whatever the reason, the teenager lit out on his own, heading first for Pittsburgh and then Philadelphia, where his career really got under way with Jack in action as many as two or three times a week.

Nat Fleischer, founder-publisher of *The Ring*, credited Blackburn with 167 fights; Jack himself estimated more than as many again. An accurate tally will forever remain a mystery, and equally obscure is an exact description of many of his contests. Jack was the archetypal black fighter in an era when there was a large percentage of no-decision results and an extraordinary number of draws awarded, and one cannot shake off the notion that many bouts were little more than glorified exhibitions.

To ensure regular work, a black fighter had to make all sorts of concessions. Against a home town white, the black opponent often had to agree to take things easy – fighting 'with the handcuffs on' was the phrase of the time. And with the blacks regularly having to box a series of bouts against one another, it would be naïve to imagine that they were out for blood every time.

An example. Blackburn boxed the renowned Sam Langford on six occasions – once was quite enough for Jack Johnson! Even today, Langford is on every short list of ring marvels and he was significantly heavier than Blackburn, and yet he never defeated him. The final score was four draws and two no decisions, and in at least some of those meetings, the suspicion has to be that both men were sporting 'the cuffs'. Who can blame them? To earn a dollar, they were adapting to harsh circumstances, and this perhaps explains why so many of them developed into scientific masters of the defensive arts rather than slam-bang attack merchants.

Legend has it that Blackburn tackled six different men, one round apiece, on the same night and knocked out three of them. That smacks of fairground booth fighting, and if he did engage in many such events, then one can begin to understand the disparity between Fleischer's records and Blackburn's own recollection. He should not, however, be written off as a carnival attraction and many of his contests were serious, often bloody affairs against the very best of his time.

At 5ft 10in, he was tall for a lightweight, never grew any heavier than a welter, but he fought all sizes, including, in 1908, a six-round no-decision match against the reigning light heavyweight champion Philadelphia Jack O'Brien, who, in the two previous years, had twice challenged Tommy Burns for the heavyweight title!

Crazy times, but black fighters could not afford to be choosy, and conceding anything between 20lb and double that was by no means rare. They did adopt dodges to redress the balance somewhat, the most popular being to soak their bandaged hands in plaster of Paris, illegal and dangerous but extremely useful in adding power to their punches. Forever the pragmatist, Blackburn freely admitted to using this subterfuge when he deemed it necessary.

But he wasn't wearing loaded gloves when, in 1908 in a Philadelphia gym, he engaged in a sparring session with Jack Johnson, who later that year was to become heavyweight champion. Because of the vast difference in weight, Johnson naturally was taking things easy and instead it was the smaller man who took the liberties. Blackburn's jab bloodied Johnson's nose and when the exchanges became more heated, his fast, evasive footwork kept him out of trouble and had the future champion looking foolish and embarrassed. Johnson had a long memory.

Almost thirty years later, when Blackburn hit the jackpot with Louis, Johnson tried to exact some revenge for that session in the gym. He became one of the young champion's fiercest critics, going to great lengths to highlight flaws in his style, and in so doing, indirectly knocking Blackburn's teaching ability. Never lacking for front, the old champion even offered to take over the responsibilities as trainer, but he never even received a reply.

If that Philadelphia gym session with Johnson proved anything, it was that Blackburn was well able to handle himself against anyone in the ring. He possessed an excellent left jab, a damaging left hook, and was a skilled all-round technician. Aside from his series with Langford and his bout with O'Brien, he beat future welterweight champion Jimmy Gardner on points over twelve rounds in Boston; boxed another future welter champ Mike (Twin) Sullivan to a fifteen-round draw in Chelsea, Massachusetts; and went six rounds to a no decision with a future fabulous middleweight title-holder, Harry Greb. And, of course, there was Joe Gans.

Though they met only three times, which was just a quick hello compared to some of the long-running serials of those days, Gans was the man Blackburn most wanted to beat because he held the lightweight title.

Gans was somebody special, a brilliant black champion, fondly titled The Old Master by the cognoscenti. Almost nine years older than Jack and vastly more experienced, he had travelled a similarly long, hard road, and had more than 100 bouts under his belt before winning the championship, when stopping Frank Erne in the first round in 1902. In those hundred-odd fights he had to make all sorts of concessions, the most notorious being a two-round loss to Terry McGovern in 1900, a tank job so blatant that for a time boxing was outlawed in Chicago. Even a genius had to do deals if he was the wrong complexion.

Gans relinquished the title in 1904, the year he fought a draw with the original Joe Walcott for the welterweight belt, then two years later, back at his own weight, he regained his title following a 42-round endurance test against Battling Nelson at Goldfield, Nevada. Nelson, battered, bleeding and thoroughly outclassed, fired a volley of low blows in the final round, preferring to be disqualified rather than knocked out. Promoter Tex Rickard had put up an extraordinary purse of $34,000 for the contest, and Gans's share was $11,000, which was by no means a generous cut.

Sadly, he was to enjoy neither his wealth nor his health for too long. The Old Master became a tuberculosis victim and in 1908, he was knocked out in seventeen rounds in a return with Nelson; two months later the Durable Dane – and he certainly was that! – repeated the dose, this time in 21 rounds. Considering the desperate state of his health, it is remarkable that Gans could survive for so long in those stamina-sapping marathons.

But the final curtain came down after one last fight (a no decision against Jabez White in New York) and he died on 10 August 1910 in his home town of Baltimore. He was 35.

Blackburn and Gans had fought two six-round no decisions in Philadelphia in 1903 and 1906, and squeezed in between was their most significant meeting, a fifteen-round non-title victory for Gans in Baltimore in 1904. That was Blackburn's first recorded defeat and he was still only twenty, but he must have shown The Master skills out of the ordinary, because in his remaining years, Gans would admit that Jack was the only lightweight against whom he would never risk his crown.

With Gans retiring from the ring in 1909, the way should have been clear for Blackburn to press for a title tilt against Nelson, but by then he was not in any position to press his pants, far less his championship aspirations. In 1909, he was doing hard time, serving the first year of a sentence for manslaughter.

Blackburn was a violent man, quick to react to any imagined insult, and he was an extremely heavy drinker – by today's classification an alcoholic. That was a lethal combination and when recalling all the fights that he'd had, maybe he was including the countless saloon brawls and street battles, in one of which he had collected his razor scar. But it was a gun, not a razor, that was the weapon when he totally flipped on a January night in Philadelphia.

There were the four of them: Blackburn and his white common-law wife Maude Pillion, and a gentleman called Alonso Polk and his wife. Their evening may have started out sociably, but as can happen, it wound up in tragic mayhem. A row flared and Blackburn, most likely drunk, produced a gun, shot Polk dead and wounded the two women before he was subdued by the police. A senseless, dreadful event, and, everything considered, the five years he spent locked up doesn't seem too severe a sentence. But those years should have been the best of his boxing career; instead he could only languish and ponder over what might have been, as the lightweight title passed from Nelson first to Ad Wolgast and then on to Willie Ritchie.

On his release in 1913, his friends in the business – and despite his volatile nature, Jack did not lack friends – organised a benefit to bankroll his return to the ring. One notable non-participant was his old enemy Johnson, now the hugely unpopular heavyweight champion of the world, who, when asked to help, publicly badmouthed Blackburn.

In later years, when the circumstances were reversed and Blackburn was flush, thanks to his association with Louis, and the old champ was down on his luck, Jack refrained from sinking in the boot, often extolling Johnson's ring brilliance. To the newspapers, he always claimed that Louis would have had few problems with Johnson, but to those in his circle, he never concealed his admiration for the ex-champion. Just another twist to a very complex character.

Blackburn was now thirty and he was to box for another ten years, but if it was difficult to sell a black fighter, then it was all but impossible to steer a black fighter with a manslaughter rap to a championship. There was no alternative but to continue on the circuit – wins, draws, no decisions – but he was never going to get rich, and after one final bout in 1923 when he was beaten by Roy Pelkey, he retired. Since his teens, he had known nothing but boxing and it was a natural progression for him to remain in the gym, sling a towel over his shoulder, and become a trainer.

Not many great fighters, however, can communicate their skills to the youthful wannabes, and Blackburn, such a hard nut and with such a short fuse, seemed a most unlikely candidate to make a successful professor of the science. But it soon seemed as if his quarter of a century in the ring was no more than an apprenticeship for his true vocation. Jack was a natural teacher, concentrating on the fundamentals of good balance and a sharp left hand. Sounds simple, but from these basics, a prospect can be developed into a serious proposition, and Jack produced serious fighters.

Not that he had journeyed along the road to Damascus. Blackburn still drank far too much, and when he drank too much he would become really nasty. And when he grew nasty, some of his gym charges would take off never to be seen again. But the ones who stayed the course were all the better for the experience.

Eddie Futch, then a young gym student and destined to become one of the most famous trainers of all time, got along with Blackburn, yet he remembered him as 'a mean person. As mean as he looked.' Another future trainer, Joe Gramby, declared that a lot of people were afraid of him, but at the same time he said, 'He was a nice man, but when he was drinking he was hell.' And Marshall Miles, who would be Louis's last manager, perhaps got to the truth of Blackburn when he said, 'He wouldn't take any foolishness.'

Three years after his last bout, Jack trained his first champion, and ironically he was a lightweight. In 1926, Sammy Mandell from Rockford, Illinois, won the title that Blackburn had so long sought, and he was to hold on to it until 1930, when he was knocked out in one round by Al Singer. In 1927, Blackburn scored another success, training Bud Taylor to win the N.B.A. version of the bantam crown against a teenage Tony Canzoneri. The styles of both Mandell and Taylor were fashioned around their ability to throw a great left hand; they were Blackburn boxers, but they were white.

Training those champions confirmed his status as a brilliant teacher but they did not make him wealthy. Nor was he going to get rich on a young black middleweight called Arnold Cream, whom he was developing in the early thirties in Philadelphia. Cream, later to enter the record books as heavyweight champion Jersey Joe Walcott, somehow got lost in the shuffle when Blackburn went to Chicago to join up with Louis, but had nothing but good to remember about his old mentor.

Now we come to Joseph Louis Barrow, the Brown Bomber, and one of the all-time great heavyweights. Would he have achieved that same greatness without the genius of Blackburn?

While conceding that he was an established amateur star and a terrific puncher before Jack had ever heard of him, throughout their partnership Louis showed such a willingness to comply with Blackburn's every instruction that he would surely have been a lesser fighter under different tuition. There must be no denying the Bomber's raw talent, but it was Blackburn who brought him down off his toes, taught him the value of his jab, and refined the economical style that was to be the Louis trademark. They were a dream team, a match made in heaven . . . and there are precious few of these in any walk of life, much less in a feud-fraught business such as boxing.

Blackburn was still the stern disciplinarian, but there was a warmth to the relationship that must have amazed many who had only seen Jack on the booze. Louis seemed to elicit the considerable good in him: they addressed one another affectionately as 'Chappie' and their conversations were monosyllabic, almost telepathic. But most of the important talking, and if need be, sharp reminders, were done one-on-one – Blackburn never slated a fighter in front of a third party, nor did he showboat for the press.

Louis, however, was no robot, programmed to destruct only when Jack pressed the buttons, and Joe enjoyed the good life. But right from his first days as a pro, his managers and trainer gave him a code of behaviour to follow, both inside and outside the ring – the list was long but basically the instructions were not to do anything that Jack Johnson had done before him. And so Louis maintained a carefully nurtured profile outside the ropes and a deadpan expression within them. It was his trainer who was still more liable to go off the rails.

The increasing years and the worsening arthritis had slowed down Jack, but he still drank more than was good for him. Heading towards the ring for the 1935 fight against Kingfish Levinsky, he warned Joe that he had been drinking and wasn't feeling so hot. Louis assured him that he would have to climb the corner steps only once and duly delivered on his promise, flattening the unfortunate Kingfish inside a round.

Far more seriously, however, Blackburn could still get into desperate trouble away from the ring. In 1935, in the lead-up to Louis's fight against Paulino Uzcudun, Blackburn and two other men were charged with the fatal shooting of one Enoch Hauser in Chicago. At a further hearing, he was indicted for perjury as well as manslaughter and the case dragged into the March of the following year when the prosecution decided not to proceed with the case. Whatever really happened that night in Chicago, Jack Blackburn was not yet a mellow old man, ready for his rocker.

On 22 June 1937, Joe Louis survived a first-round knockdown before stopping Jimmy Braddock in the eighth in Chicago to become heavyweight champion of the world. The dream that Blackburn had laughed off as impossible had come true. For the next five years, he was to bask in the happiest days of his life as his protégé steamrollered the opposition, only Tommy Farr and Arturo Godoy managing to remain upright for the full distance. But there was little he could do about his health, and for the fight against Abe Simon in March 1942, for the first time, he was too ill to train his champion or tend to him in the corner.

A month later, Blackburn was dead. Louis was devastated (the following February he named his daughter Jacqueline in honour of his old trainer) and the funeral in Chicago drew an attendance of 10,000, among them old opponents and many of the fighters that he had taught. He was 59.

But for his wonderful partnership with Louis, Blackburn would be remembered by only a handful of ring historians as just another excellent black fighter who was denied the title chance his talent deserved. He was a strange and dangerous man, sometimes very wise, sometimes very foolish, and there is no doubt that his wild streak tripled the odds already stacked against him. To this day, Jack Blackburn remains an enigma, but no question, he could really fight!

3

Charley Burley:
'Only the Lord Understands'

SUGAR RAY ROBINSON was every manager's midnight dream of the perfect fighter. His boxing was artistic, his footwork sublime; he was a dynamic puncher with a chin of granite, and, on the occasions when the going got tough, the heart of a ferocious pit bull. More than that, he was personable and marketable, and he knew how to cut himself a good deal with the shrewdest of the shrewdies.

His ring record was quite remarkable: only three defeats in his initial 137 fights before his first retirement in 1952; a life total of 202 professional bouts with only nineteen losses, and most of those coming in the winter of a career that ended in 1965; welterweight champion of the world, five times middleweight champion of the world, and beaten by the scorching heat as much as Joey Maxim when he challenged for the light heavyweight title. With the proliferation of belts on offer today, Robinson would have wound up with a roomful.

The finger-snapping, toe-tapping Sugar Ray it was who first travelled complete with an entourage, but his team bore no resemblance to today's gangs of menacing minders, uniformed in baseball caps, shades and bulging T-shirts. Robinson's crew was far more fan-friendly and, aside from his manager and his trainers and sparring help, often included his secretary and his barber, sometimes his personal golf tutor or his dance coach, and on his European sorties, a midget Parisian named Jimmy Karoubi, whose job description was vague but his memory enduring – as enduring as the clippings of the Sugarman's giant, pink Caddie, which attracted open-mouthed crowds in a Europe still dusting itself down after the war. Ray was a class act.

He died in April 1989, aged 67, his last years plagued by Alzheimer's, but he lives on as a genuine ring legend. Muhammad Ali nominated him as the greatest boxer pound-for-pound of all time, and perhaps he was. But nobody can be perfect, and if we must nit-pick through his career, Robinson fails to secure maximum marks if only for one very important omission on his record: there is no trace of his ever fighting Charley Burley.

Charley Burley? A threat to Sugar Ray? Make no mistake, he certainly would have been had he ever got the chance, but the wily Ray made sure he never got that chance.

Although over fifty years have gone since Charley's last fight, his name refuses to fade into total obscurity, his amazing exploits being passed down from generation to generation by the dwindling number of the fraternity who actually saw him box, and who regard him as at least the equal of anyone who ever ducked through the ropes.

The reverence and the affection that his memory evokes are quite astonishing, especially as the only title Burley ever held was the small-league middleweight championship of California, which he won from the very respectable Jack Chase. But whenever his name crops up, grizzled old trainers go into rhapsodies and ancient pugs roll their eyes and shake their heads in awe. Veteran managers are, understandably, less ecstatic, because Charley never turned over a minuscule fraction of the cash that a Sugar Ray could command and, of course, dosh is the name of their game. But the overall consensus is that the Pittsburgh marvel would have given Robinson nightmares.

Charles Duane Burley was born in Bessemer, Pennsylvania, on 6 September 1917, turned professional in 1936 as a nineteen-year-old welterweight with a four-round stoppage over George Leggins, and by 1938, he was already rated by *The Ring* as the third best in the world. That rapid rise was to prove misleading, however, because eight years later, he was still in the ratings, but now as number two in the middleweights, and still no nearer a title shot.

Back then, competition was fierce for a mention in Nat Fleischer's top ten, but in reality his ratings exerted little influence. They were a useful yardstick for promoters and could, on occasion, improve a fighter's earning power, but when it came to the crunch, the gentlemen who made the big decisions and who decided who was going to get lucky and who wasn't turned a dummy eye to all Fleischer's industry.

The extraordinary Archie Moore, for example, was *The Ring*'s number one middleweight behind champion Tony Zale in 1942 (Burley was next in line) but Moore was made to wait another ten long years before he received his first crack at a world title, outpointing Joey Maxim for the light heavyweight crown in St Louis – four days after his 39th birthday, though Archie always maintained he was three years younger.

Even then, nobody was handing Moore a belated birthday present. Maxim, masterminded by a most able trickster called Doc Kearns, boxed for a $100,000 guarantee; Moore was paid a ludicrous 800 bucks, from which he had to cover his expenses. That was blatant exploitation, but at least Archie finished up with the title and he would earn very well from it. However, Burley and a host of fine contemporary black fighters never even got the offer of a similar championship rip-off.

Discrimination was rife, more subtle and insidious than in the days of Sullivan, but still a terrible affront to equal opportunities. In *The Ring*'s advertising feature, Managers' Directory, some bosses bracketed their fighters as '(negro)' to ensure that there would be no misunderstandings, and in certain states, mixed-race matches were a no-no. Life for the likes of Charley Burley and Holman Williams and Lloyd Marshall and many others was no picnic.

True, Louis had come good, and the freakish triple holder Henry Armstrong ruled Burley's welter division in those immediate pre-war years; a select few others like featherweight Chalky Wright and lightweights Bob Montgomery, Beau Jack and Ike Williams were beginning to get the breaks. But for every black who somehow wangled a title deal, at least another dozen deserving candidates were callously shunted aside. If you had the wrong complexion, then the right connection was a must.

Burley never had the benefit of a smart operator like Jack Kearns supervising his affairs. From very early on it became apparent that his handlers were more interested in the quick dollar than the long term, and when he was still only a promising twenty-year-old, he found himself tossed in against a fellow Pittsburgh attraction called Fritzie Zivic, who had already been a pro for eight years with 77 fights under his belt.

Fritzie Zivic looked rough and fought rough. His nose was burst beyond restructure, but he too had bent a few beaks in his time. Zivic was a master of the illegal, be it butting, heeling, using the laces, the thumbs, hitting low, choking – almost always on the referee's blind side. His was a special art, and no manager worthy of the name would have matched a prospect against such an accomplished ruffian, but the youngster already knew enough not only to survive, but to force Zivic to pull out all the stops to win a close decision.

That bout was held on 21 March 1938 in Pittsburgh, and less than three months later, there was a rematch, with Burley this time emerging a decisive points winner. Zivic still needed convincing and the following year they met again, and this time Fritzie was overwhelmingly outpointed and badly worked over in the process. The *Pittsburgh Post Gazette* reported that Zivic 'was so far behind at the finish that a telescope would be the proper instrument to find him'.

That should have been a crossroads meeting for the battered veteran and the slick youngster, and in a sick and cynical way it was. In October of the following year, a rejuvenated Fritzie Zivic was rewarded with a title shot against the fading Henry Armstrong and after fifteen rounds became the new welterweight champion. And Charley Burley? Not only did he discover what it was like to be a victim of the fast shuffle, but he had also marked himself out as a dangerous fighter, best avoided.

Certainly Zivic, who as a rule was not too fussy about the opposition he faced, wanted nothing further to do with Charley. After thirty rounds at close quarters with Burley, he made it public that there was no way he was going to risk his crown against him. In fact, there was even a story published at the time that Fritzie had bought out Burley's contract just to ensure that he would never have to fight him again! Zivic never denied the tale.

Weird things like that could happen back then without the twitch of an eyebrow. Having Joe Louis under contract, promoter Mike

Jacobs had established himself as the most influential figure in the business, and as a result he also pulled the strings in the most lucrative of the lighter divisions. Of equal significance, a sinister New Yorker called Paul John Carbo, Frankie to some of his pals, Mr Gray to others more respectful, was beginning to flex his muscles.

In Hollywood's version of the fight game, there was always a mob guy lurking in the background, and there is no denying that heavyweight gangsters such as Owen Madden and Al Capone and Legs Diamond were linked to boxers. But more often than not, the associations were more friendships than business. With Frank Carbo, boxing was all business.

Carbo's reputation hinged on his affiliation to the Lucchese crime family and his impressive C.V. numbered arrests for all sorts of major disorder, including a couple of murder raps. Under no circumstances could he ever have been licensed as a promoter or a manager but, as the Mob's ambassador to the sport, he quickly attained great power by becoming the undercover overseer of managers, of whom he soon gathered many, all prepared to do the bidding of Mr Gray. His clique included such prominent handlers of champions as Frank (Blinky) Palermo and Hymie (The Mink) Wallman, and Al Weill, known in the trade as The Vest, and to become really rich and famous as the manager of Rocky Marciano. Eventually Carbo's fiefdom stretched from coast to coast, and even extended to London and Paris.

If a fighter hooked up with one of his favoured nominees, then he had sound chances; if not, then he was going to require a fairy godmother to become a champion, or even land a feature spot in New York's Madison Square Garden, then the centre of all matters important in boxing.

In 1942, Charley Burley finally made it to New York, but not quite to the Garden. By then he was the second-ranked middleweight; but remember this was before the television era, and so he was still something of a mystery man to the big wheels in the Big Apple. His rating could not get him a Garden fight; his influence stretched to no more than a spot at the St Nicholas Arena, a popular club used as a nursery for prospects with Garden potential.

The selected opponent was 'Showboat' Phil McQuillan, an honest trier with a sound reputation, but Burley sank the Showboat inside one round, and that was the last any New York manager wanted to know about Charley. He had proved himself too good for his own good – all the stories about the middleweight who knocked out heavyweights were true. New York had no need of a black called Charley Burley and he was never offered another fight in the boxing capital.

In his early years, Robinson had found the going equally frustrating. In fact he was drawing to the close of his seventh year as a pro, and had boxed 75 times with only one defeat, against Jake La Motta (later avenged on five occasions), before he eventually won the vacant welterweight title, outpointing another black fighter, Tommy Bell, in Madison Square Garden in December 1946. Like Burley, he had been forced to do most of his fighting on the road, and although he was based in Harlem, and had a tremendous following there since his Golden Gloves days, in his thirty bouts prior to facing Bell, he had appeared in New York only five times.

How did two blacks wind up fighting for the title in the Mecca that was the Garden, when Burley, as first a welter and now in 1946 a highly regarded middleweight, couldn't get into the building without purchasing a ticket?

Red Cochrane had been champion since 1941, but because of the war, was never called upon to make a defence until February 1946, when he was knocked out in four rounds by Marty Servo, who happened to be managed by The Vest, Al Weill. With Burley having moved up to middle, Robinson was widely recognised as the uncrowned welterweight champion (he had already beaten Servo twice) and deserved his shot, but nobody was in a hurry to offer him one.

A month later, however, the picture changed dramatically when new champion Servo suffered a brutal two rounds' beating in an overweight match with Rocky Graziano and retired soon after. Robinson could be ignored no longer and had to get one of the vacant title slots. Tommy Bell, a very good fighter who actually floored Sugar Ray, may have lacked charisma, but he clearly had the connections to fill the opposite corner stool.

This was where Robinson would always have the edge over Burley.

Ray was a born hustler and although George Gainford was employed throughout his career as his official manager, he was soon cutting his own deals, and once he became champion, he quickly earned a reputation for being a very difficult man at the conference table. Robinson would haggle not only over his wages, but over everything else right down to the size of the ring and the make and weight of the gloves. And if he didn't get his way, he could discover a virus or a muscle strain that could leave the promoter frantically searching for a last-minute top-of-the-bill.

In contrast, the placid Burley seldom planned further than his next payday, and to ensure those wages, he would never give a promoter any headaches over such trifles as the weight of an opponent or the split of the purse money. He was far too easy to deal with, believing that his ability would eventually be acknowledged and rewarded, but that was to prove a serious misjudgement. More hard-headed customers like Robinson and Moore knew that the business didn't operate that way – that possessing an exceptional talent was no guarantee of securing a square deal – and so they both became masters of the art of self-promotion.

Nobody ever really tried to sell Charley Burley in that pre-TV era. He was a devoted family man, married to the same wife, Julia, for over fifty years, and when he finally quit the ring, he then worked at the same job in the Pittsburgh sanitation department for 34 years. If he ever became frustrated that his career languished while inferior fighters prospered, then he hid it well, and he never seemed to get upset about Robinson's refusal to box him. Charley was almost too good to be true, certainly too good for the fight game.

When his career was over, Burley would shrug off all the injustices, declaring: 'Only the Lord understands.' But he was wrong. Sugar Ray understood. And so too did old Mike Jacobs and Mr Gray. They understood that nice guys seldom got a sniff at the serious money.

Without rancour, Burley maintained that Robinson's sidekick Gainford told him to his face that there would never be a fight between the pair of them, and legendary trainers Ray Arcel and Eddie Futch were also in accord, saying that Sugar Ray just didn't want to know. According to Burley, Pittsburgh promoter Jake Mintz offered him a three-fight deal against Robinson – provided he agreed to lose the first fight. Burley claimed that Mintz, who was also the co-manager of Ezzard Charles, hedged when asked about the guarantees of getting the rematch, and so the proposition came to nothing. Back then, Frankie Carbo liked to dream up those three-fight scenarios, and the chances are that this was only Mr Gray testing for reactions from both fighters with future business in mind.

In the years when they could have boxed, Robinson was tackling and beating plenty of tough customers such as Sammy Angott and Servo and Zivic and La Motta – all sometime champions and all white; wins that would look good on his record. Ray most probably believed that the rewards would never match the risk in facing a top black like Burley, and he was probably correct.

Of course, Burley always fancied his chances in a bout with Robinson but Charley fancied his chances against heavyweights! We can only speculate when discussing Charley and Ray, but the mere fact that men like Moore and Futch and Arcel regarded Burley as at least Robinson's equal is testament to his greatness.

Unfortunately, no film exists of the smooth, cultured style and the fast, destructive fists, but in a career that spanned 98 fights, there were ample opportunities for the man from Pittsburgh to demonstrate that his talent bordered on the mythical, ensuring him a place in boxing's Hall of Fame, if not its Roll of Champions.

In 1938, the year when he shared decisions with Zivic, the fledgeling Burley also outpointed another future white champion in middleweight Billy Soose. And six years later, while campaigning in California, he was brought in as a last-gasp substitute, travelling from San Diego on the day of the fight, to outpoint no less than Archie Moore in Hollywood, flooring Archie twice in the ten rounds. In his thirty-year career Moore boxed many of the greats and sampled just about every style imaginable, and he always nominated Burley as the best man that he ever fought, graphically describing his style as 'slick as lard and twice as greasy'.

The few boxers who beat Charley – there is a career tally of eleven losses – had to be equally slick. There was a seven-fight series with Holman Williams, another brilliant black who never got the breaks, and they won three apiece with one being declared a no contest. And in consecutive months in 1942, he was twice outpointed over ten rounds by Ezzard Charles, who was to go on to win the heavyweight championship.

At that time, Charles was a feared light heavyweight; Burley no more than what would be described today as a light middle. Nobody in his right mind would have considered giving Charles over a stone, yet in both fights, the Pittsburgh fans made Charley a hot favourite, though in the end, the weight concession to such a brilliant boxer proved just too much. But it is also worth noting that just six days before their return fight, Burley outpointed Holman Williams over ten rounds in Cincinnati!

Those escapades only strengthened the Burley legend. Nobody seemed too big for him and he boxed great light heavies such as Lloyd Marshall (the only man to knock him off his feet) and Jimmy Bivins, and dangerous heavyweights like Shorty Hogue and Big Boy Hogue and J.D. Turner. Archie Moore beat both the Hogues but also lost twice to Shorty, who, prior to fighting Burley, had never taken a count. Charley knocked him out in ten rounds. And against Turner, who had just lost a split decision to the brilliant Billy Conn, and who had an incredible 70lb pull in the weights, Burley scored four knockdowns before winning in the sixth.

Such unbelievable feats may have enhanced his reputation but not his career prospects. If Burley could easily handle bigger, heavier men and only lose to the very best of them, is it any wonder that fighters in his own division went walkabout?

Robinson was not the only champion who avoided Charley. There was serious money to be made in Pittsburgh with a match between Burley and the other huge local favourite, Conn. The purse offer made to Conn was his biggest up to that stage of his career, but he turned Burley down flat. And the old Bronx Bull, Jake La Motta, who had raged against most of the feared blacks, including Holman Williams and Bert Lytell and Bob Satterfield, somehow never got around to signing a deal with Burley.

Even when his hopes of a title bout had been extinguished, Burley kept on winning, but work was getting harder to find and in his last five years fighting, he could barely scrape a living, boxing only thirteen times, and losing just the once, to the excellent Lytell. And just short of his 33rd birthday, he bowed out on a winning note when on 22 July 1950 he travelled to Lima, Peru, to outpoint a light heavyweight named Pilar Bastidas. He may have never been handed the magic key, but Charley's talent never deserted him.

If Sugar Ray Robinson was every manager's dream of the perfect fighter, then Charley Burley was every trainer's fantasy. There is a million-dollar distinction between the two visions, but the bottom line is that Sugar Ray made it and Charley Burley did not. Both in and out of the ring, Charley really was too good for his own good, and maybe he was right, and only the Lord could understand.

He died on 16 October 1992, aged 75.

PART TWO

Right Time, Wrong Place

Joe Louis and his heavyweight title were waiting in New York, but Joe Baksi decided on a stop-off in Stockholm.

Laszlo Papp had won three Olympic golds and was unbeaten as a pro. A world championship beckoned, then Budapest pulled the plug.

Kirkland Laing had just outclassed the fabulous Roberto Duran and the big-money offers were pouring in, but where was Kirk?

It's not only in the ring that a
fighter requires perfect timing

4

Joe Baksi:
'No More Fooling Around'

JOE BAKSI will never be remembered as one of the great heavyweights, not even one of the great white heavyweights. He does, however, have solid claims to be included in any short list of the chumps of all time, regardless of weight, and for that fact alone, his name should never be forgotten. Joe's story is an object lesson to all of those boxers who are reaching that crucial stage when well-intentioned advice becomes just a pain in the ear.

In this particular instance, in the spring of 1947, Joe Baksi convinced himself that he knew better than the major executives from Madison Square Garden, and more than the astute London promoter Jack Solomons, and certainly more than his own long-suffering manager Nat Wolfson, who was only granted Joe's attention when he was in the humour. The big man from Pennsylvania decided he knew better than any of them, and so he opted for a modest payday in Sweden, and in so doing, scuppered a lucrative tilt at the ageing Joe Louis and his heavyweight championship of the world.

He could have become Contender No. Twenty-four for the Bomber's title; instead he became boxing's Bonehead No. One, a tag he would never live down.

Baksi did not enjoy a soft or sheltered upbringing, which makes his scant regard for a one-in-a-million opportunity all the more puzzling. He was born on 14 January 1922 in Kulpmont, Pennsylvania, the son of immigrant Czechs, and when he was ten, his father, who worked in the anthracite mines, died following an accident at the pit. When the time came to leave school, the youngster briefly sampled the mines, then, like thousands of other kids of that era, he took to the road, riding the freight trains from town to town, working at anything that would fetch the price of a meal, washing dishes, shining shoes. Anything.

He must have eaten reasonably well, for he grew to an inch over 6ft and weighed around 210lb, and he was by then able to hire himself out as a bouncer in taverns and a carnival roustabout, where he also featured in an act that saw him hoist aloft a gang of midgets. Before he had ever been in a ring, he was beginning to look the typical pug, complete with a caved-in nose, the souvenir of a football mishap, and so, when in 1940, aged eighteen, he wandered up the steep flight of stairs and into the famous Stillman's Gym on New York's Eighth Avenue, by no means did he look out of place.

Aside from the fighters working out in the two regulation-size rings and the other hopefuls pounding away at the bags, or skipping rope, or grunting their way through excruciating floor exercises, Stillman's – accurately described as America's Sock Exchange – was always buzzing with managers and would-be managers and matchmakers, all doing deals, scurrying in and out of the line of phone booths, forever searching for their next dollar, their next prospect.

Fate would decree that the teenage Baksi should first approach one of the less larcenous types in Nat Wolfson, who, when he wasn't hustling in the gym, conducted his business from room 808 in a building at 1650 Broadway. Further along The Great White Way, at 1585, Al (The Vest) Weill, then representing the rated heavyweight Arturo Godoy, could afford the luxury of a suite. Be that as it may, Wolfson's partnership with Baksi was to endure fourteen roller-coaster years and 72 fights, and the pair would make a sizeable chunk of money. But, as we shall see, not nearly as much as they ought to have earned.

With one of the Stillman legends, diminutive trainer Whitey Bimstein, tutoring him on the basics, Baksi turned pro at a time when there was no shortage of work for young white heavies. Promoter Mike Jacobs believed in keeping his champion busy, and the turnover in Louis contenders was, to say the least, brisk.

While Baksi was first learning to jab and hook, Louis was in the fourth year of his reign, and making four defences, twice against The

Vest's Godoy, and also against Johnny Paycheck and Al McCoy. Easy money. The following year saw him squeeze in seven title fights, the most memorable being the thrilling thirteen-round knockout of Billy Conn. But in 1942, the Bomber joined the army, and after stoppage wins against Buddy Baer and Abe Simon – charity events in aid of the Navy and Army Relief Funds – the title went into mothballs until 1946.

Thanks to Bimstein's perseverance, Baksi had developed an effective if ponderous style. He was never going to be a dancing master, but he could hit hard and could take a good punch, and these two attributes can carry a heavyweight a long way; by 1943 he was ranked sixth in the world. From then, right through until the early fifties, big Joe flitted up and down the heavyweight listings, at times looking sensational, as in his two visits to London, at other times disappearing altogether because of the odd upset defeat or one of his frequent spells of inactivity.

Weird things had a nasty habit of happening to Mr Wolfson's pride and joy. He was as clumsy outside the ropes as inside, and to describe him as accident-prone didn't really do Joe justice. He could be a menace to himself and a heartbreak to those around him.

Some examples. It is October 1946, and Wolfson, Bimstein and Baksi are dining at New York's La Guardia Airport, prior to flying to London for the Freddie Mills fight. The trio are in high good humour for the contracted wages are their best yet, and Mills does not shape as too daunting a task. But before they have even tucked into the main course, high drama! Baksi somehow contrives to slice himself so badly with a bread knife that he requires seven stitches in his left hand. Panic stations on both sides of the Atlantic, but somehow the promotion survives without even a postponement!

When it came to sharp instruments, there was surely a hex on big Joe. He was a D.I.Y. nut long before that became fashionable, and, doting parent that he was, one day in his basement he was making toys for his son and other neighbourhood kids when he all but severed the index finger of that abused left hand. The injury could easily have cost him his career instead of just the two fights that the harassed Wolfson had to cancel. Similar disasters seemed to happen all the time.

Then there was the curious case of his long-postponed bout against Italian Gino Buonvino. That fight was originally scheduled for March 1948, when, not for the first time, Joe was rediscovering himself. Buonvino was a crowd-pleasing but light-hitting opponent who was expected to make Baksi look good, but in his final workout, Joe tripped on the ring canvas and cracked his ankle so badly that he was left hobbling on crutches for months.

Lee Savold, considered well past his sell-by amongst the Stillman's regulars, was drafted in as a late substitute, and shocked everyone – himself included – by knocking out Buonvino in 54 seconds, the fastest ever main-event stoppage in the history of Madison Square Garden. While Baksi was still in plaster, Savold kick-started his career and went on to enjoy two big-money matches against Bruce Woodcock in London, followed by further profitable, if somewhat more painful, paynights against Louis and Marciano.

Now fast-forward three and a half years and Baksi finally gets around to fighting Buonvino. Joe is staging yet another of his comebacks, and barring one minor tune-up, he has been inactive for eighteen months, but he is still only 29 and is still an attraction. Instead of the Garden, however, he has been relegated to the St Nicholas Arena, and what happens? He too knocks out the normally durable Italian in round one, in exactly 54 seconds of the first to be precise – identical to Savold's feat and pure Baksi!

Baksi and Savold were to fight three times with Joe winning twice, and he also numbered Tami Mauriello, Gus Dorazio, Gunnar Barlund, Lou Nova and Bernie Reynolds among his victims. Those were fair fighters of that era, and Mauriello, Nova and Dorazio all earned title fights against Louis. Baksi, however, will be best remembered for his three fights in Europe, where his Jekyll-and-Hyde persona truly manifested itself.

In 1946, blitz-weary Londoners were learning how to enjoy themselves once again. Conditions were still terribly hard, but all forms of entertainment were flourishing, particularly sports, and especially boxing, thanks almost single-handedly to the efforts of a one-time East End fishmonger.

Jack Solomons puffed on giant cigars while his countrymen were queuing up for their ration of extremely dodgy ciggies. His suits were Savile Row, his motor a Roller, and he had an ear-to-ear grin that could sucker the most suspicious of his business rivals. He had been briefly a boxer, then a matchmaker and a manager; he had made money from fish, had dabbled in bookmaking, and now at 46, he was the undisputed daddy of Europe's boxing promoters. His shows were artistic masterpieces, years ahead of their time in showbiz presentation, and the promotions at the 11,000-capacity Harringay Arena invariably sold out within days of the tickets being printed. The media liked to call him Jolly Jack.

From his office in Soho's Great Windmill Street, right across the narrow road from the Windmill Theatre, whose nudes never clothed throughout the worst of the bombing, he conducted business with Mike Jacobs in New York and Gilbert Benaim in Paris, and ruled the British scene with an iron fist. Jack could have given tutorials on how to extract the last drop of juice from an orange.

Solomons paid top dollar, but he demanded his money's worth from his employees. He made heavy demands on his star attractions – excessive demands one would be forced to say, when looking back on the careers of his two major post-war earners, Mills and Woodcock, both of whom were to become terribly unstuck against Baksi. No Solomons fighter would ever lack for opportunities, but they had to learn to take their lumps when those chances came along.

In 1946, light heavyweight Mills fought only four times, but come Christmas, he had soaked up as much serious punishment as most modern boxers might accumulate in a career. Mills made good money, as did heavyweight Woodcock, but as Solomons permutated them against one another and against the trans-Atlantic importations Baksi and Gus Lesnevich, he was to subject all those men – with the exception of Baksi – to the type of rough treatment that would live with them long after the wages were spent.

In his defence, the ever-smiling Solomons could say that he had the okay from the British Boxing Board of Control (the Board of *No* Control as some wags described it) and the fighters' managers, and finally the boxers themselves, who found it hard to resist the money on offer. But to fill an arena, Solomons was prepared to throw the form book out of the window, and in so doing he would hand Joe Baksi a gilt-edged chance to hit the jackpot, though Joe would never appreciate that until it was far too late.

In the August of 1945, Baksi's championship aspirations had suffered a severe knock when he dropped a ten-round decision to Jersey Joe Walcott, then considered no more than a slippery stepping stone, in Walcott's home town of Camden. Still licking their wounds the following May, Joe and manager Wolfson were at the Garden ringside when Tami Mauriello (a Baksi victim in 1944) knocked out Woodcock in five rounds and qualified for a title crack against Louis. Understandably, the pair were cursing their luck until Solomons contacted them with an offer – not to face Woodcock, but rather the much lighter Mills. They couldn't believe their good fortune.

Of course, it is easy to be wise after the event, but Solomons staged his share of mismatches, and just as it was nigh impossible in later years to make a case for Dave Charnley beating Emile Griffith or Brian London standing a chance against Muhammad Ali, so Mills could only be regarded as cannon fodder for the Pennsylvanian. Maybe Baksi's loss to Walcott had persuaded the promoter that Mills stood a chance. But that would have made Jack a bad judge, and Solomons knew his boxing and his boxers.

In May 1946, Mills had been stopped in the tenth round of a ferocious battle for the light heavyweight title by Lesnevich – a battle in which Mills especially suffered serious damage. Disgracefully, just three weeks later, Solomons paired Freddie with Woodcock (still recuperating from the Mauriello experience) and the heavier man won after a gruelling twelve rounds. Following two months' recuperation and a one-round win against a nobody called John Nillson, Mills had to prepare for Baksi.

When the firm of Wolson, Bimstein and Baksi eventually touched down in London, the fighter's hand was still stitched up from the La Guardia mishap. Baksi, a moody individual, was on his best behaviour and said all the right things to the hordes of news-papermen, and no, the bandaged hand wasn't a problem and concealed no more than a scratch, and yes, he knew all about Mills and expected a tough scrap. Little Bimstein tongue-lashed Joe into taking his training seriously at Solomons's gym, and so he was in reasonable condition – stitches removed – when he stepped into the Harringay ring.

Mills was giving away height and just a fraction short of 28lb. He was as game as any fighter who ever lived, but after two rounds, he was badly marked up around both eyes, his best punches were having absolutely no effect on the bigger man, and at the close of the sixth, he had sufficient sense left to inform his corner that he'd had enough, and referee C.B. Thomas was called over to be told that the mismatch was over.

Freddie had never been on the canvas, but he had suffered a sickening and humiliating beating. Baksi was naturally feeling good, had collected a very healthy £5,700, and was back in contention amongst the big men. And even better, he was still on Solomons's shopping list.

Woodcock was being nursed back to credibility following the Mauriello knockout, had outpointed Mills, had won the European title against Al Renet, and had knocked out Lesnevich in a catchweights' bout at Harringay. He could again be sold as a viable challenger to Louis if he could beat Baksi, and so, before the American team had returned to the States to celebrate Christmas, Wolfson had agreed terms for another London visit.

But it was to be a different Baksi who was to return for the April 1947 showdown. This time his wife, Anne, was in the party, and, replacing Bimstein, he employed Ray Arcel as his trainer. Arcel, widely acknowledged as one of the best in the business, didn't know Baksi as Bimstein did, and he even found trouble getting Joe to do his roadwork at their Brighton camp. Baksi was acting the bigshot, finding fault with the food, his training quarters, his sparring partners, everything. His contract called for a percentage of the gate, and so his relationship with Solomons took a nosedive when he accused the promoter of selling off blocks of complimentary tickets, thus swindling him of his rightful share of the takings. Forget Woodcock and Louis, the big man from Kulpmont was already conducting himself as if he were champion of the world.

The spectators who saw him take Woodcock apart on 15 April

could have been excused for agreeing with him. The 11,000 inside Harringay – Solomons claimed he'd had 100,000 ticket applications, and he charged an incredible twenty guineas for a ringside view – witnessed an execution.

Woodcock had an accurate left hand and a fair right, but he was an extremely one-dimensional performer, and conceding 19lb to a brawler like Baksi, he was never in with a chance from only seconds after the first bell. The gutsy 26-year-old from Doncaster was bounced off the canvas three times in the first, was down again twice in the second, and was somehow allowed to continue absorbing a dreadful battering until referee Moss Deyong eventually stopped the massacre in the seventh. Post-fight, it was discovered that Woodcock had suffered a broken jaw in that disastrous first, and a bone splinter had actually pierced his eye, almost blinding him permanently. The miracle was that he had the desire, far less the ability, to box again after seventeen months on the sidelines.

Nat Rogers, matchmaker for the Madison Square Garden Corporation, had been an impressed Harringay ringsider, and he was in London to sign up the winner to box Louis in a summer outdoor extravaganza at the Yankee Stadium. The negotiations should have been a formality, and would have been if manager Wolfson had been allowed to do his job. But by that time, nobody could reason with the big man, and as the increasingly desperate Rogers, backed up by Lew Burston, another of Mike Jacobs's heavy hitters, kept raising the ante, Baksi, the one-time freight train bum from Kulpmont, kept playing even harder to get.

Then the heavyweight stunned all concerned by declaring that he would consider the Louis offer – consider! – only after he had fought Olle Tandberg in Stockholm in July. Olle Tandberg? Sweden? Admittedly, this was a very low-risk undertaking, and the £5,500 purse must have looked like a gift. But with a heavyweight title deal in the pipeline, just crossing the street, much less the North Sea, was considered a dodgy proposition, especially for a guy with such an unpredictable track record.

The original New York offer had spiralled from $30,000 to an incredible $100,000, so desperate was the need to secure an outdoor opponent for Louis, and although Solomons went on record as advising Baksi to accept the fight, he might have been secretly whispering in Joe's ear. The official promoter for the Tandberg bout was Edwin Ahlquist, later to steer Ingemar Johansson to the heavyweight crown, but in Solomons's own publication, his 1948 *Ring Annual*, he listed the Stockholm fight as one of his own promotions!

Most likely Jack, very close to Jacobs but also the main man in Europe, would have been on an earner wherever Baksi fought, but there is little doubt that serious money was made from the Swedish venture. Boxing had been made legal again in Sweden in 1943, and Tandberg, despite winning only six of his first eleven fights, was the local hero. He had won and lost the European title against Belgian Karl Sys and had somehow put together a nine-fight winning streak when he fought Baksi before a 24,000 crowd, paying $43,000 at Stockholm's Rasunda Stadium.

Baksi was a 3/1 on favourite, but despite Arcel's best efforts, he had cheated on his training, and that would prove costly. The fight was not much to watch, but the back-pedalling Swede scored often enough to damage the American's nose, open a cut above his right eye, and have him blowing heavily before the end of the ten rounds. Still, Arcel described the decision as a disgrace, and even Tandberg was surprised to get the verdict, admitting, with an extraordinary frankness, that he didn't believe he had won the fight. Baksi and Wolfson were in shock, back down to reality with a bump more painful than the pick of Olle's punches.

There was to be no major outdoor appearance for Joe Louis that year. Instead he had to wait until December, and a Garden defence against Jersey Joe Walcott, a fight in which only the two judges reckoned that the champion had retained his title. Louis was far from the Bomber of old, and Baksi would have had at least a puncher's chance against him. The champion's dismal display in the Garden only magnified Baksi's Swedish folly.

But such was the paucity of serious contenders in the division that the following year, with only one minor tune-up under his belt, he was matched against Ezzard Charles at the Garden on 10 December, in what was regarded as an important eliminator, especially with Louis mulling over his retirement plans.

A disappointing crowd of only 11,194 saw the sleek Charles, just 3lb over the light heavyweight limit, outspeed and outclass the cumbersome Baksi, who failed to take advantage of a 32½lb weight pull. Only in the sixth was Joe seen with a real chance, having Charles in severe trouble from a terrific body barrage, but he ran out of steam and for the remainder of the fight it was all Ezzard. In the eleventh, with his right eye closed and his left blinded with blood from a bad cut, Baksi was rescued by referee Ruby Goldstein. That was the only time in his career that he failed to last the distance.

Although he would still figure in the ratings, Baksi would never again get so close to a title fight. There were wins against much lighter opponents such as Maynard Jones and Jimmy Holden, but these were strictly paydays; he was being cut more easily and the lengthy absences between fights were becoming more frequent. But big Joe never stopped promising.

In 1950, he popped up at the St Nicholas Arena after six months' absence and slaughtered a popular performer called Bernie Reynolds, scoring seven knockdowns before referee Goldstein stopped the action in round seven. With a considerable weight advantage, the result was no surprise, but the enthusiastic manner in which Joe went about his work certainly was. Further encouragement to his aspirations came with the news that in London that summer, the eternal optimist Solomons would match Woodcock and Savold – two Baksi victims – for the British-recognised version of the world title!

In his dressing room, after disposing of Reynolds, a delighted Baksi told reporters, 'I don't know how far I'm going, but I'm on my way. No more fooling around, I've missed the boat for the last time.'

By that stage, Joe most likely meant every word that he said, but he was fooling nobody and he was on his way to nowhere. Over the next couple of years, he would appear sporadically and there would be the occasional headline, like the one-round demolition of Buonvino, but his career just gradually sputtered to a halt.

Baksi had indeed missed the boat, but the real shame was that he had ever caught the plane – that famous flight that took him to Stockholm and a harmless heavy called Olle. Big Joe could have been a contender, a richly paid contender, but he believed that he knew best.

He had survived slicing his hand and almost chopping off his finger, but when he turned down the guys from the Garden, he was cutting his own throat. And not even Joe Baksi could recover from that!

5

Laszlo Papp:
'Better Than Ali'

ZBIGNIEW PIETRZYKOWSKI was even more of a handful for his opponents than he was a mouthful for the ring announcers, and with a career history that included three Olympic medals, four European championships and only fourteen losses in over 350 contests, the Pole is rightly regarded as one of the all-time great amateur boxers. Ironically, he will always be best remembered for a fight that he lost – his 1960 Olympic final in Rome against a young man who would later become known as Muhammad Ali. That was the last occasion that Cassius Clay was to box without getting paid, and almost everyone has seen a clip of the fight at one time or another.

Then there is that picture that has appeared in a zillion publications. The solemn Clay, proud and erect on the winner's podium, his light heavyweight gold dangling from his neck; to his left, his beaten rival Ziggy, his singlet bloodflecked, his expression stunned and exhausted; to his right, the bronze winners, Australian Tony Madigan and Italian Giulio Saraudi, spotless and fresh for the medal ceremony.

In a few months' time, the Louisville Lip would start telling the world that he was The Greatest, but as far as Ziggy Pietrzykowski was concerned that was one crown that Cassius could never claim. A worthy winner in Rome? Certainly. A wonderful champion? Definitely. But The Greatest? According to the Pole, there was absolutely no question that that title belonged to another of his old foes, the extraordinary Hungarian, Laszlo Papp, the first fighter to strike gold at three Olympics.

Ziggy's reasoning was succinct. 'Every moment I was facing Papp could have been the last one for me. Clay gave me more opportunity. I could stand three rounds with him, but Papp was dynamic. You only get one like him every 100 years.'

Some tribute, but the light heavyweight's opinion was based strictly on amateur three-round experiences; also on facing a seasoned campaigner in Papp as opposed to a developing teenager in Clay; and of course, there is an ever-widening gulf between the amateur and professional codes which renders comparisons all but impossible. But the Polish hero studied both Papp and Clay from the heat of the battle zone, and he is more entitled than most to his assessment; so if he says Laszlo was the best ever, he is certainly worth a listen.

Papp must be one of the most exasperating imponderables in ring history. As a three-round fighter, he was awesome, and when he was eventually permitted to turn professional, he proved himself not too bad either over the longer distances. In fact, he was never beaten as a pro, and although by that time he was past his prime, negotiations were under way finally to make him a contender, when his government pulled a double-cross, ordering him back to Budapest like some dodgy diplomat brought home to account for his sins.

Different times. Now amateur boxers sport headguards, box two-minute rounds and rely on the accuracy of finger-popping computer judges; a spattering of blood or one serious belt on the chin can be enough to make the referee call a halt. And changes too in the professional ranks. Champions now only have to prepare for twelve rounds, rather than the fifteen that Papp had to travel when he was European champion; and throughout eastern Europe, the barriers are down and professional competition is now of a very reasonable standard.

But after completing his golden hat-trick in Melbourne in 1956, Papp became the only boxer from the communist bloc to be granted the okay to box for money – reluctantly given the all-clear by a political machine that was always uncomfortable with the national hero's stubborn and independent streak.

Uncomfortable and also grudging. The authorities decided that although Papp could turn professional, none of his fights would be staged in Hungary, thus denying him any home advantage. But Laszlo had enjoyed his greatest triumphs in London, Helsinki and Melbourne; so that would not prove such a great handicap. Another two provisos, however, were a lot more serious and sinister. There was going to be no chance of his stashing away his purses in a Swiss bank, because part of the arrangement was that all wages had to be converted into Hungarian currency at an unrealistic official exchange rate. And equally depressing, all bets were off, if he happened to lose even one fight! All it would take would be one bad decision, and Papp's career was over.

That pressure, coupled with the fact that Laszlo was already a 31-year-old with 230 fights to his credit when he joined the paid ranks in 1957, make his subsequent performances all the more remarkable. There were a couple of draws, narrow squeaks that might have spelt the end, but he had successfully defended his European title six times and was on the brink of a crack at world champion Joey Giardello when the Hungarians reneged on their deal and said he could fight no more.

What a sorry close to an amazing career!

Laszio Papp was born on 25 March 1926 in one of Budapest's toughest districts. His father had done some boxing, but the young Laszlo was more interested in playing soccer, and it was not until he started working with the Hungarian National Railways, spending some time in their gym, that he began to become seriously interested. Then at the age of twenty, his career really took off, when, brought in as a last-minute substitute, he knocked out the reigning national middleweight champion inside a minute, and was immediately promoted to the Hungarian international squad.

He also became acquainted with a pint-sized character named Zsiga Adler, who was to become a huge influence in his career. Pre-war, Adler had held the Hungarian flyweight championship, but his real talent lay in coaching and he developed several outstanding champions. Zsiga, however, had never toed the party line and he was also a Jew who was considered 'politically unreliable'. But when he first met Papp, such was his success that the party hacks were still prepared to go along with the man who was called the Father of Hungarian Boxing. He was to do a great job with Papp.

Laszlo was short for a middleweight, but Adler turned that into a plus because, allied to his southpaw stance, he became very difficult to reach cleanly; moreover, he was a terrific puncher with either hand. And yet, on their first major venture abroad in 1947, the partnership came unstuck at the very first hurdle.

The world amateur championships did not come into being until Havana in 1974. Until then, the Olympics were every amateur boxer's goal, although there was a school of opinion that believed the European championships were equally hard, if not harder, to win. The 1947 Europeans were staged in Dublin, and in his opening bout, the youngster had the misfortune to be outpointed by a Czech of Hungarian origin named Gyula Torma, who earlier in his career had been taught by Adler.

There was no disgrace in the loss; it was all part of the learning curve, and the following year in London, while Torma was winning Olympic gold as a welter, Papp was carrying all before him at middleweight. He had not really expected to go far in London, and would have been satisfied with one or two victories as part of his education; instead he had little trouble beating fighters from Finland, Italy, Belgium and Luxembourg to reach the final, where he beat the local hope Johnny Wright.

In the next four years, he would produce the best boxing of his life. In 1949 in Oslo, he won his first European title at middle, then two years later in Milan, he dropped down to the newly introduced light middleweight division and became a European champion for the second time. Not surprisingly, he was the hottest of hot favourites to win his second Olympic title in Helsinki in 1952.

This was the first time that there were light welter and light middleweight divisions in the Olympics, and but for the innovation, the stocky Hungarian might well have faced a teenager called Floyd Patterson. As it was, the seventeen-year-old New Yorker, later to become the two-time world heavyweight champion, blasted his way through the middleweight ranks to take gold. In an exceptionally powerful American squad, which eventually wound up with five gold medallists, the light middleweight representative was a young man from Chicago called Ellsworth Webb.

Later, as a professional, Spider Webb was an oustanding performer who went agonisingly close to becoming world champion. In fact, three of his victims in 1958 – Dick Tiger (points), Joey Giardello (stopped seven) and Terry Downes (stopped eight) – all went on to win the middleweight title. The following year, the Spider did get his chance against rugged Gene Fullmer but was outpointed in Fullmer's home state of Utah.

Back in 1952, he came within seconds of springing an enormous first-round upset against Papp. With practically the opening punches of the fight, Webb stunned the Hungarian, who was in dire trouble for the entire round and glad to hear the bell. But after the minute's break and a lecture from a furious Adler, he regained his composure and, as a confident Spider advanced to finish him off, Papp landed a terrific three-punch combination, knocking the American spark out. That was one of the outstanding performances of a high-quality tournament, and the remainder of his fights almost seemed an anticlimax as Laszlo beat a Bulgarian, a Canadian and an Argentinian, before taking care of South Africa's Theunis van Schalkwyk in the final.

But trouble was not too far away for both Papp and Adler. The feisty trainer, always on the brink of a battle with authority, refused to buckle under pressure to adopt Russian training methods for his international squad, and he was fired before the 1953 European championships in Warsaw. Papp was stunned, but his protests were in vain and he was made to travel to Poland without his friend and coach. To those closely monitoring the situation, it came as no surprise when an uninterested Papp was beaten in the first series by a fairly ordinary Russian.

He returned home totally disillusioned, his love affair with boxing seemingly over. There followed a period of almost semi-retirement, and he further estranged himself from the party hacks by refusing to box in the 1955 Berlin Europeans. But Papp was too big a name just to disappear, and with the approach of the 1956 Melbourne Olympics, secret talks got under way. Despite himself, Papp was inspired by the thought of winning a third gold; and despite themselves, Hungary's sports chiefs knew that they desperately needed Laszlo.

The stumbling block was Zsiga Adler, idolised by Papp, loathed by the powerbrokers. There was absolutely no way that Adler would be allowed to travel to Australia, but eventually a compromise was reached. If Papp went to Melbourne and won another gold, he would be allowed to turn professional, and he could even have Adler as his trainer!

Now that makes a great story and it has been retold many times and in many quarters. But was that really how Laszlo Papp was allowed, against all the odds, to turn professional? Consider an alternative theory.

In the October of 1956, there was a dramatic and bloody uprising against the Soviet domination in Hungary. The world watched with a mixture of wonder and horror as the Hungarian people battled against impossible odds, but their resistance was finally crushed on 5 November, when an estimated 1,000 Soviet tanks surrounded, then entered, Budapest, flattening entire streets in the search for outposts of snipers. Around the world, the Magyars were martyrs, the Soviet system seen at its most brutal.

Just seventeen days later in Melbourne, the Duke of Edinburgh performed the opening ceremony to a Games where feelings were still at fever pitch, and where every Hungarian competitor earned a sympathetic cheer, especially the water polo squad, who eventually won gold after beating the might of the U.S.S.R. in a memorably fractious semi-final. The Hungarian party machine desperately needed good P.R., and isn't it possible that the scheme to permit Papp to box pro was principally a cosmetic exercise, aimed at making the communist regime appear more tolerant than before?

Whatever the reason, there was to be one final hiccup before Laszlo went to Australia – he got himself stopped for the first and only time in his career. And the perpetrator of this shocking upset? None other than Ziggy Pietrzykowski!

There were, however, legitimate excuses. Papp had been sidelined due to a bout of pneumonia, and had been back in training for only a week, when he was ordered to box for his country in a prestige international against Poland in Warsaw. He protested that he was nowhere near ready, and he knew he would not get an easy ride against Pietrzykowski, whom he had already beaten, but apparently a ringside packed with party dignitaries was expected, and the appearance of Papp was mandatory. Doubting that his legs would carry him through three rounds, Laszlo went all out for a quick finish and had the Pole down in the first, but Ziggy's strength was decisive in the second, and the Hungarian took two counts before he was stopped.

Papp was to gain massive revenge in Australia, but the Warsaw misadventure was hardly the ideal tune-up, and he was anything but a raging-hot favourite when he arrived in Melbourne. Since the glories of Helsinki, his career had been under a cloud; he had just been stopped for the first time; and, of course, he was now a thirty-year-old.

Many sound judges opted for Pietrzykowski to beat him again; the Americans strongly fancied their entry, a young Puerto Rican called Jose Torres; and the Brits considered themselves no forlorn hopes with their entry, John (Cowboy) McCormack from Glasgow. This was the perfect stage for Papp to underline his greatness.

In the semi-finals, Torres was made to go all the way by McCormack, and in an all-southpaw battle, Papp demonstrated that the Warsaw result was a complete one-off, by flooring the outclassed Ziggy twice and winning by a landslide points margin. The twenty-year-old Torres, a smart boxer and a fast, damaging puncher, would go on to win the world light heavyweight championship under the guidance of Cus D'Amato, but in Melbourne, in a hard and close final, Papp was always one smart move ahead. He had completed the golden hat-trick!

Today, almost any Olympic gold medallist can write his or her own ticket. Millions are on offer, depending on the marketability of the star, but it was possibly the boxers who first cashed in on their status and, typically, it was Cassius Clay in 1960 who led the way by returning home to Louisville and signing up with a home-town syndicate of millionaires who paid him an initial $10,000, a guaranteed monthly wage against earnings, full expenses, and an arrangement whereby a percentage of his earnings was set aside in a pension fund. Back then, it was considered a mighty smart deal for young Cassius.

But after the Montreal Games in 1976, Sugar Ray Leonard could afford to turn down a $200,000 offer from promoter Don King in favour of an agreement with a lawyer named Mike Trainer, which included a purse of $40,000 for his début appearance as a professional against somebody called Luis (Bull) Vega, who incidentally was paid $650 for his pains.

By Barcelona 1992, the price of Olympic gold had gone into orbit. The only U.S. boxing winner in Spain was lightweight Oscar De La Hoya, and his package for turning professional included a $500,000 lump sum, half the cost of a luxury house, a van, a car, and God knows what else. Unbelievable, but Oscar has gone on to make some serious money since then!

But back in 1957, when Laszlo Papp set out on the pro trail, his three golds wouldn't even have caused a stir in a pawnshop. His government may have granted him permission to turn pro, but it withheld its good wishes, and there were no grants or sponsorship deals offered. Worse, there was no rush of entrepreneurs from the capitalist West, intent on tossing wads of cash in his direction. Europe's major brokers were totally underwhelmed by the news that there was a new middleweight on the circuit. Europe, it appeared, was quite well off for 31-year-old itinerant southpaws.

And so, with a total absence of fanfare, and for pitifully little pay, Papp made his pro début on 19 May 1957 in Cologne, outpointing one Alois Brand over four rounds. The following month, in Dortmund, he outpointed Herbert Sowa, again over four, and a fortnight later, in Hamburg, he stepped up to six rounds to beat Gerhard Moll. The Germans were far from impressed, and Adler, a smart trainer but as much a novice as his fighter in the professional game, decided they should return home and rethink their strategy. But in Budapest, things became even worse when Papp, who had long suffered from fragile hands, broke his right during a sparring session.

Considering the hostility at home and the apathy abroad; considering the dodgy state of his hands and his mediocre start in Germany; considering all that, and most importantly the fact that time was running out for him, it speaks volumes for Papp's incredible self-belief, that he started out all over again, after a full sixteen months of inactivity.

He resumed with a six-round knockout of Hugo Koehler in October 1958 in Vienna, a city where he was to become a huge favourite. And before the end of that year, he had created a stir in Paris when he demolished the French champion François Anewy in three rounds. This was more like the Papp of old and now he was in big demand.

Through the next four years, his perfect record was marred only by draws of the home-town variety, against Germinal Ballarin in Paris and Giancarlo Garbelli in Milan, and then, after outpointing the veteran American Ralph Tiger Jones, in 1962 he won the European middleweight title in his twentieth contest by stopping the rugged Dane Chris Christiansen in seven rounds in Vienna.

He would make six successful defences of the title against fair-class opposition, stopping Hippolite Annex, George Aldridge (televised throughout Europe), Peter Mueller, Luis Folledo, Christiansen again, and finally a televised fifteen-round points win over the tough Irishman Mick Leahy. That bout took place in October 1964 in Vienna, and at the time *The Ring* rated Laszlo at number four. Champion Joey Giardello beckoned.

Could Papp have beaten Giardello? He certainly would have stood a far better chance than some of today's so-called contenders, who are often plucked from obscurity to fill a television date and whose qualifications are so remote that bookmakers don't even bother quoting odds against them. The bookies' price against Papp beating Giardello would not have been overgenerous.

Admittedly, the Hungarian was an ancient at thirty-eight, but he had made steady improvement throughout his time as a pro. And it must also be remembered that he was only four years older than a champion who had had a very long and taxing career. Born Carmine Tilelli on 16 July 1930, Giardello made his pro début in 1948 – the year Papp triumphed in London. He was 33 and fighting his 124th contest when he outpointed Dick Tiger for the title; and it is significant that from 1965 (the year following Papp's enforced retirement) he boxed only six times and lost three of them.

At that stage, Giardello was most definitely vulnerable and Papp's awkwardly clever style would certainly have caused him problems. Common opponents? Both outpointed the useful Randy Sandy and Tiger Jones; Papp knocked out Spider Webb at the Olympics, six years later Webb stopped Giardello; the Hungarian three times stopped Peter Mueller, who in 1960 outpointed Giardello in Cologne. You can go bats studying stats, but all the signs suggest there wouldn't have been too much between the two old men.

Why then did the Hungarian government break its word to the nation's sporting icon, cancelling his career when once again it had soared to such an extraordinary height?

That treacherous move could only have been brought about by the rampant jealousy and pure spite of the bureaucrats, the guys with the long memories whom Papp and Adler had crossed so many times down the years. For a start, they hadn't believed they were granting the fighter all that much when first allowing him his professional freedom – at the best, a few years scuffling around for peanuts before his age caught up with him. And for a time, they appeared to have read the scenario perfectly.

But then Laszlo started to win the important fights, get wide television coverage and earn significant purse money. He was fast becoming an embarrassment, and how would it have looked if Hungary were to gain a world champion who couldn't perform in his own country?

And so, after the win over Leahy, his government retired him. No appeals, no deals, no real reason down on paper. Just the bare information that his permit to travel abroad had been revoked. End of story. He was allowed to hold on to enough of his money to build a comfortable villa in the Buda hills, would later travel the world as the national boxing coach, and of course, his ring exploits guaranteed him superstar status at home.

But Laszlo Papp will best be remembered as the fabulous fighter whose country did not want him to be a contender, much less know him as a champion. Politically he had become a red face to an already outdated red regime.

6

Kirkland Laing:
'The Gifted One'

KIRKLAND LAING was so laid back that there was always the danger that his trademark dreadlocks might brush the canvas behind him. In the ring and out, the marvellously talented Kirk was the epitome of supercool, even though his antics transformed normally hard-headed promoters and managers and trainers into a sad collection of basket cases. Being closely associated to a virtuoso can often have a serious downside.

When considering wayward genius and squandered opportunity, the Nottingham welterweight must figure in any top ten of sporting eccentrics. No question, he could have been a contender, indeed would have been, had his manager been able to track him down and haul him back to reality. But at a time when he could have dictated his own terms, quirky Kirk opted for a sabbatical, and walked away from a business that was waiting to hand him a fortune. Not just walked away, but rather disappeared, with the scalp of the illustrious Roberto Duran still dangling fresh from his belt.

Over eighteen years on, and the sheer effrontery of what Laing did – or rather didn't do! – is still quite breathtaking in its apparent lack of logic. Perhaps notorious soccer prodigals such as Best and Gascoigne will have an inkling of what passed through the fighter's head; and the story of Kirk's walkabout might ring a few bells in Hollywood with the likes of a Mickey Rourke or maybe a Robert Downey Jr; and of course, Mike Tyson has been dying to pull a similar stroke for years, but the world has grown too small for Iron Mike to vanish off the planet.

So why did Kirkland Laing turn his back on the big bucks? In his autobiography, manager Mickey Duff ascribed the whole mystery to the fighter getting involved with a woman, but that would appear an over-simplification. Laing was just . . . well, just Laing. Why did he box with that crazy, impudent style that always courted disaster? And why did he find it so hard to buckle down to serious work in the gym? And why did it take him over eight years to win a Lord Lonsdale Belt outright? And why did he never fight even once for a world title? And why . . .?

Geniuses can seldom explain themselves, and make no mistake, there were some magic moments in the ring when Kirk qualified as a true master of the Science. But although he was proud of his ability, sadly, he would frequently neglect that one attribute that made him special, leaving him as just another mortal, just another welterweight.

Laing was born in Jamaica on 20 June 1954, reared in Nottingham, and first discovered boxing when visiting a Y.M.C.A. as a curious eight-year-old. He possessed a natural talent and investigated the sport more seriously, eventually joining the Clifton A.B.C., where he was trained by Ernie Mann. His progress was swift and in 1972 – Munich Olympics year – as a precocious seventeen-year-old, he created a huge stir in the A.B.A. featherweight final when outpointing Edinburgh's Vernon Sollas, then regarded the hottest amateur in the country. Even boxing in that final was something of a feat, for a week before his bout, Laing was seven pounds over the limit, and he had to skip off the final two pounds at the official weigh-in – an arduous task for a teenager. That probably accounted for his fading badly in the second half of the fight, but the judges, albeit controversially, still decided he had done enough to beat Sollas.

As champion, Laing should have been looking forward to a place on the Olympic squad, but even back then nothing was simple for Kirkland, and officialdom deemed that he must box a final trial, which he lost narrowly to Tommy Wright. Not surprisingly, the massive disappointment hit him badly for a time, but he bounced back and in 1974 he won a bronze at the Under-21 European Championships in Kiev, being voted 'The Unluckiest Loser'. But then he suffered a broken jaw in a multi-nations tournament in Holland, and decided that it was time he started getting paid for his boxing.

His long-range plan had always been to box for a living, and Kirk's choice of manager showed that at times he could be anything but slapdash about the direction of his career. Rather than sign with any of the Midlands managers who would have taken him on gladly, he opted to make the big move with Terry Lawless, even though that meant switching bases and moving to London.

The year was 1975, and before its conclusion, Lawless would manage his first world champion when another welter, John H. Stracey, created a huge upset by stopping José Napoles in six rounds in Mexico City. From his gym at the Royal Oak in Canning Town, he would go on to enjoy a remarkable run of success, also guiding light-middle Maurice Hope, lightweight Jim Watt and flyweight Charlie Magri to world titles; for a time he handled welter Lloyd Honeyghan, who would win the world championship under Mickey Duff, and also Frank Bruno for much of his career. Equally important, he enjoyed a lucrative relationship with the influential Duff, and promoters Harry Levene, Mike Barrett and Jarvis Astaire – the men who had effectively taken over from Jack Solomons as the major players in Britain.

Laing certainly wouldn't lack for opportunities in joining the Lawless camp, nor would there be any risk of his being overmatched, because the Londoner had a reputation of being cautious in the extreme when selecting the opponents for his fighters. Kirk had chosen well, and if there was going to be a problem then it would be in how the twenty-year-old would adapt to working and living in London.

At first all went well as Laing trained harder than he had ever done in his life, mostly working alongside fellow West Indian Mo Hope – an excellent role model – and on 14 April 1975, he made an impressive introduction, stopping Joe Hannaford in two rounds back in his native Nottingham. That early super fitness, allied to Lawless's sensible matching, may have given Kirk the wrong idea about the pro business, for although he continued to win, he began to take liberties with his training, frequently disappearing home to Nottingham and soon only doing enough to scrape by. After all, wasn't he now being hailed as the best prospect to emerge from the Midlands since Randolph Turpin?

Yet even the brightest of prospects must put in the hours in the gym.

There were warning signs, such as a ten-round draw in Wolverhampton against Peter Morris, a boxer who had beaten him in the amateurs but who Laing was now expected to beat comfortably. Not for the first time, he ran out of steam in that fight and some thought him fortunate to get even a share. Kirk appeared to have got the message, for in the rematch later that year, he was much more motivated and readily stopped Morris in five rounds.

A pattern was being set, but despite being increasingly hard to handle, he was still undefeated in fifteen starts when he was awarded his first chance at a British title, and that night in Birmingham – 4 April 1979 – Laing was definitely in the right mood, stopping Henry Rhiney in ten rounds, and in the process flooring his opponent six times. Again, Kirk had fancied the job, had prepared well, and the results were obvious.

Almost exactly a year later, however, he was a former champion, and it is ironic that his first defence, against Colin Jones at Wembley, was staged on April Fools' Day. Ringsiders saw the two Kirkland Laings that night . . . the brilliant and the bewildering.

Colin Jones was a 21-year-old from Wales, still quite short on experience, but a methodical boxer and a seriously damaging puncher. He would later prove his worth in two memorable, but vain, tries for the W.B.C. title against Milton McCrory in America before suffering a cuts stoppage against Don Curry for the W.B.A. and I.B.F. versions of the championship in Birmingham. For eight rounds at Wembley, Laing made Jones appear a novice, building up a substantial lead, and then in the ninth, the Welshman caught him, dropped him, and the fight was stopped.

Was he tiring? Had he become too cocky? Or, when showing his chin, was this merely the case of a guy who was enjoying displaying his talents, being a millimetre adrift in his calculations? Perhaps a combination of all three, but his connections were stunned and Kirkland distraught. He could not believe that he had lost a fight that he was winning so easily. Yet, a year later, after three unremarkable wins, he was back against Jones with an opportunity to set the record straight, and the Albert Hall crowd witnessed a rerun of their first meeting – Laing dominating for eight rounds and being stopped in the ninth.

Only with Kirkland Laing could lightning strike twice. All sorts of theories can be put forward for a loss, but two identical losses? Jones's walk-forward style should have been ideal for Laing and for sixteen rounds it was, but on both occasions it was the Welshman's hand that was raised. Kirk's career was in tatters and fans who liked to back their judgement with a few pounds were fast despairing of him.

He was now 26. He had been an amateur champion and a professional champion, if only at the domestic level, and after two such ego-shattering defeats, there are many boxers who would have been satisfied with what they had achieved, bought a case for their trophies, pasted the final cuttings in the scrapbook, and buckled down to the day job. But for Kirk, boxing *was* the day job, and like so many other contrary artists, he could find reasons, not excuses, for his peccadilloes. He would soldier on, but an uninspiring twelve-round points win in a title eliminator against Cliff Gilpin, followed by a points defeat against Reggie Ford at the Albert Hall, did not bode well.

The long-suffering Lawless, rather than experience a coronary, had decided that enough was enough, and now Mickey Duff took over Laing's management. The mere fact that Duff was prepared to persevere with The Wayward One speaks volumes for the fighter's ability. Mickey never had the time to spare on lost causes; he also had an old fighter's admiration for natural talent.

Duff must rank alongside any of boxing's great characters and hustlers on either side of the Atlantic. Industrious, encyclopaedic, opinionated, eager, ruthless, shrewd, Mickey Duff, from the early forties right through to the close of the century, was to be the Sammy Glick of the fight game.

Born Monek Prager in Tarnow, Poland, on 7 June 1929, this son of a rabbi arrived in London in 1938, started boxing as a twelve-year-old, adopted the name of a film character and turned pro under-age at fifteen, boxed 69 times, losing only eight, and retired at the ripe old age of nineteen. Whew! But, of course, he couldn't leave the sport alone and first became a matchmaker, subsequently being involved in all facets of the business, working corners, managing, promoting, staging shows all over Britain, and operating with his colleagues Astaire, Levene and Barrett in producing the major events in London. Throughout his career, in one capacity or another, he worked closely with no fewer than nineteen world champions.

Kirkland Laing was not to be one of them, but in the league of what-ifs, their partnership has to be right up there with the top challengers.

It was 1982 and Laing had earned a confidence-boosting win, stopping Joey Mack in Solihull. No big deal, but at least there was something to work on, and Duff could always travel a long way on very little. He had a hundred ears to the ground and the two of his pricked up when he heard that in the States, promoter Don King was searching for an opponent for Roberto Duran – a credible opponent, but not one that would likely queer the long-range objective to pair Roberto with Tony Ayala in a money-spinner.

At that time, not too many boxers would have thanked their manager for the offer of a face-up with Duran. Kirkland Laing might have been a natural talent, but Roberto came straight from the womb snarling and slugging, and would develop into one of the finest and most popular fighters of all time.

Roberto Duran was born in Guarare, Panama, on 16 June 1951, made his professional début as a sixteen-year-old, and by 21, was unbeaten in 28 contests when he challenged Scotland's Ken Buchanan for the W.B.A. lightweight belt in New York on 26 June 1972. There were two great fighters in the Madison Square Garden ring that night, but Buchanan failed to recover from a low blow in round thirteen and a legend was born. Duran could be a no-holds brawler but he was also an excellent boxer and, especially as a lightweight, a concussive puncher. One black mark remains that he never gave a return to Buchanan, whom he regarded as his toughest ever opponent, but he wiped out all the other challengers in the division, until he outgrew the weight and in 1980 handed Sugar Ray Leonard his first defeat when outpointing him for the W.B.C. welterweight title in Montreal.

There followed the notorious rematch in New Orleans when the fearsome Duran waved his glove in disgust, cried 'No mas' and quit in round eight. The shock waves from that astonishing capitulation reverberated throughout boxing for a long, long time; Leonard had been outpointing him, showboating, and making the Panamanian look foolish. Like Sonny Liston, another ring ogre, Roberto would fight any man, but he could never handle a public humiliation.

To win back the affection of his shell-shocked countrymen and the respect of the boxing world at large was never going to be easy, and after two low-key victories, he then lost in a bid for the W.B.C. light middleweight title, being outpointed by the excellent Wilfred Benitez in Las Vegas in January 1982. He was 31, had lost only three times in 77 contests, and as later events would prove (he subsequently won versions of two world titles and earned vast sums) he was anything but a punched-out wreck. But he desperately needed a good win.

Why pick Laing? Don King would never have had the time or inclination to delve into the nuances of the Science; probably the Duran camp took a rapid glance through Kirkland's record, spotted two losses from his last four fights and said okay; and Mickey Duff would have been the last man to put any innocent wise as to just what his mercurial charge might deliver. And so the match was made for Detroit on 4 September 1982.

Students of Scottish international soccer will be familiar with the scenario: often dire and disappointing against the most ordinary teams, but on occasion, outstanding when given no chance. That was Laing and this was the perfect showcase for him to demonstrate his skills. He never went into the ring more confident or better prepared physically, and for ten rounds he produced quality boxing and punching against a Duran who found himself deep in another Leonard nightmare. The verdict was beyond dispute.

As it turned out, that was to be the highlight of Laing's career, but it need not have been that way. Beating Duran had rocketed him into the major league. Even better from his point of view, Ray Leonard was on the brink of retiring for the first time because of eye problems (his official announcement came in November) and both the W.B.C. and the W.B.A. were in the market for contenders for what were soon going to be vacant championships. Opportunities abounded and there was nobody better in the business to exploit the situation than manager Duff . . . but for six frustrating months he couldn't make contact with his fighter.

Kirkland had vanished and by the time he resurfaced, Don Curry had outpointed Jun-Sok Hwang for the W.B.A. belt, and his old hoodoo Colin Jones had boxed a stirring draw in the first of his fights against Milton McCrory for the W.B.C. version. Had he been around, Laing would surely have been awarded one of those contender slots and the considerable money that accompanied such a chance.

No matter what domestic delights or traumas Kirk experienced when he went underground, he should have kept at least one eye on business. Maybe he felt that having beaten Duran, he deserved a break before relaunching his drive to the world title; perhaps he was just enjoying his money. But in boxing, hot properties soon cool off, and there was no doubt he had blown it bigtime.

One year and several days would pass before Laing would fight again, and all the credibility he had so brilliantly earned against Duran was destroyed when he was knocked out by a heavy hitter called Fred Hutchings in the tenth round in Atlantic City. Hutchings would progress to a well-paid, if short-lived, world challenge against Thomas Hearns; Kirk had to go to hospital for repairs. Another fourteen months out of the ring, and then he was back with a stoppage win against Darwin Brewster at Wembley. No question, Laing could still deliver, and even if a world title shot was now not much better than a pipe dream, there were still lesser championships to be won. And curiously, now dreadlocked, and with his stance adapted and akin to that of an arrogant matador, he started to develop a cult following.

Boxing is awash with championship belts, usually tawdry eyesores which reflect the organisations who present them. But the Lonsdale Belt, on offer to British champions, is still a beautiful prize that any boxer would be proud to own. The original belts were launched in 1909 and the first 22 struck were donated by the Club's president, Lord Lonsdale. In 1936, the British Boxing Board reintroduced a less valuable, but still extremely attractive, belt, and for a fighter to own one outright, he had to win three title fights at the one weight. In the nineties, the Sheffield light middleweight Ryan Rhodes raced to his Lonsdale in a record ninety days. Kirkland Laing can also claim a Lonsdale record, taking eight years and seven months finally to make one his own property!

On 14 March 1987, he rewon the British championship that Jones had so stunningly removed from him such a long time back, halting Sylvester Mittee in five rounds in London; and the following November, he finally won the belt outright when referee Larry O'Connell had to rescue the youthful Rocky Kelly in the fifth round at Fulham, after Laing had floored him with a fast, perfectly timed right.

But he was still on that roller-coaster. There was only one appearance in 1988 – a Wembley win against Sammy Floyd – and the following year he lost an iffy verdict in a European bid against Nino La Rocca in Italy. He still knew far too much for his British contenders such as George Collins, but 1990 got off to a horrendous start when an American import, Buck Smith, got a clean shot at his chin and knocked him out in six rounds. Two months later, however, the irrepressible Laing, following another successful British defence against Trevor Smith, found himself European champion after stopping Antoine Fernandez in the second at Wembley. It was the most important title he was ever to hold, but he kept it for only six months.

Strange things can happen in Italy, and following the La Rocca experience, Laing knew he could expect few favours. But his defence against a former Olympic gold, Patrizio Oliva, was to prove bizarre even by Kirkland Laing standards.

The timekeeper must have had a liking for the local vino because every one of the scheduled twelve rounds lasted well over the stipulated three minutes, the final round actually being timed at an incredible four minutes and 37 seconds! But it wasn't lack of stamina over what turned out in reality to be a fourteen-rounds fight that cost Laing the decision. True, he had had to make three visits to the scales at the weigh-in; also true that he suffered a bad cut to his left eye from a butt in the sixth; and true again that he was frequently badgered by a Spanish referee who also allowed Oliva many liberties None of all that could have helped his cause, but the bottom line was that, on the other guy's turf, he had failed to do enough work against an inferior opponent. Once more, he had blown it.

Had he beaten Oliva, who had a solid reputation, there is little doubt that even although he was now 36, Duff could still have engineered a shot at one of the big belts. But that had been the story of Laing's career, right from his amateur days . . . if only.

Kirk had always relied on his razor-like reflexes to make opponents miss and set up his own counters, but these were beginning to erode alarmingly and in his next contest – what should have been another routine British defence against a tough southpaw Del Bryan in London – he looked lethargic and lost his title on points. That was the first time he had been beaten in consecutive fights as a professional, and exactly three months later, back in his home town of Nottingham, he was to complete a sad hat-trick when Canada's Donovan Boucher knocked him out in the ninth in a Commonwealth championship bout. The magic had gone for good.

But it was boxing that paid the bills and he would continue until 1994 when he was a forty-year-old. He had won 43 of his 56 pro fights, had been a European champion, a two-times British champion, had his own Lonsdale Belt, and had beaten the great Roberto Duran. Some might describe that as a glittering career, but in reality, Laing should have been able to boast of much, much more.

Kirkland always liked to think of himself as The Gifted One and few would quibble with that. But all too often he thumbed his nose at those special presents, and after that magic night when he turned over Duran, he did not bother even to open the gift box. What a waste!

PART THREE

Bad Boys

Tony Janiro loved to box, but he also loved the ladies. By the time he was twenty-two both his loves had left their scars.

Mitch Green was a bossman on the street until Mike Tyson fought a 4 a.m. return with him. After that, he was the boss of nowhere.

Tony Ayala spent sixteen years paying for his desperate crimes, but still he thinks he can be a contender.

For fighters, old habits can die hard

7

Tony Janiro:
'He Drank Scotch Very Well'

ROCKY GRAZIANO and Jake La Motta were the leaders of the pack; the original Dead End Kids who completed the trek from the slums and the streets and the reform schools and the jails all the way to the middleweight championship of the world. Old cellmates, they both took a turn at being the champ. Later Paul Newman would portray Graziano, and later again, Robert De Niro would be unforgettable as La Motta, and after that, it wasn't only the aficionados who were experts about The Rock and The Bull.

Their prime time was the forties, a decade when Joe Louis went into gradual decline and his heavyweight division was increasingly being forced to take a back seat to several of the more exciting lighter weights, from where emerged a group of highly colourful attractions who started regularly to pack out the cavernous Madison Square Garden.

There was tough Terry Young, a hugely popular lightweight from New York's East Side, who actually introduced Graziano to the business, but who, unlike Rocky, could never leave the mean streets behind him. And there was Young's cousin, Lulu Costantino, who battled fine lightweight champions like Beau Jack and Bob Montgomery and Ike Williams and who somehow avoided the mayhem that cousin Terry was doomed to search out.

There was Tony Pellone, a hardcase welter from Greenwich Village, and there was the rumbustious Al Davis, Boomy to his friends, Bummy to the fans who used to boo him in the Garden. And then there was the teenage Tony Janiro, as flashily talented as any of those Garden headliners, and with a drawing power almost as magnetic as that of the extraordinary Beau Jack or the great Graziano himself. Janiro, with his babyface good looks and his cheering section of adoring females: the undisputed playboy champion of forties boxing.

Janiro wasn't reared alongside budding career gangsters, unlike Bummy Davis, who was born Abraham Davidoff in Brooklyn's Brownsville district, and who palled around with Bo Weinberg, until Bo was cemented to the bottom of the East River, courtesy of Dutch Schultz. Nor had he a pedigree of juvenile crime like the young Rocco Barbella, who would become Graziano. And in contrast to the surly, suspicious La Motta, everybody had a good word for Tony. He wasn't even a New Yorker, originating from Youngstown, Ohio, which had a history of producing decent fighting men.

Yet like his contemporaries, he had known the rough days of the Depression. His father had walked out on the family and did not resurface until Tony was earning the big purses in the Garden; the five children were put in care, but eventually his hard-working mother reunited them. Tony had had it tough, but whereas Graziano and La Motta quickly grew to appreciate the value of a dollar, the young man from Ohio could not spend his fortune fast enough.

Tony Janiro was a fresh-faced seventeen-year-old when, in 1943, he arrived in New York with an introduction to one of the more prominent managers, Frankie Jacobs, also part owner of The Neutral Corner, a popular hangout for the boxing fraternity. Sportswriters liked to refer to characters such as Frankie Jay, as he was known in the trade, as 'colourful', a euphemism that could cover a lot of territory, but Jacobs certainly was well connected and could guarantee the youngster plenty of work.

Back then, it was the norm for a fighter to box at least once a month, keeping busy, building up first a neighbourhood following, then hopefully a city-wide support that would attract the attention of the Garden scouts. Al Davis, for example, started out as a teenager in 1937, and in his first three years fought 39 times, winning 24 inside the distance thanks to his devastating left hook, and going undefeated until the reigning lightweight champion Lou Ambers outpointed him in a

Garden non-title fight in February 1940. Nothing much would go right for Bummy after that.

In 1943, Janiro's début year, Graziano was fighting eighteen times at the small clubs in and around New York, and La Motta was in action thirteen times, but only twice in the Big Apple. Manager Jacobs did not waste any time in getting young Tony earning, and in his first eighteen months as a professional, he won 23 times, mostly in New Jersey, before he suffered his first defeat, a points loss to Al Guido in New York.

In those early years, the new welterweight sensation had so much going for him. Janiro was a beautiful boxer and mover who could throw bewilderingly fast and accurate combinations. He had a terrific chin, oozed both courage and confidence, and was blessed to have a conscientious, patient training team in Ray Arcel and his partner Freddie Brown. *The Ring*'s Nat Fleischer labelled Tony 'another Benny Leonard' and the fans flocked to see him.

Although he was not an especially hard puncher, his other attributes should have guaranteed him a relatively smooth path to a title fight; instead his new Broadway pals pointed him out the well-lit road to the best bars and brothels in town. Janiro was not even old enough to drink legally; could not even box a ten-rounder in New York because he was too young, but that wasn't going to stop Tony. He had discovered women and Scotch and was wondering how he had survived for so long without them!

Trainer Arcel, who tried to dampen some of boxing's finest free spirits, awarded his all-time vote to Janiro. 'When it came to the ladies,' he recalled, 'he was the champ.' And manager Jacobs, much later trying to explain some of their complex financial exchanges, remembered, 'He'd call and say "I'm flying home", which would cost $60 round trip. I'd have $200 and he'd want a thousand. And it would take another thousand to bring him back. He drank Scotch very well.'

Janiro was not the only headstrong kid in town. The Depression dropouts finally had money in their pockets, and they had never taken kindly to authority. Keeping them in check during their fighting careers, particularly during those madcap war years, was all but impossible, and compared to some of the lapses of his Stillman Gym colleagues, the young Janiro's indiscretions could have been viewed as little more than boyish, though costly, high jinks.

Terry Young, who once climbed as high as number three in *The Ring*'s lightweight category, was frequently at odds with the law: on bookmaking charges, then break-in offences, eventually spiralling to much worse. And his good pal Graziano's career was seriously interrupted early on by a sorry stint in the army, culminating in a dishonourable discharge.

Bummy Davis earned his 'dishonourable' about the same time and from the same stockade as Graziano, and his tale is the most pathetic of them all. After that first defeat by champion Ambers, Davis got his show back on the road; then in November 1940, he was matched in the Garden against Fritzie Zivic, the doyen of dirty fighters and the reigning welterweight champion. Both fighters fouled repeatedly in a savage opening round, and in the second, Davis, infuriated by Zivic's superior arsenal of dirty tricks, started punching low and wild until he was disqualified. By now, Bummy had totally lost the plot, started kicking the referee, and a minor riot ensued. The New York Athletic Commission suspended him for life.

Shortly after, he was called into the army, but behind the scenes a scheme evolved for him to box a return with Zivic in New York's Polo Grounds. The bait was that the promotion would be in aid of the Army Relief Fund, and after much wrangling, Athletic Commission chairman General John J. Phelan was persuaded to lift the ban. Davis, however, suffered a terrible beating from Zivic, was stopped in the tenth, and went AWOL from the army. A furious General Phelan immediately reimposed his ban, the M.P.s finally captured Bummy, and not long after, Uncle Sam slung him out for good.

The New York ban lasted three years, but Davis kept busy 'out of town', as Whitey Bimstein might have said, and when in the summer of 1943, after some intense politicking, his licence was returned, some great nights still awaited him. The biggest was a shock one-round Garden knockout of Bob Montgomery, who the following month won the lightweight belt from Beau Jack. But both Henry Armstrong and Beau Jack beat him, and when in May 1945 his fellow dishonourable, the much heavier Graziano, knocked him out in four rounds, Bummy was all but finished.

Ironically, in September of that year he won his very last fight on a second-round foul against Johnny Jones, and then announced his retirement. He never got the opportunity to change his mind and make a comeback for two months later, he was dead. On the evening of 21 November 1945 he returned to a bar that he had once owned to talk some business with the new proprietor. Four armed stick-up men walked in and once again Bummy saw red. He dropped one of the bandits with a left hook, but as he chased the partners out of the door he was shot several times and died on the pavement. He was 27 years old.

If 1945 signalled a tragic finish to Al Davis, the year also saw the emergence of both Janiro and Graziano as confirmed Madison Square Garden headliners, genuine Friday night heroes. On 9 March, Rocky, considered no better than a heavy-punching club fighter until then, went into the ring a 7/1 outsider against a red-hot Billy Arnold and knocked him out in three sensational rounds. And in the chief supporting contest, the youthful Janiro boxed like a dream to beat Monty Pignatore. Terry Young was also in the Garden that night, cheering on Graziano, and afterwards the two pals and title hopes were pictured together. But a month later, Terry Young was Sing Sing-bound after being nabbed during a hold-up.

Janiro was flying high and such was his popularity that the Garden executives broke with tradition and elevated him to main-event status, even though he could box only a maximum of eight rounds because of his age. For the remainder of 1945, he was to be involved in a tremendously exciting three-bout war against the uncompromising and hard-hitting Canadian champion Johnny Greco. The Montreal welter won their first meeting on points, Janiro got his revenge in the second, and both were close affairs.

The word was that Tony would get a non-title match with champion Red Cochrane if he won the decider, but this time Greco handed Janiro a terrific beating, a beating so severe that many ringsiders voiced concern that he was taking too many punches. He passed blood for a week, but then simply put the result down to experience, and concentrated on the serious business of enjoying life.

Tony Janiro was earning plenty and spending more; and now he had discovered the joys of horseracing, soon relishing a bet almost as much as he loved a drink or a woman. Almost. Everybody loved Tony, not only the bloodsuckers and the layabouts forever looking for a touch, but also the biggest stars of the era. There was none bigger at the time than Frank Sinatra and he counted himself a friend and a fan; the same went for Perry Como and Mickey Rooney. The pace was frenetic but somehow Janiro still managed to deliver in the ring. And then came that magic day when he was even old enough to engage in ten-rounders!

Amazingly, the babyface from Ohio had already fought 57 pro fights. But now, on 11 January 1947, three months after his twentieth birthday, he boxed his first scheduled ten-round contest, easily outpointing the rough and tough Tony Pellone, who had built up a following of his own in the small clubs.

The Garden chiefs could not get enough of Tony and no wonder! A month after Pellone, Janiro and Beau Jack attracted a crowd of over 18,000 for a match that carried no title label. For three sizzling rounds, Janiro might have just had the edge, but there was huge drama and anticlimax in the fourth when Beau collapsed with a broken knee – an injury that was to cause him grief for the rest of his career. Perhaps it could be described as a hollow victory, but still Tony pocketed $30,000.

Looking back, it is difficult to understand what sort of championship blueprint manager Jacobs was mapping out for his protégé, other than have him box regularly for big money. Certainly Tony's spend-spend lifestyle dictated that he had to keep earning, but often the selection of opponent was curious to say the least – one fight, he was boxing a lightweight, Beau Jack, next he was being thrown in with one of the roughest middleweights of all time, none other than the Bronx Bull, La Motta.

In Martin Scorsese's movie, *Raging Bull*, considerable dialogue and action centres on the La Motta–Janiro clash on 6 June 1947: how La Motta had to starve down to 155lb to accommodate his much lighter opponent or pay a forfeit of $15,000; how Jake's wife Vickie had him scenting blood when she referred to Tony as 'good-looking, attractive'; how Janiro wound up like the victim of a car wreck; how the mob chieftain remarked, 'He ain't pretty no more.'

Had it not been for a chance meeting between La Motta, Janiro and Frankie Jay in the Garden one morning when they were hunting up work, the fight would never have come about. Tony and Jake kidded back and forth, then the kidding grew to serious and Jake said he would train down to 155lb or stump up the fifteen grand, and the deal was struck. Jay and Janiro were gambling that La Motta – a heavy middleweight – could never scale so light and remain strong, but somehow the stubborn Jake managed to sweat off the pounds and still retain enough stamina to hammer out a decision. Janiro just didn't have the power to keep The Bull at bay, yet he finished on his feet.

Before that year's end, La Motta would play the villain in one of boxing's most shameful nights, and Janiro would find himself in a rather messy situation over a proposed fix.

This was a period when Frankie Carbo and his minions were making themselves particularly busy. Tales abounded of tank jobs and crooked judges and gambling coups, and there were plenty of wild rumours, but very few bent fights were ever proved. La Motta's appearance in the Garden on the evening of 14 November 1947, when he was stopped in four rounds by Blackjack Billy Fox, was, without doubt, a fraud. There had been wild fluctuations in the pre-fight betting, suggesting that something was seriously fishy, and so inept was La Motta's performance that there was little argument that he had lost deliberately. The knowledgeable Garden regulars howled their fury, and the following day in his *New York Daily Mirror* column, heavyweight writer Dan Parker blasted La Motta and his ham acting.

In the subsequent inquiry, Jake claimed that he had boxed while suffering from a ruptured spleen and had the medical evidence to back him up, and so the New York State Athletic Commision could fine him only $1,000 and suspend him for seven months for failing to report an injury. But in 1961, when the Statute of Limitations had expired and he was guaranteed immunity, a tearful La Motta confessed before a U.S. Senate Committee that he had indeed taken a dive, in order to facilitate getting a shot at the world title.

To make matters worse for boxing's image, La Motta's fellow delinquent, Graziano, was also in deep trouble with the Commission and barred from fighting in his home state. But there is no doubt now that Rocky was a victim of political chicanery, a conveniently soft target because of his bad record for a headline-hunting district attorney named Frank Hogan.

Graziano had cancelled a tune-up bout against a modest performer called Cowboy Reuben Shank because of a back injury. The D.A.'s office maintained that Graziano had been offered a $100,000 bribe to lose to Shank and had faked the injury rather than take the dive. There was absolutely no evidence to back up the allegations and no criminal charges were ever filed, but Hogan got his headlines, and then Colonel Eddie Eagan, the chairman of the New York Athletic Commission, decided to grab some of his own. He instigated a fresh investigation and barred Graziano for failing to report a bribe – a bribe that may never have been made for a fight that never took place.

No matter that Rocky had received a bum rap: he was exiled from New York and would have to win his title from Tony Zale in Chicago and then lose it back to Zale in Newark, New Jersey, and he didn't box again in his home town until 1949, when he knocked out Charley Fusari.

The attempt to nobble Janiro came three months after his loss to La Motta and there was considerable rumour and counter-rumour, but the Commission never got involved. The supposed bribe came in the build-up to Tony's return with Pellone, a match that, according to the newspapers, would see the winner get a crack at Sugar Ray Robinson's welterweight title. The incentive to lose was $35,000.

Aside from being a soft touch for five bucks here, a ten-spot there, the 21-year-old young man about Broadway had also made himself naïvely vulnerable to more sinister approaches. Sex and booze are the two principal no-nos when a boxer is in training, and knowing Janiro's predilection for both, invariably there were characters seeking him out, urging him to forget what those killjoys Ray Arcel and Freddie Brown were saying; guys who could set him up with this gorgeous girl or take him to that fabulous new bar. These were gambling men, looking for an edge when betting against their boozing buddy, hoping that the drink and the dames would take their toll. From there, it was only a short shuffle to offering the wide-eyed youngster a fistful of dollars outright to take a dive.

Thirty-five grand was a fortune in 1947, and it was never established if Janiro initially agreed to the proposition, or hedged on turning it down out of hand, but when Jacobs and Arcel heard the rumours, they confronted their fighter, who in turn contacted the bribe merchants, telling them he would be fighting to win. On 19 September, he boxed rings around Tony Pellone to win a unanimous decision.

He did not get any title match with Robinson, but then, neither did he wind up face down in a Jersey swamp, and the chances are that Janiro's bribe came from freelance gamblers rather than the Mob. When Carbo made one of his suggestions, there was never any physical danger in turning it down flat; but once having said yes to The Man, there could be no reneging. Even such a popular high-flier as Tony would have been checking for broken bones had he crossed Mr Gray.

But life in the fast lane was at last having its effect. The endless merry-go-round of partying and drinking sprees, the cavalier attitude to getting into proper shape, and the sheer accumulation of fights – many of them desperately tough – were ageing the youngster. At 22, he was a seasoned professional and had he taken care of himself, he should have been ready to launch a bid for the championship. But the punishment his body was soaking up outside the ropes was slowing him down inside them, and now, for the first time, there were real money pressures.

Janiro had always carried around a large roll and was famous throughout the city for his crazy generosity, but now there was a wife, Rita, and a son, young Anthony, to look after as well as the usual gang of backslappers and bartenders and bookmakers and blondes. For sure, Tony hadn't mended his ways, but now the lucrative Garden appearances were becoming less frequent, and although he was still winning, victories over guys like Indian Gomez and Joe Agosta and Lou Valles and Frankie Cordino only provided him with betting and drinking money, and did nothing for his ranking.

In his biggest fight in 1948, he was outpointed by *The Ring*'s Rookie of the Year, Laverne Roach, before a 12,000 crowd in the Garden. Twelve months earlier, Janiro would have been a hot favourite to outclass the Texan, but much had happened in that year. In the following months, there were a couple of decent pay-nights in Britain, losing to the local welter champion Henry Hall and stopping a Welshman, Gwyn Williams, but by now the slide could not be stemmed.

There was, however, to be one last hurrah – which developed into three last hurrahs! – against none other than his old buddy, Graziano. Like Janiro, Rocky's great fighting days were long gone, and although he was comfortably fixed financially, he saw no harm in accepting the large sums he could still command. And, of course, Tony would be a perfect opponent: considerably lighter, no great shakes as a puncher, and definitely past his best.

On Friday, 31 March 1950, Janiro came agonisingly close to queering the script. Before a boisterous crowd of 16,983, which paid a whopping $81,049 to see Graziano in his first Garden appearance since getting reinstated in New York, the seven-pounds-lighter Janiro ran the ex-champ ragged for half the fight, before tiring badly in the late rounds. Many thought he had done just enough to win, but on such a gala night, few quibbled with the announced draw. Tony's purse was a very healthy $14,000 (in his very next fight – a tune-up against an old rival Al Guido in Elizabeth, New Jersey – he earned $300!); he was delighted to be asked to do it all over again in the October, and this time Graziano was awarded the verdict.

If not exactly hot again, Janiro was better than lukewarm and in June 1951 he caused a big upset when outpointing Charley Fusari. That set the stage for yet another Graziano fight in September, this time in Detroit, and this time Rocky won in the tenth. Janiro was played out, but two months later he was back at the Detroit Olympia, losing in four rounds to Kid Gavilan. Tony was all washed up and he was only 25.

Especially back then, it was more the rule than the exception for a boxer to wind up broke, but most managed to survive at least a year or two of bad investments and freeloading friends before the tank ran dry. Not Janiro. Right after the Gavilan defeat, he was stony; not only penniless but seriously in debt to the Internal Revenue Service. He had earned the best part of half a million dollars in his meteoric career, but his manager hadn't even taken care of his tax affairs.

Frankie Jay was no prize, but could anyone have put a rein on Janiro? Extremely unlikely, for, terrific guy that he was, Tony was no

Einstein. Master of the magnanimous gesture, Frankie provided him with a job in his bar, The Neutral Corner, and that must have been really hard at first for Janiro, who was on drinking terms with the majority of the clientele.

However, in the summer of 1952, there came the chance of some decent money when he was offered a fight in France against a durable performer called Charles Humez. With difficulty, he worked himself into some sort of shape, somehow lasted four rounds in Paris, and returned to New York with $7,000. But he blew the lot within a couple of weeks, and in the long years to come, Janiro would pay dearly for those mad days when he was the hottest ticket on Broadway. Son Anthony died a junkie, then wife Rita died, and after many years tending bar in New York, his own health failed, and he finally went home to Youngstown, where he lived modestly and reasonably content until his death on 19 February 1985. He was 58.

Unlike Graziano and La Motta, who were always alert to everything around them, Terry Young and Bummy Davis and Tony Janiro were forever doomed to self-destruct. Those wild Dead End Kids were certainly no role models, but they brought a pulsating life to the fight game in those vintage long-gone Friday nights at the Garden, and provided some of boxing's most exciting moments . . . though, alas, never when a title was at stake.

8

Mitch Green:
'King of the Jailhouse'

DON KING has always known the secret password into the minds of black fighters, particularly black fighters from the ghetto, and especially black fighters from the ghetto who also happen to be large, intimidating heavyweights. Long before he restyled his hair to shock-horror chic and carved out his huge personal fortune from promoting some of the most spectacular boxing events ever staged, Don could talk the talk and walk the walk, and like so many of the boxers who would come under his spell, he was a product of the streets who acquired his education in the joint. Of equal significance, he was the first black promoter of championship boxing.

This shamelessly amoral buccaneer – a one-time Cleveland numbers boss responsible for the deaths of two men – has been pursued relentlessly by the F.B.I. and investigated by the I.R.S., while at the same time, wining, dining and cutting deals with heads of state and television moguls. He has been beaten up by vengeful Black Muslims; has battled in the courts with a seemingly endless stream of irate, former partners and sad, disillusioned boxers; can bluster for an hour without pausing for breath, but when required, he can muzzle up and plead the Fifth like a grand old trouper.

In thirty years of scheming and conniving and ducking and diving, Don King has proved himself time after time to be boxing's greatest survivor.

His first killing, a shooting in 1954, was ruled 'justifiable homicide' and when, in September 1971, he was released from Ohio's Marion Correctional Institution, having served three years and eleven months of a manslaughter rap after stamping to death one Sam Garrett, he decided to move into boxing, and typically, opted to start at the top.

Thanks to a combination of exuberant imagination, brilliant opportunism, and an unbelievable brass neck, he staged a benefit promotion, ostensibly to avert the closure of a Cleveland hospital, and succeeded in persuading no less a personage than Muhammad Ali to top the bill in an exhibition. This was a major coup, and almost a decade and millions of dollars later, King was still sweet-talking Ali – not to mention seriously short-changing him – when he promoted Muhammad's pathetic, penultimate appearance against Larry Holmes in Las Vegas on 2 October 1980. For a considerable time thereafter, King, employing his stepson Carl as a managerial stooge, would control the destiny of practically every worthwhile heavyweight in the ratings, and with almost no exceptions, they would all part company from the Kings chorusing 'robbery'.

Some of those heavyweights – big, dangerous men in the ring, it must be remembered – would cope better than others with the trauma.

The Easton Assassin, Larry Holmes, owns considerable chunks of his home town thanks to the millions he earned boxing for King, but there were millions more that he maintained were siphoned off, and the bitterness lingers on. Terrible Tim Witherspoon fought his longest and bravest battle in the courts before eventually seeing justice done; and Michael Dokes, Greg Page, Tony Tubbs, Pinklon Thomas, Trevor Berbick, Bonecrusher Smith and Tony Tucker all went through agonies after experiencing life with the Kings.

Some of those fighters lost their ambition, cheated on their training, and grew fat; others sought solace in heroin and crack; but those made of sterner stuff just bit harder on the mouthpiece and got on with making a living. Until Tyson arrived on the scene, King was running the only heavyweight game in town, and in a bewildering spell in the eighties, all his men contrived to hold one version or another of the heavyweight championship. At least they would have some good memories, however fleeting.

A large New Yorker called Mitchell Green might well have qualified for membership of that band of belt holders; so too might one of King's earliest heavyweight hopefuls, Jeff Merritt; and given the breaks, there were many more who instead wound up as supporting players in the big Las Vegas extravaganzas and as sparring help at the training camps. That they finished up residents of Palookaville is not, of course, all down to the Don; some were simply not good enough, others lacked the drive and the discipline. But as Schulberg's former pug, Terry Malloy, might have said, 'King could've looked out for them a little bit. Could've taken care of them. Just a little bit.'

Admittedly, watching over either Green or Merritt could have developed quickly into a full-time occupation. Far from the most stable of characters, Mitch Green could neither forgive nor forget after sampling King's sleight-of-contract just before the biggest fight of his life. What had been no more than a routine exercise in purse-cutting for the promoter became an obsession for the big man they called Blood on the streets and, in a flood of paranoia, he simply allowed his career to vanish down the tubes, ranting and raving for a kind of fair play that he was unlikely ever to find in the merciless world of boxing. King probably could have appeased him with a few grand; instead, he chose to ignore Green, which only inflamed the fighter's frustration.

Jeff Merritt was also talented but flaky. The boxer they called Candy Slim graduated from Missouri State Prison – its most famous alumnus was ex-champ Sonny Liston – to go on to break Earnie Shavers's jaw, and knock out Ernie Terrell in one round at the Garden. But he couldn't stay on the straight, nor could he resist the dope, and nobody can drop that baggage at the door of his then manager D.K. But perhaps with a little more care, a little more attention . . .? King, however, has a smile that somehow never reaches to his eyes, and he possesses an extraordinary indifference to those around him needing a hand up. Whatever his talents, and he has many, counselling is not one of them.

In his early years, Mitch Green certainly did not lack for opportunity, affection or attention. The would-be tough guy from the Jamaica section of Queens enjoyed the support of a loving and loyal mother, Charlene, and a caring, college graduate younger brother, Jerry. But out on the streets, he transformed into Blood, president of the Black Spades; nobody messed with the bossman and he discovered he could also box a bit. And as he grew into a 6ft 5in 225lb giant, complete with moustache, whiskers, long, straggly hair, and a trade-mark toothpick, he learned to move and punch well enough to win four New York Golden Gloves titles and attract professional interest. Big bucks were awaiting.

From a bundle of offers, the 24-year-old chose to go pro with Shelly Finkel, who had made his money promoting pop concerts, and Lou Duva, a squat, hardcore boxing veteran. Along with other members of the Duva clan, they formed a highly successful organisation which would later include such luminaries as Evander Holyfield, Pernell Whitaker and many other class acts from the amateurs.

Green had done well for himself, and he was delighted with his first purse – a very respectable $10,000 for a one-round blowout of Jerry Foley at Lake Tahoe in November 1980. But as he remained undefeated through his first three years of fighting, this born rabble-rouser began to plague Finkel and Duva with complaints over the size of his wages. Mitch claimed he was worth more than the television networks were prepared to offer his management, and he grew increasingly hard to handle.

This has been a scenario played and replayed throughout the history of boxing: the fighter starts earning some decent money, but his friends tell him he should be making much more, and, of course, he starts to listen; inevitably a bad situation arises that often results in a strained relationship, but just as often winds up in litigation. Only the lawyers are winners. Mitch Green, naturally, thought he knew best. After all, wasn't he the guy with the street smarts, the big, bad dude who spelt grim tidings for anyone who crossed him? Mitch loved role playing, whether he cast himself as the toughest guy on the block or the hottest prospect in the ring; what he did not love was the application and dedication required to be the latter. A divorce from Finkel and Duva became inevitable.

Within the business, he was acquiring the reputation of being a troublesome headbanger, but nevertheless an extremely marketable headbanger, and it was no surprise when he joined King's heavyweight circus, stepson Carl becoming his official manager; nor was it a surprise when he was soon bitching louder than ever about his earnings. He had enlisted in a heavyweight army that was always on the brink of mutiny, and it wasn't long before he became one of its noisiest agitators. The bellyaching abated, however, when King booked him to headline in the main arena at Madison Square Garden against a young, unbeaten prospect named Mike Tyson. A chance at the championship was a distinct possibility if he could only do the business on 20 May 1986.

Tyson was the sensational protégé of boxing guru Cus D'Amato, bankrolled by the millions of co-managers Jim Jacobs and Bill Cayton; and considering all the grief that has enveloped him in recent years, it is rather sad to recall that back then no fighter had ever enjoyed such a privileged and meticulously orchestrated build-up towards winning the championship. Every future opponent was thoroughly scrutinised, his training programme was scrupulous in its attention to detail; no expense was spared, and even if the young Mike did occasionally stray offside, then the problems were handled without any media embarrassment. When he signed to box Green, Tyson was nineteen, and had won twenty in a row.

But on paper at least, Blood was no lost cause. He had been beaten only once in eighteen fights – a 1985 points loss to Trevor Berbick for the U.S.B.A. title (two fights later Berbick would win the W.B.C. belt) – and was ranked seventh by the W.B.C. He had significant advantages in height and reach, was a smart boxer, a good puncher with a sound chin, and to give him real encouragement, only seventeen days earlier, Tyson had been forced to travel the full distance for the first time, against James Tillis.

This would be the first occasion that King would promote one of Iron Mike's fights, and no doubt, when he made the match he was hoping that his fighter would ruin all the dreams of Team Tyson. But by the time the boxers stepped into the ring, both Kings were wishing more hurt on Mitch than even Tyson might be expected to inflict.

The reason, of course, was dosh. Naturally, Tyson was the attraction, and as such was going to collect the bulk of the money. He was on a $200,000 guarantee, off which a number of expenses were to be deducted, and this would also be his first fight in a package deal with Home Box Office, who were paying him $450,000, a handsome renumeration. Green was originally on a flat $50,000, but in the lead-up to the fight, this was reduced to $30,000 by the Kings. Aside from the hit to his pocket, the enormous disparity in the wages was a savage blow to Mitch's ego and at the Garden weighing-in ceremony he started to rumble.

At first he appeared to be mumbling through his toothpick, but only to himself, 'They ain't been paying me'; and as the assembled media started shoving microphones and tape recorders under his nose, the fighter built up to full tempo and volume. 'I have no manager to negotiate for me. I've got Don King's son as a manager. Whatever Don King decides to give me is all right with my manager. And whatever they give me, I have to take. That's why I don't fight much.'

When Carl King arrived, Green started waving a finger in his face and the manager pushed it aside, insisting that the fighter had long known that his purse was going to be $30,000. The situation was bordering on the chaotic, and former light heavyweight champion Jose Torres, in his capacity as chairman of the New York State Athletic Commission, warned Green that he faced a possible life ban if he pulled out of the fight.

Being such an erratic customer, there was always the danger of Blood heading off on a trip, but he arrived on schedule at the Garden, and in his dressing room he was calm and collected, in fact extremely laid back. Unfortunately, his passivity accompanied him into the ring, and instead of employing his considerable attributes, it was soon apparent that his prime concern was survival. He held and wrestled and spoiled, but in the third, Tyson still managed to knock his mouthpiece – complete with bridgework and two false teeth embedded in it – on to the ring apron. For the full ten rounds, Mitch stood up under a comprehensive beating from a methodical Tyson, who seemed to be enjoying his workout, especially as he was taking little in return. The spectacle was eminently forgettable, the decision unanimous and lopsided.

Don King had been furious at Green's outburst at the weigh-in, particularly as he had been trying to ingratiate himself with Jacobs and Cayton, and contemplating doing future business with Tyson; he had even felt the need to hire a couple of bodyguards just in case his heavyweight tried to deliver on his threats, and the entire episode, he decided, might have put him in a bad light with Mike's managers. But D.K. had always regarded his fighters as commodities and Green still had some value; the promoter was not yet ready to cut him loose.

And so it came about that later that year Blood would be a bit player – with one or two memorable lines! – in an extraordinary heavyweight wrangle, and once again, he would wind up as one of the victims of the Don's machinations.

Tim Witherspoon had been scheduled to defend his W.B.A. belt against Tony Tubbs in the Garden on 12 December, but Tubbs called off because of a shoulder injury, and in order that the precious television date would not be lost, King drafted in James Bonecrusher Smith as a substitute. An unpublicised proviso was that the ubiquitous Carl King would become his co-manager, despite the fact that he was also the manager of Witherspoon! This was in total contravention of the Commission's rules, but the rules were not going to scupper a big fight. A troubled Witherspoon, unhappy at the turn of events, sought legal counsel and tried to get out of the match, but the pressure on him proved too great. He went into the ring confused and disillusioned, and was knocked down three times in the first round before the bout was stopped.

Smith was a big winner and Mitchell Green a medium-sized loser, because that same weekend, he had been booked to box the Bonecrusher on the supporting card, before Smith was upgraded to the championship gig. He had been robbed of a pay day, and at a pre-fight Garden press conference, he once again vented his fury against the Kings, demanding all the money he claimed he was owed, and threatening to break the promoter's neck. King, smiling nervously, called for security and kept a safe distance until the demented Mitch was persuaded to leave.

The Kings were finally done with Green, but Mitch could not shake the Don loose from his head, an extremely confused head that increasingly was fuelled by booze or angel dust or a variety of other prohibited substances. The giant guy who liked to boast that he was king of the jailhouse whenever he enjoyed one of his sojourns at Rikers Island, the New York City Penitentiary, was in fact no great shakes as a criminal: most of his misdeeds could be described as mad rather than bad. For all manner of infractions, he had had his driving licence suspended over sixty times; he was forever getting into senseless scuffles with the police; and in one highly publicised jape, he chased away the attendant from a filling station, commandeered the pumps, started selling to customers, and pocketed the takings. Hardly the work of a budding Lucky Luciano.

Jeff Merritt, on the other hand, was a far more dangerous lawbreaker. One of ten children, Candy Slim, like his hero Liston, learned his boxing in Missouri State, where he was serving a lengthy stretch for armed robbery. He had completed 29 months and was still a month short of his 21st birthday when he was paroled in December 1967; and having gone unbeaten as an amateur, there were plenty on the outside prepared to lend him a hand in turning pro – including former champions Liston, Joe Louis and Sandy Saddler. Bill Perry was appointed manager; he knocked out Ronnie Williams in one round on his début in New York on 23 February 1968; and apart from a hiccup in his sixth contest against John Gause, he compiled a promising sequence of victories.

The same height and weight as Mitch Green, Merritt threw a dynamite left hook, but also like Green, he was a nightmare to control. There were unexplained disappearances, rows over money, domestic beefs, heartache over heroin, and not surprisingly, Perry finally gave up on him. Bob Arum, then the foremost promoter, displayed a fleeting interest, and there was a spell in Florida at Angelo Dundee's gym but that also failed to work out. The heavyweight's career was headed nowhere, but in Miami, his punching had impressed Ali's soul mate Bundini Brown, who contacted Don King with a good word.

At that time, the Don was still just a voracious student of the business, and along with another Cleveland entrepreneur, Blackie Gennaro, he was doing quite nicely, co-managing a leading heavyweight contender, Earnie Shavers, who was fresh from a one-round knockout over Jimmy Ellis in the Garden.

Bundini sold King on Merritt's capabilities, but before D.K. could sign him to a contract and get him licensed in New York, there were a number of problems to be ironed out, not least an outstanding burglary charge in Manhattan, which was finally plea-bargained down to the time already served by the boxer. And then, before Candy Slim had even earned a dollar for his new mentor, he unintentionally sabotaged King's summer plans by hospitalising his star performer Shavers, breaking his jaw in two places during a training session at Grossingers, a Catskills resort, long used by boxers as a training camp. Former great Archie Moore, who was supervising the session, was summarily fired by King; Shavers's Garden date against Jerry Quarry was postponed; and Merritt's debut for his new promoter was delayed until September.

The publicity generated by the Shavers incident was priceless, and Merritt's newest campaign gathered momentum when, on 10 September 1973, he knocked out former W.B.A. champion Ernest Terrell in one round in the Garden; and when he performed another quick job on a tough, one-time contender, Ron Stander, in Cleveland, it appeared that Candy Slim was at last getting his act together. Wishful thinking. He was still running wild, doing drugs, skipping training, and when he was knocked out by Henry Clark – a fighter he had already beaten – he found himself once again at the bottom of the ladder, once more in the twilight world of guns and dope and robberies and jail sentences. He was washed up as a fighter and all but washed up as a human being; when he was out of jail, he would roam the Las Vegas hotel lobbies before the big fights, begging for a few bucks, complaining about King and how he had robbed him. But it was Candy Slim who had been the robber and the deceiver.

Mitchell Green would also be a regular whenever the fight crowd gathered and invariably he would badmouth King and deride Tyson: not only had he been financially fleeced, but Tyson hadn't really beaten him, because his head had been too screwed up to concentrate on his big night. Mitch had never officially announced his retirement, although he hadn't boxed since Tyson, and occasionally he would talk to a trainer or a manager about his future; around the gyms, however, he was fast becoming a bad joke. But that all changed in the early hours of 23 August 1988, when suddenly he became one of the hottest properties in boxing.

It was four o'clock in the morning, a time when boxers should be enjoying their last hours of sleep before rising for roadwork, but in

Harlem, Mike Tyson and friends were pulling up in a Rolls-Royce outside Dapper Dan's, an all-night boutique on East 125th Street; just a few blocks away, Blood Green was on a nocturnal prowl, and on getting the word that the champ was in the area, he hurried to confront his old foe.

Outside Dapper Dan's, Mitch went through his complete repertoire, all but hysterical and incoherent: how Tyson hadn't really beaten him; how King would have to pay; how because he (Tyson) was tied in with King, they both owed him money. There are conflicting stories about what happened next, but the upshot was that Tyson suffered a torn shirt, a broken wing mirror on his Rolls, and a hand fracture that led to the postponement of his defence against Frank Bruno. Green's left eye had been shut tight and he required five stitches to close a deep gash between his eyes. The story made headlines around the world, and once again Mitch Green was an extremely marketable heavyweight, even though all the evidence had suggested he had been a clear second-best in the street.

A natural grudge match, a Tyson–Green return became a serious possibility. There was only one snag: Green had not fought since their 1986 bout and had been dropped from all the ratings. He would have to beat somebody in the top ten to qualify for the title shot, but that should not have been an insurmountable obstacle. And when manager Bill Cayton gave Green a letter of agreement saying he could have a fight with the champion, in exchange for Mitch dropping charges he had filed against Tyson, the deal looked as if it was all but done.

For a couple of weeks, Green preened and postured, gave smart-ass interviews and basked in the publicity. But somehow all the offers to match him with the required contender weren't good enough, and in his sporadic visits to the gym, he conned and kidded but never got down to any serious work. He was throwing away the opportunity of a lifetime – a possible shot at the undisputed heavyweight championship of the world – and as the days passed, the media frenzy died down, and the loyal few who still genuinely cared about Mitch just shook their heads and got on with their lives.

About four weeks later, the reluctant heavyweight was arrested for causing a traffic jam while once again ranting and raving about what he was going to do to Mike Tyson. Officers had to subdue him with electric stun guns.

Jeff Merritt and Mitch Green would have been gigantic misfits in any walk of life. They both liked to think of themselves as fighters, but in truth, neither of them really belonged in the ring, although they both came so close to boxing for the richest prize in sport. Perhaps Don King could have looked after them a little better, but not even the Don should take the rap for what befell Candy Slim and Blood. Nobody should.

9

Tony Ayala Jr:
'A Cinch to Be Champion'

TONY AYALA JR may be able to boast the longest unbeaten streak in the history of boxing, but this is one record of more relevance to the anoraks and pub quiz specialists than it is to the sports purists. True, Ayala never experienced defeat in the ring from when he was a precociously talented eight-year-old until he was a balding, thick-set pro of 37 but for sixteen of those intervening years, he was what you might describe as inactive: Tony Ayala Jr had been a guest of the state of New Jersey for the most desperate crimes.

On 20 April 1999, when he walked free from Bayside State Prison, having served the sixteen of a thirty-five-year sentence for the rape of a thirty-year-old schoolteacher, burgalry, and possession of a knife, there to meet him were his father Tony Sr, his mother, Pauline, and his attractive former wife, Lisa, who was prepared to give marriage another fling; also in attendance was his one-time psychologist from Trenton State Prison, Dr Brian Raditz, now his friend and manager; and, of course, there were the inevitable television crews and packs of journalists. Despite his long time away, Ayala still commanded major attention.

And perhaps that has always been the problem. From the moment he tossed his first left hook, which was not too long after he could balance himself on two tiny feet, Ayala has seldom been free of intense public scrutiny – as a freakishly destructive baby boxer; as a spoiled twelve-year-old, driving his own car around the streets of San Antonio; as a ferocious professional fighter, almost unanimously tipped as a certain future champ; as a confessed drunk and dope user; as a convicted rapist and celebrity inmate; and eventually as a boxing curiosity on a comeback mission, both inside and outside the ropes. The horror story that has been the life of El Torito – The Little Bull – has always insisted on banner headlines.

These are not the opening lines in an apologia for the tough guy from Texas, and even if, as was disclosed after his release, he was sexually abused as a child by someone close to the family, that should not be used as an excuse or a plea bargain for his crimes: Tony did what he did, and superior intellects can delve into the reasons why. Yet even when analysing his extraordinary boxing life, one quickly discovers that we are dealing with a subject who, despite the obvious love of his family, was never granted the usual carefree years enjoyed by most little boys.

The Ayalas were not your average folks next door, and little Tony was always going to be a fighter. His father, big Tony, had decided that was how it must be.

El Torito was born on 13 February 1963, the third son of the clan. The oldest boy, Mike, would later develop into a very good featherweight and would survive into the fifteenth round of a world title challenge against Danny Lopez, while brother Sammy became a decent performer around the welter mark. Big Tony, a bulky ex-Marine, was a staunch believer in the macho, no-tears culture and also in the theory that boxing was the surest way for his sons to improve their lot and escape from the hardships of life in the barrio. So it was not too long before toddler Tony was strutting his stuff alongside his big brothers in the improvised gym in their backyard, and then, in what were described as 'peewee' boxing tournaments, in venues all over the state.

Right from the start, Tony could punch with the force of a hobnailed boot to the head, and soon had to face much older aspirants, his landmark loss coming at the age of eight against a youngster three years older. But his rate of progress was remarkable, and in one celebrated sparring session when he was fourteen, he floored no less than Pipino Cuevas, who was then the reigning W.B.A. welterweight champion and a hero with the boxing-mad Mexicans.

In 1979, The Little Bull won the National Golden Gloves championship, and he would have been a snip for selection for the 1980 U.S. Olympic squad until Jimmy Carter insisted on an American boycott of the Moscow Games. That only served to bring forward the long-formulated plans for Tony's introduction into the professional ranks.

No surprise that the Ayalas chose to sign contracts with Shelly Finkel and Lou Duva – the Main Events partnership who had given Mitch Green his professional start, but who had also collared some of America's finest young talents and were boxing's flavour of the month. They would do the managing and the promoting, while Big Tony would continue as trainer, but they were taking on a teenager who was already carrying excess baggage.

As early as twelve, Torito had discovered drink, which he couldn't handle, and drugs, which very few can handle; and although he still maintained a strict gym routine, he could, when he slipped the leash, discover a darker side that would ultimately cause destruction and self-destruction. At the age of fifteen, he was convicted, fined, and awarded ten years' probation for an assault on a teenage girl. But there are few choirboys who stumble into the hard world of boxing, and flat-faced Lou Duva, who had seen just about all there was to see, shaped as a good bet to straighten him out.

For a time it appeared that the partnership was going to be all right. As a professional, immediately seen by an awe-struck television audience, Ayala was electric: a clone of the great Roberto Duran, but even nastier if that were possible. Torito did not just go out to win his fights: he wanted to ruin his opponents, wreck them, humiliate them. The barrel-like light-middle may have been trying to exorcise inner demons, but it was big box-office.

He was uncaged on the professionals in his home town on 17 June 1980 and Zip Castillo failed to hear the bell for the end of the first round; neither did opponents two, three and four; ringwise veteran Mike Baker took him the full eight rounds at Lake Tahoe, in his fifth outing, and for the remainder of his 'first' career, only two more adversaries would be around to hear the points divvied up. But it was the manner in which Ayala dispensed with some of his rivals that had the guys who monitor the viewing figures smacking their lips.

January 1981 in San Antonio, and El Torito knocks out Jose Luis Baltazar in the second, leans over and spits on him. Macho words had been exchanged at the weigh-in, and Ayala hotly denied the expectoration, but E.S.P.N. viewers saw it otherwise.

March 1981 in Syracuse and Mario Maldonado has the insolence to record a flash knockdown at the end of the first round. Ayala rises as the bell rings and screams, 'I'm gonna kill you' as Duva hauls him back to the corner and has to restrain him for the full minute's respite. Maldonado manages to survive until the third.

June 1981 in Houston, and an enraged Bull has to be held back from attacking opponent Jerry Cheetham before the bout is even under way. Cheetham does better than most and lasts out until the sixth.

August 1982 in San Antonio, and Ayala keeps throwing heavy shots after referee Dickie Cole has stopped his fight against a helpless Ronnie Epps in the first. Epps had been an amateur gym mate, but had left to turn pro elsewhere, and later described the Ayalas as 'animals'.

Those incidents could be written off as macho gone mad, a dip into the wrestling gig, but they send out eerie echoes when thinking about the latter-day Mike Tyson and his craziness in the ring. The young Ayala was just about in control of himself and his powerful P.R. machine was always on red alert, and there was no question that he really was an exceptional fighter. So much so that serious negotiations opened for a match against Roberto Duran, then without a title to call his own. The Hands of Stone against The Little Bull; the two ultimate macho men nose to nose. The viewing figures might have gone to the moon, but the fight would never happen.

Fifteen days after caving in Ronnie Epps, Ayala was arrested for breaking into and ransacking a neighbour's house. Very serious, and more serious, taking into account that he was currently on ten years' parole. Torito's story was that he had gone out drinking to celebrate the Epps victory, had had a big blow-up with his wife, Lisa, and so maintained the binge of booze. He claimed that he was so drunk that he did not realise he wasn't in his own house until he tried to go upstairs to bed and discovered there were no stairs!

Lawyer Dan Duva, son of Lou, dismissed the notion that Ayala was on a burglary mission, pointing out that a fighter who was on the brink of a $750,000 match against Duran would be an unlikely burglar. What was he going to do? Steal a watch? Nevertheless, on 25 August, the boxer was whisked off to a care unit in Orange, California, where he was diagnosed an alcoholic who could not even drink a little without catastrophic repercussions. He remained in the unit for four weeks, during which time Duran was amazingly turned over in a tune-up against Kirkland Laing, and the big-money match went up in smoke. But come October, there was much better news for Ayala, when the owner of the house dropped the charges against him. The risk of the parole violation was lifted.

On 20 November in Atlantic City, El Torito returned to the ring for the most important fight of his career, against the W.B.A.'s number one challenger for the light-middleweight championship, Carlos Herrera. The winner would be nominated as the mandatory contender for the title held by Davey Moore, and Herrera was hammered to defeat in three rounds. At the age of nineteen, and unbeaten in twenty-two contests, nineteen of them failing to go the distance, Ayala was being offered the best part of a million dollars and an odds-on chance of becoming champion of the world.

Tony Ayala should have been all set to celebrate his merriest Christmas ever. There seemed no bounds to his future in the ring; Lou Duva forecast he was 'a cinch to be a champion' and estimated his future earnings in mega-millions; and because of his youth, he was sure to develop into an even more accomplished fighter. He had been extremely fortunate to escape a court case that could have sent him off to prison, and he should have been learning his lessons and counting his blessings. And although he had been diagnosed as a guy who would self-destruct on alcohol, that wasn't the end of the world. Surely it was much better to discover the truth about himself, make the necessary adjustments such as attending his weekly treatment and counselling sessions in New York, and get on with living what still should have been a highly productive life.

Torito, however, despite being reared on the strict disciplines required for boxing, had also been pampered; when he got himself into scrapes, there were always people around prepared to clean up the mess. Again shades of Tyson, but there was no shortage of back-up players willing to write off his escapades as just those of a high-voltage youngster going through the growing-up process. They did him no favours, and in the end might have played a part in putting the public at risk.

What should have been a carefree holiday, before the serious business of beating Davey Moore, was shattered by another night of mindless horror.

In the early hours of New Year's Day 1983, Ayala attacked a thirty-year-old schoolteacher at knifepoint in her West Paterson, New Jersey, home. On 13 April, a jury found him guilty of rape, and he was packed off to Passaic County Jail to await sentencing. That was delivered on 22 June, when Judge Amos Saunders handed down a term of 35 years with Ayala having to serve a mandatory fifteen years before becoming eligible for parole. The hottest property in boxing was now inmate No. 69765, and for the first time he found himself in a bind from which nobody could set him free.

From behind bars, he would learn that Duran would replace him for the title challenge against Moore, score a sensational eight-round stoppage in New York and recharge his career; what could have been Torito's had become the property of Roberto. And yet, there remained one slim hope that Ayala could continue boxing from inside the walls. After all, there was a famous precedent in the state of New Jersey.

James Scott, a 6ft 1in hardcase from Newark, had sampled life in many of the state's jails and had learned to box in Trenton State Prison, where he was serving a stretch for armed robbery. When he was paroled in 1974, he headed south to Florida, where he signed up with a promotional outfit called the Mendoza Group, which was spear-headed by Murray Gaby and also included Ferdie Pacheco, known as The Fight Doctor, most famous for his lengthy association with Muhammad Ali.

Working out at Miami's 5th Street gym, Scott impressed his new connections, made a winning debut against John L. Johnson on 22 January 1974, and went through the year unbeaten in ten fights, marred only by a draw against Lee Royster. The future looked particularly rosy when Scott outpointed the highly regarded Jesse Burnett on 25 February 1975 in Miami and gained sixth spot in the light heavyweight ratings, but that was to prove his last contest for three years.

Scott had been complaining about his meagre earnings – sounds familiar? – and, against the advice of his management, had started to make visits back to his old haunts in New Jersey, believing he could promote his career better on home turf. His aim was to secure a title fight against W.B.C. champion John Conteh, but those ambitions were quickly shattered. On 7 May, his car was used during the fatal shooting of one Everitt Russ, and the following day – hearing that the Newark police wanted to talk to him – he turned himself in. Scott's story was that he had loaned out the car, but nevertheless, he was charged with murder and armed robbery; a jury failed to agree on the murder charge but found him guilty of armed robbery; and because of his prior record, the sentence was a stiff thirty to forty years.

His one stroke of luck was that he was sent to the state prison at Rahway, where the warden, Robert Hatrack, turned out to be a man always open to fresh ideas.

Not only did he put Scott in charge of the prison's boxing programme, but he consented to the fighter continuing his career from the inside, provided a suitable promoter could be found, and also provided that a percentage of Scott's earnings would be donated to the Victims of Violent Crimes. The promoter came in the form of Newark entrepreneur Murad Muhammad; the television companies showed an interest because of the unique locale; and on 24 May 1978, the career of the now thirty-year-old resumed with a two-round stoppage of Joe Roberson.

When, the following October, he outpointed Eddie Gregory, who, as Eddie Mustafa Muhammad, would later win the W.B.A. light heavyweight championship, Scott and Rahway were truly on the map and no longer just on the sports pages. Other notable wins followed against Richie Kates and British import Bunny Johnson, and Alvaro Yaqui Lopez, but it was becoming increasingly evident that if Scott was ever going to get a shot at the championship, then some manner of parole deal would have to be arranged. A title holder would be naturally reluctant to risk his belt in such a hostile environment.

The World Boxing Association acted with typically classic indecision. They had Scott rated as high as number two in their light-heavy list, but when the pressure began to mount for the convict to get his chance, they simply removed him from their rankings. Just like that!

Scott's legal team was making strenuous efforts to get him out – however briefly – for a title shot, but New Jersey wasn't having any, and the hullabaloo quietened somewhat when Scott got himself knocked down twice in the opening round against Jerry (The Bull) Martin and convincingly outpointed over ten. And when, in September 1981, he suffered another points loss, this time to Dwight Braxton, who would win the W.B.C. championship in his very next bout, James Scott's career simply ground to a halt, and the brave Rahway experiment lost all momentum.

The state of New Jersey showed little interest in reviving a similar boxing project for Tony Ayala, and the fighter, looking at all those years ahead of him, did not appear overly concerned. He had other matters on his mind, such as getting his head straight and, if possible, coming to terms with just what he had done. To help him achieve that, in prison he met a man who was prepared to put in the hours of talking and listening and trying to discover if there could be another Tony Ayala, other than the beast of the streets.

Dr Brian Raditz had experienced an extremely brief pro boxing career, had managed a well-known lightweight, Tracy Spann, and when he first met Ayala a few months after his incarceration in Trenton, he was working as the prison psychologist. It was a fellow inmate, noting Ayala's disturbed state, who suggested that he could do worse than have a talk with the doc.

Raditz quickly appreciated that the boxer was willing to give their sessions a chance, and soon they were meeting as many as five times a week. That programme carried on for over four years until the doctor left to enter private practice, but they never lost touch. Only Tony knows the true value of all that work, but a few days before his release, Raditz told the *Philadelphia News*: 'He's won the war. He's turned his life around, regardless of what happens with the boxing thing.'

The boxing thing. Even as a teenager, Ayala had been a bulky light-middle, always liable to pile on the pounds, but there had been few problems in working off the weight back then. He had stayed reasonably fit – not boxing fit – by doing plenty of running and calisthenics, but he was no longer El Torito: this Bull had fattened to about 30lb over his once fighting weight. As a parole date began to loom as a probability, however, the idea of boxing began to emerge as a reality. He would be 36 when he got out, but hadn't George Foreman – every old fighter's fantasy role model – been much older when he announced his impossible dream and made mugs out of all the experts?

For better or worse, boxing now boasted a number of not-so-golden oldies, some of them earning a fair whack, and though his hairline had retreated and his waist had thickened, Ayala could not be considered a nut for wanting to give the game another fling.

Exactly four months after being released from Bayside, Ayala returned to the ring as a beefy middleweight, back in San Antonio in the Freeman Coliseum before a 10,000 crowd. The opponent Manuel Esparza was five when the Bull had gone inside and he wasn't expected to do much. He didn't, but Ayala at least proved that if his movements were more deliberate, his hands were still fast and packed plenty of power.

And as he rattled off five inside-the-distance victories, there were still flashes of the old nasty Torito. Against a 27-year-old Nebraskan journeyman, Tony Menefee, who had a rather misleading 67 wins to his credit, Ayala twice threw heavy shots after the bell, one of them flooring the unfortunate Menefee, who gamely absorbed a beating until he was rescued in the eighth.

The comeback was gathering speed and was being billed as the 'To Hell And Back Tour', but for all the ballyhoo and the carefully selected opposition, there was no denying that Ayala was looking like a serious proposition once again. So much so that his connections decided to step up the calibre of opponent and match him with the former I.B.F. light middleweight champion Yory Boy Campas in San Antonio on 28 July 2000. Although he was only 28 and had been beaten only four times in 78 fights, the word was out that Campas was on the slide and losing his appetite for the business. Somebody had fed the Ayalas bum information, for, before a 9,000 crowd, Yory Boy chose to battle as if his life depended on it.

Ayala failed to come out for the ninth, but that bare statistic does not reveal the thrilling battle staged by both boxers; or how the bloodied Yory Boy had to dig deep to stave off defeat; or how Ayala, both eyes swollen almost shut, had fought with a broken left hand. The result does not tell how it was Big Tony, the disciple of all things macho, who decided that his son's cause had become hopeless; nor does it tell how Little Tony wept bitterly in disappointment.

An Ayala crying in front of his father and a crowd of 9,000? Perhaps the two Tonys would never get that title shot that once seemed such a formality, but just maybe, they were both beginning to learn how to live like your average folks next door.

And that should have been a pleasant, upbeat note on which to wave farewell to Tony Ayala, but in the lead-up to Christmas in San Antonio, once again, he succumbed to his demons, and was shot in the left shoulder whilst breaking into a young woman's house. He was charged with intent to commit burglary and assault, was released on $100,000 bail, fitted with an electronic monitoring device round his ankle, and had a breath alcohol detector hooked up to his home phone.

If convicted, he could spend the rest of his life in prison . . . few bothered to find out if the gunshot wound might threaten his career.

PART FOUR

Ain't Your Night

Tommy Campbell had all the right moves but the wrong connections. To get the purse, they said he had to be a loser.

Billy Collins was going places, a real prospect . . . until he was the victim of a mugging in the Garden.

Willie Classen had seen better days but nobody seemed to notice much until it was too late.

No secret that boxing's worst enemies
have invariably come from within

10

Tommy Campbell:
'I Needed the Money'

TERRY MALLOY was in his dressing room, deep in the bowels of the Garden, when brother Charley The Gent arrived with the news: this was not to be Terry's night; the boys were going for the price on Wilson. The fighter was not getting much notice, because usually such operations needed a modicum of planning, most likely a deal of persuasion, and of prime importance, adequate time to get all the bets down in a fittingly discreet fashion.

Back in May 1950, for example, an extremely capable lightweight called Tommy Campbell had all of two weeks to become accustomed to the idea that he was about to lose a fight that he felt certain he could win, against Art Aragon, the Golden Boy of Californian boxing.

At best, the fight game has always suffered from a scruffy image, and as we have already noted, many of its participants have been less than upright, and, of course, that has not helped. But movieland has also done its bit to shape the perceived notion that every second bout is a tank job, and that behind every other manager lurks a gangster wielding a lead pipe. Those old black and white melodramas may have been great entertainment and boxing has always lent itself to the screen better than any other sport, but the price has been high and the memories linger on.

In the past, soccer players have gone to jail for match rigging, and not too long ago several big names were heavily investigated. A gambler named Arnold Rothstein got the credit for fixing the 1919 baseball World Series between the Chicago White Sox and the

Cincinnati Reds, admittedly with the help of a boxer, the dapper former featherweight champion Abe Attell. Athletics and cycling are awash with drugs; jockeys are frequently under the microscope; and even the grand old game of cricket has been rocked of late by betting scandals at the highest level. In comparison, boxing is not doing too badly these days – at least inside the ropes. The backroom machinations and the often inexplicable judging, however, are an entirely different affair.

Today, there is little incentive to mastermind an old-fashioned betting coup, as the gambling industry has become so sophisticated and betting trends so carefully monitored that any significant activity would be quickly spotted. The days have also gone when a fighter, such as Primo Carnera under the control of gangsters Owen Madden and Bill Duffy, had his record bolstered with a string of phoney wins. Today a prospect is simply matched against a much inferior opponent who is free to try his best; surprises can happen, but not too often, and there is no illegality.

But back in 1950, when Tommy Campbell still daydreamed about being given a title shot against Ike Williams, the bad guys infested the business, and though bent fights were not a weekly occurrence, they did take place, although there must have been few more unlikely candidates for taking a dive than the classy 28-year-old lightweight.

Tommy Campbell was born in Kansas City on 25 August 1921, was outstanding at track and basketball in high school, and started boxing amateur in 1939. The following year he won the National A.A.U. lightweight title, became the National Golden Gloves champion in 1941, and lost only five of seventy contests. But professional ambitions had to be shelved when he joined the Air Corps in 1942 for a stint that included duty in the Pacific and was to last almost four years. He was a 24-year-old with a wife when he came out in January 1946, and he might never have pulled on a glove again, but for the fact that no employer was interested in the skills he had learned at radio and communications school in the forces.

By this time, he was living in Rock Island, Illinois, married to Minnie and about to start a family. The impetus to turn pro was provided by a local enthusiast, Ritchie Smith, who offered Campbell

$200 to sign with him. The two hundred bucks looked extremely good to the Campbells, especially as there appeared to be so few alternatives, and so in 1946, Tommy made his professional debut in Chicago, knocked out Whitman Buress in the first round, and collected a purse of $45.

For the next eighteen months, he averaged a fight a month, winning fifteen, drawing one, but nobody was getting overly excited about another smart, black lightweight. The gyms were full of them and most of the others had better connections than Ritchie Smith, who could find his fighter work at the minor locations but who lacked an in with any of Chicago's major operators.

The partnership was going nowhere, but Smith was not yet disillusioned and suggested they should head for California, where there seemed to be plenty of activity at all weights. This was a huge step for a scarcely known fighter with a family, not to mention a raw manager, but Campbell decided to gamble on his ability, and the pair set out on the long drive to Los Angeles, wife Minnie planning to follow once he had become established.

If anything, however, Smith packed even less clout with the regulars at the Main Street Gym in L.A. than he did back in Chicago, and it was not too long before Campbell arrived down from his hotel room one morning to find his manager gone and his board paid only until the end of the week. He was in a desperate predicament, totally broke in a strange city, but a fighter he had befriended in the gym gave him a roof. That boxer was Harold Dade, who for a brief period in 1947 borrowed the world bantamweight title from Manuel Ortiz; and not only did Dade share his accommodation, but he also discovered that Campbell had a new manager!

Before setting off home, Ritchie Smith had passed on power of attorney to a local manager, a one-time fighter by the name of Soldier Eddie Stanley, and as Stanley was reputed to be close to a character called Babe McCoy, the move seemed a sensible one for Campbell. No matter that he had never been consulted about his new manager, who was a complete stranger; Tommy could not afford to be picky, and anyway, back then, such transactions were not unusual. Archie Moore remembered several times waking up to find himself under new management, and plenty of boxers were traded on like second-hand motors.

Campbell had not been in Los Angeles long, but already he recognised that having a connection to McCoy, however tenuous, just might provide the break that he so desperately needed. Babe McCoy was the matchmaker for the fights at the Olympic Auditorium, and as such he wielded tremendous influence; he could make and break careers on a whim, and very often did just that. A balding, jowly, cigar-smoking fat man, the Babe's word was L.A. law among the managers and boxers in the city, and if he decided now and then to help himself to a share of the purse money – to which, of course, he was not entitled – who was going to give him an argument?

Thus the lightweight was soon busy enough to afford to send for his family, and though his wages were meagre, he was boxing regularly, always hoping that the big money was just one bout away. He was comfortably beating local attractions like Tony Marr and Arturo Barron and Rudy Cruz (twice) and John L. Davis (three times) and he was steadily climbing the ratings, but still he was barely scraping a living. It was not long before he came to the unpalatable conclusion that he was just another black fighter scuffling for a buck, rather than a prospective contender being carefully nursed along.

That fact was hammered home when, on only ten hours' notice, he was told to fly to San Francisco to fill in against a tough welter called Johnny Williams. He fought well to earn a draw, but the warning bells were ringing about why his management should hand him such a thankless task. Then in November 1948, McCoy made it even clearer that he regarded Tommy as just an opponent, no more than a handy guy to call upon.

In those days, there was a long queue just to break into the ratings, but even a busy champion such as Ike Williams might defend his title only three times in a year. Opportunities were scarce and an 'opponent' was not necessarily a spent boxer, easy to beat. Like Tommy Campbell, he could just as easily be a highly ranked pro, a clever boxer and a dangerous puncher, who for some reason had never developed into an automatic attraction, a guaranteed ticket-seller. Such a performer was seldom going to be given easy matches and would certainly never benefit from a cautious build-up. More often than not, he would find himself in desperate, dog-eat-dog encounters where the promoters were not too fussed about the outcome as long as the action was entertaining, and he would often be called upon as a late substitute, as Campbell was in San Francisco.

In early November, he knocked out Tommy Stenhouse, but sustained a badly cut eyebrow, which took eight stitches, and just a few days later Eddie Stanley brought him the news that he had been booked to box Enrique Bolanos in a major promotion at the Olympic on 30 November. Tommy was naturally delighted, because Bolanos was the biggest Mexican attraction of the era, had already lost in one challenge against lightweight champion Williams earlier that year, and was now being groomed for a second try. If Campbell could beat Bolanos then it would be difficult to deny him a rightful crack at the title. The big problem was the torn eyebrow.

The boxer – not his manager – approached McCoy, explained how the eyebrow was taking time to heal, and asked for two weeks' postponement, which did not seem unreasonable. But his request was met with complete indifference and the matchmaker made it clear that if Campbell could not make the 30 November date, then he would have to find somebody else. Take it or leave it. Economics dictated that he must take it, and that night, sure enough, the cut reopened early and Bolanos went on to cop a twelve-round decision, retain his California championship, and confirm his position as number one world challenger. The fight had been all square at the end of the tenth, but a tiring Campbell took a count in the eleventh, and that was enough to give the Mexican the edge. But who is to say what might have happened had Tommy not fought with the damaged eye?

The show drew a sell-out 10,200 crowd and Campbell's purse out of the $41,778 gate receipts came to $3,000 – easily the most he was ever to earn in one night. That was some consolation, but when McCoy then paid him a miserly $600 to face a terror named Freddie Dawson, then packed him off to the Midwest for a series of fights with only trainer Chalky Wright, the former featherweight champion, for company, Tommy knew that he now did not figure large in anybody's long-range plans.

He was fighting all the tough guys for joke money and even Soldier

Eddie, his not-so-busy manager and the supposed buddy of McCoy, was becoming disgusted. The Soldier even suggested that they should take off for the east coast and try their luck there, but somehow the Babe got wind of a possible mutiny, and the next thing Campbell knew was that Stanley had been replaced as his manager by a veteran called George Moore. Once again, power of attorney!

Moore had been associated with the fabulous Henry Armstrong for a time, knew the score as well as anyone, would extend an advance to the habitually hungry fighter, but in reality, he was no more than a lackey for the Babe. The situation was getting worse and Campbell's frustrations finally boiled over when, after fighting another exceedingly tough customer in Luther Rawlings, he discovered that $70 had been deducted from his promised $500. He was incensed, especially after Moore explained that the cut had come at McCoy's explicit instruction, and he decided to confront the matchmaker, who simply told him that the fight had not drawn well and that he (Campbell) had to help defray the expense of bringing Rawlings all the way from Chicago. That was the signal for Campbell to start shouting, and finally McCoy peeled $70 from his roll and handed it to the fighter. With the dough came the message that he would never fight again in the state of California.

This was crazy! Campbell was still *The Ring*'s number three rated lightweight, but he had to take all description of odd jobs to put food on the table. Times were becoming increasingly desperate for his family, but then two months after the showdown with McCoy, Moore phoned to say that the Babe wanted to see him . . . no more details. Tommy was hoping for a break, hoping for the best, hoping for just about anything, but the fat matchmaker soon put him wise. Sure, he could fight again, a big fight against Art Aragon, and the money would be good. But he would have to lose this one, and the fourth was the designated round for splashdown.

Campbell was devastated but he was also cleaned out. This was not a subject for lengthy discussion and, numbly, he consented to the arrangement, yet all the time thinking that come the night, he could double-cross McCoy, which would give him great satisfaction, and go out and beat Aragon, which he was sure he could accomplish. That was how Hollywood might have treated the script, but old George Moore quickly set him straight on that fantasy: considerable money had already been deposited guaranteeing the loss and there could be no turning back after that. Tommy Campbell, a model family man and an honest boxer, was about to play the starring role in a fraud, because, as he told the Investigating Committee six years later, 'I needed the money.'

Nobody should be too harsh or too quick to judge the boxer. His first priority was to provide for his family; McCoy had squeezed him into a corner after keeping him going on promises and pittances, and had then frozen him out of his profession. There comes a time when a man has got to do . . . and all that stuff, but not everybody can be a John Wayne.

Campbell had made his choice and was stuck with it, and that must have been particularly vexing, for he was convinced that he had already beaten Aragon once. The pair had first fought two years earlier in Oakland and the referee had announced a technical draw after Art had suffered a bad cut in the second round. Campbell always maintained that he had burst the eye with a left hook, but the referee insisted that the injury had been brought about by a butt. A difference of opinion, but it has to be said that Aragon regularly got the benefit of the doubt back in his golden years.

The Golden Boy . . . not William Holden fighting and fiddling in the best pre-war Hollywood tradition, but rather a tough, hard-punching Mexican lightweight who was fast becoming the red-hot favourite with the stars who were ringside regulars at the Hollywood Stadium. Aragon was being brought along as the logical successor to Bolanos with the Mexican fans and, from very early in his career, he was afforded the big build-up that Tommy Campbell and so many others had always craved.

Art got his fair share of easy jobs as befitted a future star – early stoppages against outclassed opponents such as Tony Chavez and Chucho Ruiz and Alfredo Pescatore. But there were also times when he was made to struggle, as against Harold (Baby Face) Jones, and many ringsiders booed when he was given a split decision against John L. Davis – the same John L. who had been beaten three times by

Campbell. The youngster might not have been the most gifted at his weight, but he brought to the ring a charisma that forced promoters and fans alike to forgive his shortcomings. Sooner, rather than later, Art Aragon was a certainty to get his shot at the lightweight championship.

The countdown to any fight is never easy for a boxer; and when that boxer has decided that he is deliberately going to lose, then it can become sheer hell. Yet why so, if the guy already knows the outcome, and probably even the round? No true fighter can go into the ring to lose intentionally without a feeling of shame and dread, unless he is a total bandit who has become adept at the art – but then, he is not a true fighter.

Nobody came tougher or more cynical than Jake La Motta, but when the time came actually to throw his fight against Billy Fox, La Motta was dreadful, staggering around the Garden ring more like a Saturday night drunk than a Friday night hero. His act fooled nobody. And many years before The Bull, one of the finest of all technicians, the great Joe Gans failed to make the fix look realistic when losing in two rounds to Terry McGovern in Chicago. We have already discussed the pressure on black fighters back then, but despite all his artistry Gans's performance was so bad that he almost spelt the end of boxing in the Windy City. Fine fighter that he was, Tommy Campbell also turned out to be a dud when it came to staging a convincing fake fight.

He had told his wife what he had to do, and at first she had tried to dissuade him, but then for the final week before the fight, the subject was just never mentioned. On the evening of 16 May, however, when he left his home to make the ten-minute drive to the Olympic, she still could not believe he would deliberately lose. He felt he had no option, though in round two he almost ruined the complete scenario.

Years after the event, he told writer Dick Friendlich: 'I botched the job . . . Near the end of the second round I had him near the ropes and saw him start a right hand. Automatically I slipped it over my left shoulder and there was his chin wide open. I hit him flush with the straight right and he went flying through the ropes on to the ring apron.'

He had only done what came naturally, but Campbell vividly

recalled his panic. How he actually reached through the ropes and tried to help up the stricken Aragon; how referee Reggie Gilmore had to manhandle him to a neutral corner; how, to his relief, Aragon rose at the count of eight; how Gilmore shouted at him to resume fighting; and how he stayed in close, throwing only body shots until the bell rang.

In the corner, trainer Chalky Wright said nothing, but he knew. And the fans knew and they were saying plenty. Campbell wanted an end to the charade and in the third, he walked out, took a few shots to the head, went down a couple of times and was counted out. He was jeered all the way to the dressing room, where the Commisssion inspector, Clayton Frye, grilled him about failing to go after Aragon in the second. Campbell, who had experienced mild eye problems in the past, claimed that he had suffered blurred vision and could not see his opponent properly, but the inspector was not convinced.

The following day there was a full Commission hearing. Tommy stuck to his story, which this time was accepted – he was suspended because of the eye trouble – and his purse money was released. McCoy's 'good payday' amounted to $800. And Art Aragon? He was busy telling anyone who would listen that the knockout punch was one of the hardest left hooks he had ever thrown.

Art did not have to wait long for his big chance, and in 1951 he outpointed the new champion James Carter in a non-title fight in Los Angeles, but almost three months later with his title on the line, the New Yorker convincingly beat Aragon over fifteen rounds.

Nevertheless, Aragon would have his moments. He beat future champions Don Jordan (twice) and Lauro Salas, and in the twilight of his career, he survived until the eighth against the rugged Carmen Basilio. No question, he was a genuine fighter and he would always be the Golden Boy. A 1956 match against another California favourite, Cisco Andrade, attracted a gate of $95,000, and Art's whack was a whopping $24,000 – more than Tommy Campbell earned throughout his entire career.

Despite the California suspension, Campbell continued to box. Naturally, he was totally disillusioned but he still thought there was a chance he might gather some money together. Moore arranged a series

of fights in New Orleans, which was a thriving boxing town, but
Campbell went accompanied by neither manager nor trainer, which
was scarcely a boost to his ego. He fought six times, including a ten-
round draw with Carter, who eight months later would beat a weight-
weakened Ike Williams for the title. Just as easily, it could have been
Campbell beating the ailing Ike, but unlike Carter, he had nobody to
press his claims.

When, in early 1951, the California ban was lifted, he outpointed
another future world lightweight champion, Joe Brown, in Los Angeles
(though Old Bones would gain a knockout revenge in New Orleans)
and then lost to Virgil Akins, who would become a welterweight
champion. The pattern was so familiar: no easy fights, no big purses.
Then, once again, Babe McCoy decided to take a special interest.

On the morning after the Akins fight in New Orleans, when
Campbell went to collect his wages from the promoter, he was told
that there was a plane ticket for him (courtesy of McCoy) to fly to
Minneapolis, where he would box the local hero, Del Flanagan.
Waiting at his hotel was the Babe, who informed him that there would
be an additional $500 if he let Flanagan win. More streetwise now,
Campbell just nodded, and McCoy, satisfied that the deal had been
done, headed back to L.A., not even waiting to see the fight.

This time, Tommy didn't obey orders. He handed Del Flanagan his
first defeat, and so pleased the promoters, who were clearly not in on
the scam, that they matched him the next week against Flanagan's
brother Glen, who also got a lesson. When he eventually returned to
Los Angeles and a seething McCoy, Campbell had his story prepared:
how both the local Commission and the newspapers had voiced their
suspicions about him before the fight, and how he'd had no option but
to box on the up; like all good stories, there was a hint of truth to it,
and McCoy was powerless to take any action.

But that one rainbow purse that would give him a fresh start was no
nearer; he was still just one of the Babe's chattels, and even before he
was sent to Davenport, Iowa, to face Wallace Bud Smith, he had
decided to quit the business.

On 11 September 1951, he gave a polished exhibition to outpoint
Bud Smith – yet another opponent who would wind up a champion

– and walked away from boxing. He had just turned thirty, had fought 63 fights, lost eleven, and had only bitter and guilty memories.

It was in February 1956 that Campbell's past came back to haunt him. Working as a technician in an aeroplane factory, he was approached by a representative of California governor Knight's special committee investigating boxing in the state. He wanted to know the truth about the Aragon fight and his relationship with Babe McCoy. Reluctant at first, Campbell finally agreed to testify; so too did a handful of other fighters, and even his old manager Soldier Eddie Stanley. At a March hearing, they all told their stories about McCoy and crooked fights and the illegal cuts he took from purses; they repeated their testimony before a new boxing commission in November, and the outcome was that Babe McCoy was banned from boxing for life. A degree of justice.

Tommy Campbell was neither a hero nor a villain, just a very good lightweight who was denied the breaks until he became so desperate that he committed the boxer's ultimate sin against Art Aragon . . . we can only plead extremely extenuating circumstances. And what about Aragon? Ever the Golden Boy, he resurfaced in 1972, when he landed a prominent role in John Huston's celebrated movie, *Fat City*.

Art played a trainer, and the film was all about boxing's losers. There should have been a part somewhere written for Tommy Campbell.

11

Billy Collins:
'He's Hitting Me with Rocks'

BILLY COLLINS had so much going for him. He was an undefeated light middleweight prospect, bubbling with that special brand of health and vitality which marks apart ambitious and dedicated young fighters from other mortals. He enjoyed the patronage of Bob Arum's Top Rank promotional organisation, which meant that if he could just keep delivering in the ring, then it would be only a matter of time before he would gain his shot at a world championship. But before that, he was looking forward to playing his part in a gala birthday celebration due to be staged at Madison Square Garden.

On 16 June 1983, the extraordinary Roberto Duran would mark his 32nd birthday by challenging the precocious Davey Moore for the W.B.A. light middleweight title in the same ring in which Roberto had won his first world championship eleven years earlier. This was going to be a memorable occasion, in front of a 20,000 sell-out crowd, and, in the principal supporting contest, Collins would have the ideal opportunity to showcase his talents against Luis Resto, a seasoned pro, originally from Puerto Rico, but now resident in New York.

Instead, the evening of 16 June became one of the most infamous in the history of boxing, and would be the last time that either Billy Collins or Luis Resto fought in public.

It is a given that boxing pays homage to the code of one-upmanship: the less than noble art of being able to put one over on a rival. The talent to pull a stroke – even one that is legally a mite iffy – is applauded and always has been; many managers and trainers go hunting for that

Peter Jackson – Lord Lonsdale's favourite fighter, but one of the earliest victims of the colour bar.

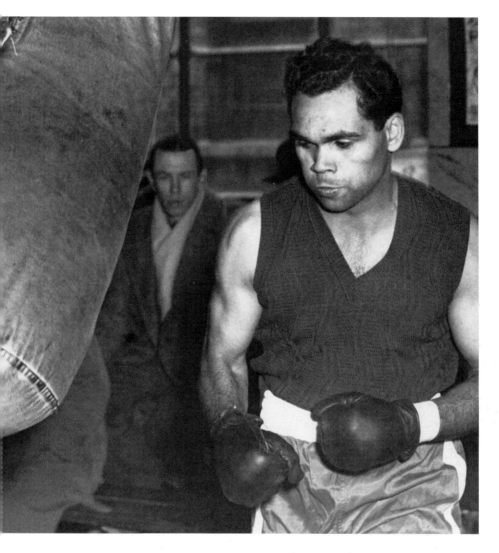

Above: Dave Sands – in line for a middleweight title showdown when his truck crashed off the road.
Courtesy of Corbis

Left: Jack Blackburn – a deadly character, but his protégé Joe Louis could always give him a lift.
Courtesy of Corbis

Al Weill – a shrewd manipulator, a cunning manager, and never happier than when raising the arm of Rocky Marciano.

Frankie Carbo – mobster and manager of managers. For too many years the man who called the shots in boxing.
Courtesy of Corbis

Above: Teofilio Stevenson – a proud Cuban, a marvellous Olympian and the one fighter money could not buy.

Courtesy of All Sports Inc.

Mickey Rourke – a headliner on the screen, a bit player in the ring, but a great trier nonetheless.

Courtest of All Sports Inc.

special edge that can make the difference between winning and losing; and if there are times when they might not be playing pure Marquis of Queensberry, then so what?

Veteran cornerman Angelo Dundee, for example, dined out for years on his story of how, in London in 1963, he deliberately widened the tear in the glove of the young Cassius Clay in order to buy him extra time between rounds and allow him to recover from a Henry Cooper left hook. A good after-dinner story and importantly, nobody got hurt because of Angelo's chicanery.

But the same Dundee and Clay were almost the victims of a more sinister incident, when, during his title challenge against Sonny Liston in Miami, Cassius was ready to quit on his stool at the end of the fourth because some foreign substance – most likely liniment from Liston's injured shoulder – had temporarily blinded him. Dundee had to push a reluctant Clay out for the fifth and then had to sponge his own eyes to satisfy suspicious and threatening Black Muslims that he had done nothing to sabotage his fighter's chances.

Of course, all ended well for Clay, but when playing for such high stakes, suspicion can quickly develop into paranoia and on from there to God knows what. The weight of evidence suggested that what befell young Cassius was accidental and was by no means unique. In fact, Rocky Marciano had suffered similar sight problems when beating Jersey Joe Walcott in their memorable battle for the same title. That time also, the accusations and denials flew like a Ray Robinson combination.

But there could be no argument that what happened in the Garden on that 16 June evening was not only deliberate, but diabolical in its planning and execution, plummeting the notion of trying to gain an edge to depths hitherto unexplored. First, however, let us examine some of the principal players in that night of shame.

Billy Collins hailed from Nashville, Tennessee, the son of a former pro fighter of the same name who became his manager and trainer, and he made his professional debut in Atlantic City on 2 December 1981, stopping Kevin Griffin in three rounds. He had a busy and successful 1982, only two of his ten contests lasting the distance, and the tough and aggressive red-head, now being billed as 'Irish' Billy Collins, was beginning to attract a growing television fan following. On the eve of St Patrick's Day 1983, he scored his biggest victory to date when, at the Sands Casino in Atlantic City, he won – for what it was worth – the vacant E.S.P.N. light middleweight title, stopping Steve (Rattlesnake) Johnson when referee Paul Venti intervened with 45 seconds still remaining of the first round. The E.S.P.N. belt was no big deal, but it was another rung up the ladder for an unbeaten white fighter – every promoter's pipe dream.

Despite the brevity of the fight, there had been some exciting exchanges and before his departure, the Rattlesnake had actually managed to rock Collins. Some critics thought that the boy from Nashville was too easily hit and there was no doubt that he would have to tighten up his defence as he stepped up in class. The crazy thing was that although he had fought only fourteen times when he went in against Resto, Collins actually had more ring experience than the reigning champion of his division, Davey Moore.

Moore, a 24-year-old New Yorker, had created shock waves when, travelling all the way to Tokyo for only his ninth professional fight, he stopped Tadashi Mihara in six rounds to become a most unlikely W.B.A. champion, and a couple of months later, he again upset the odds – this time in Johannesburg – when he took a round fewer to beat the local favourite Charlie Weir. Further defences against Ayub Kalule and Gary Guiden proved that Davey was the genuine article, and despite Duran's massive popularity in New York, there was a load of money backing the champion, eventually down to favourite.

Moore's meteoric rise had been an inspiration to Collins, and now he was about to fight on the same card as him, against an opponent who most certainly had not been selected at random. If there was some concern about Billy's defence after the Johnson fight, then the Collins camp was not looking to face a puncher. The 29-year-old Resto seemed to fit the bill, and if Irish Billy did get careless, then he was unlikely to experience too much grief against such a recognised non-hitter. At least, that was the pre-fight logic.

The winner of a pair of New York Golden Gloves titles and a participant in the 1976 U.S. Olympic Trials, Resto had made his debut the following February with a points win against Julio Chevalier, and had gone on to accumulate a so-so record of twenty wins and two draws from twenty-nine fights. Five years earlier his limitations had been exposed when a future champion, Bruce Curry, had taken him out in two rounds in Las Vegas, but just that previous December, he had shown a resurgence of form when beating Robert Sawyer in Atlantic City for yet another of those E.S.P.N. baubles, this time the welter version.

Luis had been around, fighting in such far-flung locales as San Remo and St Thomas and Caracas and Guyana. He was a tough, game performer, handicapped by his lack of power, but he invariably put up a pleasing show. For winning his E.S.P.N. belt, he had been paid $3,500 but he was on an additional four grand for his date with Collins. That was big money to Luis, and he knew that a win would put him in the market for even bigger purses. The pairing of Collins and Resto shaped up as an attractive proposition for both fighters.

Resto was managed and trained by a 37-year-old called Carlos Lewis, 'Panama' to all who knew him around the gyms, that being his country of origin. A Vietnam veteran, Lewis – easily spotted in the corner thanks to his trademark headband – was looked upon in the business as one of the brightest of the younger crop of trainers, with an increasing demand on his services, and there was no doubt that he had learned from the top men. Panama was fast becoming flavour of the month.

He had started out assisting Chickie Ferrara, one of the old-school greats from the Stillman's era, and then he began to get some work by hanging out with his fellow countryman Duran. Lewis should have picked up plenty, just watching and listening to Roberto's legendary trainers, the amazing ancients, Ray Arcel and Freddie Brown, who both thought highly of him; and thanks to Brown, he gained further valuable experience, helping prepare the tough middleweight champion Vito Antuofermo. When Arcel and Brown split with Duran, disillusioned after the second Ray Leonard fight, Lewis took charge of his countryman's training, but Duran was suffering a bad spell, and the relationship was brief. He struck gold, however, when he landed the job as chief trainer to the brilliant and mega-earning light welterweight champion Aaron Pryor, and quickly became a personality in his own right.

In November 1982 in Miami, however, Panama Lewis gained a certain notoriety that he could never quite shake off, after a huge television audience eavesdropped on his corner instructions during Pryor's epic against Alexis Arguello. Between the thirteenth and fourteenth rounds, the microphones in Pryor's corner picked up Lewis ordering his assistants: 'Don't give me that bottle. Give me the one I mixed.'

The one he mixed? Some magic potion? Some illegal stimulant? This was big news although Lewis protested that the mixture was no more than a combination of mineral water and tap water; cornerman Artie Curley said that there might have been some peppermint schnapps in the bottle to settle Pryor's stomach, which had been acting up before and during the fight; and Panama was never called upon to give an official explanation. But rightly or wrongly he became tagged as a guy who was familiar with all the dodges.

The trainer may have joined the major league with Pryor, but he did not neglect his responsibilities to Resto and the forthcoming Collins fight. He realised just what was at stake for his boxer, and for the two weeks before the fight, the pair lived together in a Manhattan hotel; endured together the grind of the roadwork in Central Park; travelled back and forth together for the sessions in the gym; took their meals together and kept discussing what a win over Collins might do for Luis's career. Physically and mentally, Resto may have been in his best shape for years when he arrived at the Garden on 16 June.

The packed tiers who awarded ringside dignitary Muhammad Ali a standing ovation also hailed their other great idol, after the rejuvenated Duran had halted brave Davey Moore in round eight to become a champion yet again. And they witnessed Luis Resto outpunch Billy Collins to cop an upset unanimous ten-round decision – at least that is how it must have looked from the cheap seats. For those much closer to the action, a stranger contest was unfolding: every time the supposedly light-hitting Resto landed a punch, the normally tough Collins would wince; ugly welts began to appear around the prospect's eyes; and returning to his corner after yet another pain-filled round, he complained to his father: 'It feels like he's hitting me with rocks.'

Not lacking for courage or determination, Collins kept battling

back, but somehow the pre-fight scenario had gone haywire. The elder
Collins was at a total loss; it was obvious that something was seriously
wrong, but what? Everything started to make sense at the fight's end
when Resto approached the shell-shocked father for the traditional
handshake, and the trainer immediately felt the absence of padding
across the knuckle part of the glove. He felt, then felt again, then held
on tight and started yelling for the Commission inspectors.

The chief inspector, John Squeri, along with the distraught dad, led
the protesting Resto back to his dressing room and took charge of the
gloves. Squeri, in turn, gave them in a box to Commission chairman
Jack Prenderville, and small holes were subsequently found in the
palms of the gloves. The holes were ¾in in diameter and from them an
ounce of horsehair padding had been removed from each 8oz glove.
For ten rounds, Resto had been punching Collins with the full force
of his taped fists, unhindered by any padding across the knuckles. Little
wonder that when, the following morning, *The Ring*'s Ben Sharav
went to the Statler Hotel to take some close-up pictures of the beaten-
up boxer, Collins looked like the victim of a particularly brutal Central
Park mugging.

The odyssey of the gloves . . . from ringside inspector Squeri to
chairman Prenderville, then on to another inspector who left them
overnight in the boot of his car before taking them for examination to
the manufacturers, Everlast, and from there the gloves were sent to the
New York State police laboratory . . . there was not the slightest doubt
that somebody had taken liberties with them.

Thirteen days after the fight, the New York State Athletic
Commission held its inquiry: Panama Lewis had his manager's and
trainer's licences revoked 'immediately and permanently'; another
Resto cornerman, Pedro Alvarado, also lost his licence. And the
fighter? Resto was suspended indefinitely, but for at least a period of a
year. The Commission also altered the result of the fight to 'No
Decision.'

They might have seemed to have done their duty with commendable speed and decisiveness, but in fact, on the infamous night, they
had failed miserably to perform their duties. Inspectors are supposed to
be on hand in the dressing room when a boxer's hands are being taped

and the gloves laced on, but for some unexplained reason, no inspector was present when Resto was being readied for the ring. Chairman Prenderville had to admit this horribly embarrassing gaffe in a televised interview days after the fight, yet the two inspectors on duty that evening did not even attend the subsequent inquiry.

With all the attendant publicity, several managers recalled occasions when no officials had turned up at the dressing rooms; at the time their absence had gone unremarked. Then there was another disconcerting story about a recent contest in which one boxer wore standard 8oz gloves while his opponent had been allowed into the ring wearing 16oz training gloves! There were loud calls for the Commission to get its act together, but that was all too late for the busted-up Billy Collins. And questions even had to be asked about Collins's own camp, because again incredibly, they had failed to send a representative to the opposition's changing room to ensure that all was kosher.

Down the years, there has been a custom of representatives of the opposing factions paying a pre-fight visit into enemy territory. This exercise provides reassurance that nothing shady is about to happen, is most often conducted with humour and without fuss, but can, on occasion, become fractious. Some opportunists regard it as a last chance to engage in some psychological warfare but that ploy can backfire. When an upbeat Butch Lewis (no relation to Panama) was looking after the interests of his fighter Michael Spinks and entered Mike Tyson's dressing room, he was hoping to cause some mischief and have some fun. Instead he watched in awe as a focused and ferocious Tyson punched a hole in the wall! Butch broke out in a sweat, made a quick exit, and whether he transmitted his anxiety to his boxer is unknown, but Spinks failed to get past round one.

Nobody will ever know if Luis Resto was fit to punch holes in the Garden walls, for the people who mattered most were not there. In the bad old days, black fighters would sometimes soak their bandaged hands in plaster of Paris to offset the weight they might have to concede, and old heavyweight champion Jess Willard maintained for years that Jack Dempsey had fought with loaded gloves in their Toledo bout, which turned into a three-round slaughter. Willard wound up with a broken cheekbone, missing teeth, burst ribs, and every right to feel sore. But two of his men, Walter Monaghan and Ike O'Neil, had supervised the bandaging of Dempsey's hands in the dressing room, and there had been no skullduggery.

What went on in the Garden on 16 June 1983 just had to be a one-off. Ancient trainers like Arcel and Brown who always played it straight themselves, but who had seen just about all the good and bad there was to see, could recall nothing comparable from the past; their main sense of shock was that nobody had been on the lookout in Resto's dressing room. And the hard cases who frequent the gyms were genuinely shocked when they saw reporter Sharav's horror pictures of Collins's battered features. Then the entire business paused for a minute and took a deep breath when the word came through that the young man from Tennessee would not be able to box again.

As part of the dreadful beating he had absorbed, Billy had suffered serious eye damage – permanently blurred vision, brought about because of a torn iris. He was never going to be a contender, and tragically, he would never be able to come to terms with his terrible misfortune.

The law would pursue its own course and in its own time, and in October 1986, Luis Resto was convicted of assault, conspiracy, and criminal possession of a deadly weapon (his fists). He served two and a half years of a three-year sentence. Panama Lewis was found guilty of similar crimes, plus tampering with a sports contest, and was given six years. Like his boxer, he was released after two and a half years.

What made them do it? What made them think that they could ever get away with such a plot? How could they know that the inspectors would not be in their dressing room? Or that Collins's people would not turn up? How were they so sure that referee Tony Perez wouldn't notice something?

Questions and more questions, and even after all these years, precious few definitive answers. No blame could be attached to referee Perez because when he gave both boxers' gloves a quick once-over in the ring, he would be checking only that the laces were safely taped over and the glove surface was clean. The last thing on his mind would have been minute holes.

Panama Lewis tossed away a blossoming career, but for what? A share of a $7,500 purse and the promise of perhaps two or three more of the same? This guy was doing all right living off a percentage of Aaron Pryor's wages and at that time, those could be a million-plus a fight. And, after all, Resto was no stranger to defeat. Admittedly this was a crossroads fight, one that might have dispatched him to Palookaville, but were the stakes high enough to take such desperate and despicable measures?

Luis Resto has still to admit to any wrongdoing, even after serving his time. He maintains that the gloves were switched some time between the end of the fight and four days later when they wound up at the police laboratory. But for what reason, Luis? Why?

In an interview with Steve Farhood for *Boxing Monthly*, Resto claimed the gloves felt the same as always. 'If the padding was out, when you hit somebody, you'd feel pain. You'd break your hands. My hands were fine. And if I knew the gloves had been tampered with, why would I have gone to Collins's corner after the fight to congratulate him? That's when the father said what he said. He's lucky I didn't hit him.'

Lucky? Nobody should ever describe Billy Collins Sr as lucky. As late as 1998, he told *Sports Illustrated*: 'You don't think Resto knew he didn't have padding in his gloves? You don't think Panama Lewis took it out? I've had fifteen years to think about it, and I know – I know – that they did it. They killed him. They killed my son.'

Billy Collins did not live long after his night in the Garden. Following the beating and then the brain-numbing news that he could never fight again, the once vibrant young prospect simply fell apart. First there was the drinking, and when that got worse, he left his wife, and then – just nine months after the fight – drunk, and with his mind still probably in an uproar, Collins drove his Oldsmobile off the road, crashed into a creek, and his death came instantly. He was 22 years old.

Could Resto have fought ten rounds without noticing that the gloves were somehow different from normal? The experts are split, some saying that in the heat of battle, there is a possibility that the fighter might not have been aware of the removal; others, however, are dismissive, asserting that he must have known after landing his first hard shot.

Resto still displays the E.S.P.N. belt that he won after beating Robert Sawyer in Atlantic City; he works out in the gym as if one day he will defend his title; and he fantasises about boxing again. He lives frugally and alone and the ten rounds with Billy Collins must often return to haunt him.

If those ghosts remind him of the part he played in a shocking crime, then we hope they are fearsome and frequent visitors. But if, as he still claims, Resto somehow knew nothing of the foul trickery being played around him, then he too becomes another victim of that June night in the Garden.

Roberto Duran's 32nd birthday bash proved to be a bummer for all but the flamboyant Panamanian. Even young Davey Moore, who lost his title that night, would die in freakish circumstances just five years later. In the driveway of his own house, his unoccupied van started to roll downhill towards him and, in trying to bring it to a halt, he was knocked over and crushed. Davey was 28.

Moore had been a champion and Collins almost a contender, and, granted different circumstances, one day they might have met in the ring. Fate took out Davey Moore, but a much more malevolent being finished off Billy Collins.

12

Willie Classen:
'Took His Defeats Badly'

EMILE ALPHONSE GRIFFITH was a tremendous fighter: a three-times world welterweight champion and a two-time middleweight holder who survived 112 ring battles to claim rightfully his place alongside boxing's other legends in the International Hall Of Fame at Canastota, New York. Sadly, however, Griffith will always be best remembered for the one fight that he would rather forget – the March night in the Garden when his fierce rival Benny Paret never recovered from a twelfth-round battering.

Not only has Griffith had to live with the memory of what happened to Benny The Kid, but he was also subjected to the horror of a close-up action replay seventeen years later, when he worked as a cornerman for Wilfred Scypion on the sorry night that middleweight Willie Classen was fatally injured in the Garden's Felt Forum. Unlike Paret, Willie Classen was no world champion, no longer even a fringe challenger, but the Puerto Rican and the Cuban shared a love of the sport and a crazy kind of courage that ultimately cost both of them their lives . . . lives that, with the benefit of hindsight, should never have been put at risk. Hindsight, however, has always been a most powerful weapon in the armoury of the enemies of boxing.

The British and American Medical Associations have been long and loud opponents of The Science and seldom fail to demand its abolition whenever a fatality or a serious mishap occurs; politicians, too, are aware that taking a wild swipe at the business will invariably attract for them considerable media coverage – let us call it the old soft-target syndrome. Yet, Britain's Boxing Board of Control can boast doctors and members of Parliament and eminent Queen's Counsels amongst the ranks of its stewards, and despite the endless sniping, the game's casualty rate is not nearly as high as that of many other sports.

But, of course, boxing must stand alone since the objective is deliberately to inflict punishment on an opponent, and so it should always be ultra-vigilant in the application of its rules and safeguards. Unfortunately, that has not always been the case.

Safety standards have improved out of all recognition compared to the pre-war days when regulation was basic beyond belief: mandatory CAT scans, paramedics on standby at the ringside, and ambulances in attendance at promotions are just three of the many advancements, but there is never room for complacency, and the obvious risk to every fighter ducking through the ropes should never be minimised. There is always scope for further progress without tampering with the essence of what, to so many, is both a wonderfully challenging activity and an engrossing spectacle; but particularly in America, where each state is responsible for its own administration and some states do not even have a boxing commission to oversee promotions, there is still much to be done.

Yet no matter what fresh measures are introduced, the bottom line is that there will be deaths in the future, and they are certain to come under the microscope much more than, for example, a similar tragedy to a jockey or a motorcyclist or a racing driver, if only because of the stark and dramatic nature of two men battling one-on-one in the ring.

Away back in 1947, Sugar Ray Robinson, had a dream on the night before he defended his welterweight title against Jimmy Doyle in Cleveland. In the dream Doyle died, and so unnerved was the normally ice-cool Robinson, that at the weigh-in the following day, he tried to call off the fight. The promoters scoffed at his dream and he was persuaded to be sensible and go ahead, but that night Jimmy Doyle was stopped in round eight and he never recovered. At the subsequent inquest, the coroner naïvely asked the champion if he had intended to get Doyle in trouble, and Robinson replied: 'Mister, it's my business to get him in trouble.'

Sugar Ray was simply telling it as it really is and there can be no shame in that. Champions like the fine featherweight Davey Moore against Sugar Ramos, and Kid Paret against Griffith, died defending their titles; young hopefuls like the Londoner, Bradley Stone, and the Scot, James Murray, died attempting to realise their ambitions. Death is indiscriminate in its selection, but there have been a few dark occasions when tragedies should have been averted, and boxing rightly suffered two black eyes and a bloody nose.

Human nature being what it is, there will always be men, hungry for a buck or a quid, who will be prepared to flout the safety regulations, and unfortunately, there will always be misguided fighters, just as prepared to go along with them, well aware that they are putting themselves at even greater jeopardy than usual. Willie Classen was such a boxer, and how he came to be fighting in that ten-rounder against Wilfred Scypion on 23 November 1979 is a tale that damaged the business to its roots.

Willie Classen was born in Santurce, Puerto Rico, in 1950 and arrived in New York as a nine-year-old. He was brought up in a tough neighbourhood in East Harlem and, like so many budding fighters, he found trouble in the streets, eventually being sent to the Spofford Youth House in the Bronx. Spofford was a medium-security facility and many wild youngsters experienced the tough regime, not least in later years, a twelve-year-old Mike Tyson, who had frequent short stays there until he was finally moved upstate to the Tryon School For Boys, which led to an introduction to his guru, Cus D'Amato. There was to be no similar Svengali for Classen.

Willie, however, showed a talent in the ring, bright enough to win a New York Golden Gloves championship in 1971, and it was inevitable that he would try his luck against the professionals. He loved to fight, enjoyed the sparring sessions, and the nights in the ring with the fans cheering him on, even if his wages were never great. Classen was value for money, but around the gyms there were stories that sometimes Willie could go off the rails, dabbling in drugs when things were not going well. The word was that Willie took his defeats badly.

He was managed by a gentleman called Marco Minuto, the proprietor of a Bronx pizza parlour, and by no means one of the New York fight scene's leading lights. The pair had first met shortly after Willie's Golden Gloves success and Minuto somehow became an unofficial adviser. He did not, however, become his registered manager until 1977. The pizza man did not enjoy a great reputation among his peers, but much of that would not emerge until after the tragedy – that old devil hindsight.

By 1978, Classen was still scuffling around the periphery of the big time, and his make-or-break match came on 25 August when he was booked into the Garden against the rugged Vito Antuofermo, who had lost only three times in 46 fights up until then. A native of Bari, Italy, Antuofermo had moved to Brooklyn as a fourteen-year-old, was a popular attraction with the Italian fraternity, and was in fact only two fights away from winning the world middleweight title. He was, however, known more for his staying power than his punch, and he also cut easily, making him a hopeful target for every opponent.

Willie and Vito knew one another well from regular sparring sessions; they had worked together often enough for Classen to become convinced that he had the Italian's number, and so the match was made. A win, even a cut-eye victory, would have been an enormous boost for the Puerto Rican, but it was not to be.

Antuofermo later recalled in a Randy Gordon interview in *The Ring*: 'I pounded him good. Hundreds of punches. I believe the beating I gave him took a lot out of him – physically and mentally. He lost three weeks later to Al Styles and from then on it was all downhill. In our fight he got hurt.'

Joseph Bruno, one of the ringside judges for the fatal night against Scypion, remembered the Antuofermo contest as a 'fairly close fight with Vito a unanimous winner'. In writing his version of the Classen–Scypion tragedy for *The Ring*, he recalled the Antuofermo win more for the antics of Marco Minuto.

'As is customary in close fights when a Latin fighter loses, the bottles began their descent. Then an even more intolerable event occurred. Marco Minuto re-entered the ring carrying Willie Classen on his shoulders. They waved frantically to the crowd and in minutes the ring was filled with unruly – and probably intoxicated – fight fans. The Garden was in bedlam as chairs were heaved all over the arena. Finally the police "riot squad" was called in and order was restored.'

The fight may have been close as Bruno said, but Antuofermo was also correct: Willie Classen's best days were now history. The next important milestone in his slide came on 6 April 1979 in New York, when he was stopped by John Locicero in eight rounds. In New York State a boxer must undergo a neurological examination following a stoppage, but Classen failed to take the test. And so, come October, when he was called in at short notice to box Britain's Tony Sibson in London, he was not carrying a valid licence from his home state – just the kind of subterfuge that gives boxing a rotten name. The British Boxing Board allowed Minuto and Classen to slip through their net, and that was inexcusable. On 9 October, at the Albert Hall, Sibson, then the reigning British champion and a powerful puncher, floored Classen three times before knocking him out in the second round.

A manager is supposed to look after his fighter, always first checking out for his charge's best interests, and following the blow-out against Sibson, after which Classen complained of double vision, the possibility of retirement should have been discussed, or at the very least, a lengthy rest period prescribed in order to recharge the batteries. Instead, back in New York, Willie finally took the tests that he should have undergone months before, and manager Minuto informed the Commission that his middleweight had been stopped on cuts in London – instead of suffering the shattering knockout – and so Classen was granted back his licence. Just as his manager had hoodwinked the British Board of Control, now he had conned the New York equivalent. Looking back, the lack of correspondence and co-operation between the two regulatory bodies now seems hard to credit.

But Willie Classen was free again to box in his home state, and on ten days' notice, Minuto signed him to box the unbeaten Wilfred Scypion as one of three ten-round headliners at the Felt Forum; again the pay would not be exceptional, and there was little doubt that Scypion would prove a handful; but this was still quite a high-profile pairing. The Houston middleweight was an above-average puncher, and during that year, none of his other six opponents had managed to last the distance. In 1983, he – and Tony Sibson – would be considered good enough to challenge the superb Marvin Hagler for the title, but back in 1979, just like Sibson, Scypion was still climbing the ladder and

Willie Classen was a convenient rung. The Texan's camp, however, were taking no chances, and sought out the assistance of Emile Griffith for the final stages of preparation in New York, and also to work in the corner.

Griffith had fought his last contest just two years earlier – a points loss to Alan Minter in Monte Carlo – and now he was earning his bread coaching and training some of New York's better prospects. Everybody in the game had a fond word for Emile, and not just because of his warm nature and his wonderful fighting record. There had been fewer than 8,000 in the Garden that night when Benny Paret was damaged beyond repair, but for some strange reason, the industry that mourned the stricken Cuban also demonstrated an extraordinary compassion for the shell-shocked Virgin Islander.

In a professional career spanning nineteen years, Griffith had exchanged punches with the greatest names of his generation – champions such as Luis Rodriguez and Dick Tiger and Nino Benvenuti and José Napoles and Carlos Monzon – and on no fewer than five occasions, the ring announcer, had raised his hand and bellowed: '. . . and new champion!'

But it is because of his three-fight series with Paret that Griffith is most remembered, and especially for that crushing final showdown on 24 March 1962. In their first fight eleven months earlier in Miami, Griffith had come from behind to execute a perfect left-hook–right-hand combination to knock out champion Paret in the thirteenth; and in the rematch, five months later in New York, Benny The Kid was awarded a split, and highly controversial, decision. That there was going to be a deciding third match was a certainty, but the Paret management decided to cash in before that.

Just over two months after that strength-sapping, and what many thought, losing fight against Griffith, Paret's manager, Manny Alfaro, arranged for Paret to step up a weight and challenge a prime hardcase in Gene Fullmer for his middleweight title. Our old pal, hindsight, tells us that this was a match made in hell, and even at the time, eyebrows went into orbit following the announcement. Paret, displaying all his inbred macho, absorbed a beating before being stopped in the tenth in Las Vegas. The alarm bells should have been ringing loud for Benny, but nobody was listening. The Kid would be okay for the 24 March date with Griffith.

Most of the claptrap perpetuated after that fight centres on an incident at the weigh-in, where a nude Paret pressed himself close to Griffith on the scales, and whispered 'maricon' – homosexual. Griffith was naturally angry, and he was supposed to have been so incensed, that hours later, he battered Paret to death. Think about it . . . in two previous title fights those guys had exchanged their best shots for almost the length of time that it takes to play a football match; the hype at the weigh-in was mild compared to the slanderous rantings that are commonplace today, and remembering the disappointing crowd that turned out that night, Paret's performance was most likely stage-managed to nudge along the slow ticket sales.

In the actual fight, Griffith overcame an early knockdown to take complete control, and in the twelfth, he unleashed a tremendous barrage which trapped the helpless Benny on the ropes, and by the time that referee Ruby Goldstein intervened, Paret had been critically hurt, and Emile Griffith permanently scarred.

But seventeen long years after the heartache of Benny's death, Griffith was feeling good when he accompanied Scypion down the aisle and into the Forum ring. In comparison, the Classen faction, far from being confident, had already been at odds and had been voicing certain misgivings. In his *Ring* article, judge Joseph Bruno wrote that veteran manager and vastly experienced cornerman Mike Capriano had expressed misgivings in the dressing room when preparing Classen.

'I didn't like the way Classen looked before the fight. I was taping his hands and didn't like what I was seeing, and so I went to Minuto and asked him if something was wrong. I told him that he [Classen] looked bad but he wouldn't take responsibility. You can be sure if I had the responsibility, he would be alive today.'

Perhaps, Mike. And perhaps hindsight, pal.

From Bruno's prime vantage point, he judged the first round to Classen, the second to Scypion, and then after Willie took a four-count on his knees in the third, he saw Classen come back into the fight. Going into the eighth, Bruno was scoring the bout four-three in rounds for the Texan, but Classen suffered a sustained body assault throughout the eighth, and there was much of the same in the ninth, until Scypion switched to the head, and Willie sagged on to the bottom rope. Referee Lew Eskin deemed it a knockdown and gave him the mandatory eight count, and at the bell, Willie tottered back to his corner on legs that were going walkabout. Time for foresight.

In his corner, Classen was surrounded, all but engulfed by carers: there was manager Minuto and the two seconds, and the two ringside doctors, and referee Eskin; one of the doctors, Richard Izquierdo, was also Classen's personal physician, and at that stage there was little doubt that there were too many chiefs . . . someone ought to have taken responsibility and cried enough for there was no way that Classen could still win the fight, and nobody should have paid the slightest heed to the middleweight warrior who kept nodding his head to affirm that he wanted to box on. But remember, there are only sixty fleeting seconds between rounds.

The bell rang for the final three minutes, and the Classen corner was late in clearing as Willie slowly rose from his stool. Scypion came out like an express and there was no traditional touching of gloves before he landed a rapid three-punch combination; Classen was knocked out of the ring and Eskin caught his head and the seconds, still clambering from the ring, cushioned his fall and lowered him to the ring apron; and from the far corner, Emile Griffith was already reliving his night of anguish against Paret. That was it for Willie Classen; he had answered the bell for the final time, though typically, he kept battling on for five days in Bellevue hospital before he accepted the final count.

Judge Bruno, at ringside but with no authority to call a halt, was of the opinion that Classen had looked more exhausted than seriously hurt; the doctors had been satisfied that Willie had known where he was, and, of course, Minuto and the fighter himself had wanted him to come out for that final round.

Could Willie have still been aware that a stoppage would have resulted in another neurological examination? Would similar thoughts have passed through Minuto's mind? And what about the medical men whose brief was not to worry about the outcome of the fight, but the welfare of the fighter? But again remember that sixty seconds flash past.

Tune in now to referee Eskin, who recorded his thoughts in an article for the South African *Boxing World*, subsequently appearing in the British *Boxing News*. Eskin had spent a lifetime in the business, had written authoritatively about the sport, and had officiated at the highest level, including refereeing Muhammad Ali' s Dublin appearance seven years earlier against Al Blue Lewis. Eskin was no novice and his words must be respected.

'At no time during the fight did I consider stopping it before I did. When Classen was knocked down in the third, he was up at the count of four. He came back in the sixth round and had Scypion holding on after landing a solid left hook.

'In the ninth round he was hurt by a series of punches, backed into a corner and bent over sitting on the bottom rope which under the rules of the New York Commission is considered a knockdown and I counted it as such.

'Just as soon as he realised that he was being given a count, he straightened up, wiped his nose with his glove, answered me both verbally and by shaking his head that he was okay and wanted to continue. He was both clear-eyed and coherent and he finished the remaining fifty seconds of the round by bobbing and weaving to avoid the punches thrown at him.'

And of those last desperate seconds between the ninth and the fatal tenth round?

'Between rounds two doctors – one of whom by the twists of fate was his own personal physician – examined him and decided that he was fit to continue. Classen's manager and his cornermen also felt he was okay. I talked to him and he was coherent, and in the final analysis he himself wanted to go on.'

That would appear to be a clinical assessment from an experienced referee, but Lew Eskin, in the follow-up inquiry by the New York State Athletic Commission, copped six months' suspension because 'the Commission feels that an official of Eskin's experience should have acknowledged the custom and practice in boxing that boxers come to the middle of the ring, particularly in the last round of a fight, and he did not do so'.

Really? Would Scypion's three-punch combo been less lethal delivered from the centre of the ring?

The Commission also weighed off Marco Minuto with a one-year ban and the cornermen Mike Capriano and Al La Cava with six months' suspension. According to the Commission, Capriano and La Cava were culpable because 'they both admitted they did not see the lethal punches Classen received in the ninth round. The feeling of the Commission is that in order to best protect their fighter, it is the duty of any Second to be fully aware of what transpires in the ring at all times.'

Really? But referee Eskin had not thought the ninth-round punches 'lethal'.

The two ringside doctors resigned from the Commission, and then the chairman Jack Prenderville suspended boxing in the state for a period of one month and issued a lengthy document calling for improvements: 'to upgrade the sport of boxing and provide for the safety and well-being of those involved'.

Really? But wasn't this just the Commission slamming the stable door . . .?

The New York authorities had dished out suspensions to four licence holders – in the light of the details surrounding Classen's stoppage in London, Minuto's year seemed lenient in the extreme – had accepted the resignations of another two, and had produced a manifesto for the betterment of the sport. They had been seen to do their duty, but the story of Willie Classen had developed into an embarrassment and would not be dusted into a corner. In death, Willie became more of a celebrity than he had ever been as a tough, game middleweight. In Britain, the *Sunday Times* initiated an investigation into just how come Classen was allowed to box in the country without holding a valid licence from his home state; and in America, the lawyers got busy. But it was nine years after that night in the Garden before Classen's widow Marilyn reached an out-of-court settlement with the two ringside doctors in attendance at the fight.

Manhattan Supreme Court Justice Helen Freedman proclaimed that Classen 'knew or should have known the risks of injury inherent in the sport of professional boxing'. But she added that 'Classen could not be expected to assume the risk of injury from negligent medical care'.

Whenever a boxer dies in the ring, there is always more than one victim, not least his immediate family. But Wilfred Scypion was also a victim, and he prayed for forgiveness though there was nothing to forgive. And before him, Emile Griffith had been a victim who suffered recurring nightmares, and then witnessed a horrific re-run. And before him, Sugar Ray Robinson had been a victim who saw a dream come terribly true. Every boxer accepts the risks, but very few contemplate that one dreadful day when they might be responsible for the death of an opponent.

But, of course, Willie Classen was the greatest victim of all because he should not have been fighting in that Garden ring in the first place; it should not have been his night. Hindsight . . .

PART FIVE

Blackballed (2)

Nobody would defend a title against Sam Langford, not even Jack Johnson, who would have been favourite to beat him. Little Sam spelt trouble.

Harry Wills had the backing of the New York commission for a title shot. So Dempsey went off to Philadelphia and fought Tunney.

Jimmy Bivins could beat the champs and he even won something called the 'duration' heavyweight title. But when it came to the real thing, nobody wanted to know him.

> Politics and prejudice would always
> score the heaviest punches

13

Sam Langford:
'Every Fight Was a Pleasure'

JACK JOHNSON, in his day, was a hugely controversial heavyweight champion; as big a front-page sensation as either Ali or Tyson would become; probably more so, because time-travelling back ninety years to his prime, a black in the United States was still widely regarded as a fourth-rate citizen, and big Jack never considered himself second best to anyone or anything. Like Ali, when making his stand against enlistment during the Vietnam conflict, Johnson brought down upon himself the wrath of a nation, if for far less noble reasons. And, like Tyson, he fought a long, running battle with the law, if for far less odious crimes.

The White America of the time could never come to terms with the extraordinary news that a black was the world's supreme fighter after the man from Galveston had thrashed Tommy Burns for the heavyweight title on Boxing Day 1908 at Sydney's Rushcutters Bay; the old, undefeated hero Jim Jeffries was press-ganged into a comeback, following huge public pressure, fuelled by the likes of the racist writer Jack London, and two years later in Reno, he was humiliated in fifteen painful rounds. And so came about the era of 'The White Hope', which offered an opportunity to every overgrown farm boy who could lick the local yokels to tug on the gloves and go for gold and glory.

For a time, Johnson, who blossomed in the company of white women and who delighted in dodging his many creditors, was in wonderland. After beating Burns and before meeting Jeffries, Jack made such unlikely defences as a no-decision in Vancouver against

Victor McLaglen (much more famous as John Wayne's sidekick in so many movies) and the middleweight Stanley Ketchel, the renowned Michigan Assassin. Ketchel, a murderous puncher, did succeed in flooring a careless champion, but was promptly repaid with a knockout blow, so concussive that two of his teeth were left embedded in Johnson's glove.

The truth – unpalatable as it must have been to the likes of Jack London – was that no white heavyweight could extend the champion. All the best big men, and some who stood not so big, were black, but Johnson did not want even to consider them. And why? Against staggering odds, he had become the first black heavyweight champion in history, and even the most remote possibility of a black successor would, in his eyes, have cheapened his achievement. Jack had no time for anything cheap, and so, like John L. Sullivan before him, he drew the colour line – but against his own race.

There was a host of talented black fighters competing at the time: Sam McVey from the West Coast and Joe Jeannette from the East Coast; there was the Joplin Ghost, Jeff Clark, only a middleweight, but exceptional against all sizes; there was Denver Ed Martin and Frank Childs and Jim Barry and Black Bill. And then, there was Sam Langford, whose awesome reputation in the ring has survived for almost a century.

Now, before examining Langford's amazing career, an important point ought to be made on Johnson's behalf. He boxed Sam once and beat him; and he also took care of Jeannette and McVey and Denver Ed and Childs and Black Bill . . . but all before he became champion. In the seven years he held the title, he made only one defence against a black, a laborious fifteen-rounder against Battling Jim Johnson in Paris. He would have been a betting favourite to retain his title against the rest, but McVey and Jeannette were certainly worthy of a championship opportunity. And Langford? Artful Jack considered him an unacceptable risk, and because the two men intensely disliked each other, Johnson took a particular pleasure in deriding Sam's efforts to secure a rematch.

Sam Langford was born in Weymouth, Nova Scotia, in 1883, according to some on 12 February, others 4 March – perhaps he was a difficult birth. Fully grown, he barely stood 5ft 8in, but this was offset by enormous shoulders and chest and a tremendously long reach. He left home at fifteen, drifted down to the States, and settled in Boston, where he attracted the attention of Joe Woodman, who owned a drugstore and a gym and who staged fights around the city. The pair were to enjoy a long and reasonably amicable partnership.

In his prime, Langford was known around the world as The Boston Tar Baby and Sambo, nicknames that today would have the P.C. police drawing their truncheons. But those were the days when words such as 'nigger' and 'coon' and 'shine' frequently appeared in print; days when many misguideds saw blacks as creatures from another planet; days when the newspapers felt free to comment on a black fighter's looks, or rather the lack of them.

Sam McVey was indeed no pretty boy and he was well aware of the fact. But that should have been no reason for a *Los Angeles Times* journalist to write: 'Any man who could look at McVey for twenty rounds deserves a good reputation for bravery, for the fighter's countenance would scare back the rising moon.' Unbelievable! Luckily McVey had a sense of humour.

He and Langford were to share many adventures all over the world, and when they were first introduced in a promoter's office, it was McVey who scored a decisive points victory. After shaking hands, he produced from his pocket a handsome, silver-mounted pipe and presented it to a puzzled Langford explaining: 'My dad gave me this and told me to keep it until I met an uglier nigger than myself. I reckon that pipe, Mr Langford, has been won by you.'

So Langford, too, would have been an also-ran in the beauty stakes, but it was those massive shoulders and that terrific reach that were important and filled Joe Woodman so full of hope. On 11 April 1902, Woodman launched the career that would span 24 years, when he booked Sam to box Jack McVicker in Boston. Langford, then scaling around light welterweight, knocked out McVicker in six rounds; he was off and running, and incredibly, by the following year, he had fought around thirty times and had climbed high enough not only to box, but to outpoint the reigning world lightweight champion Joe Gans over fifteen rounds in their December match-up in Boston. No title was at stake that evening, yet now there was no question that Langford had arrived. But arrived where? For over twenty years he would continue to astound against much bigger and heavier men, but no champion would ever risk his crown against him.

In September 1904, he fought a draw with the original Joe Walcott, a pint-sized marvel known as the Barbados Demon, who had just lost his welterweight championship on a disqualification, but who would lay claim to it again. Langford might have been entitled to the decision, but anyway, he would have been pushed to make the welter limit. He was conceding lumps of weight, however, when he toyed with the former light heavyweight holder Philadelphia Jack O'Brien before stopping him in five rounds in New York, and he played his part in a hectic brawl against the fearsome middleweight champion Ketchel only just months after The Assassin's vain try against Johnson for the heavyweight title.

Sam and Stanley got it on over six rounds in Philadelphia on 27 April 1910 and at the close it was mighty tight. Langford had controlled the early exchanges, but Ketchel had been the boss in the second half of the fight. The majority of the newspapers (wagers were settled on press accounts of no-decision contests) decided that the champion had just about done enough. Manager Woodman immediately pressed for a return with the title at stake, but Stanley played coy and instead opted for quick defences, first against Willie Lewis and then Jim Smith. And that, sadly, was that for The Assassin, who, on 15 October, contrived to get himself assassinated! On a farm in Conway, Missouri, a hand called Walter Dipley, jealous that Ketchel was being over-attentive to his wife, shot him dead. Ketchel was 24.

Over the title route, and especially at middleweight, Langford would have carried an outstanding chance against Ketchel or any other 160-pounder. As late as 1922, his best days a memory and his sight beginning to cause him serious problems, Sam was still sharp enough to knock out the future champion Tiger Flowers in two rounds. He was that good.

Langford was at his best from the time that he beat Gans as an ambitious twenty-year-old in 1903 and throughout the next ten years. After that, he would still be a crafty and dangerous opponent, a cunning boxer with a chilling punch in either hand, but by then, the ambition had been dulled and reality had taught him that he was never going to get the rematch with Johnson; that chance to avenge the one defeat that really hurt.

Chelsea, Massachusetts, was the unlikely and remote venue for their one and only meeting, on 26 April 1906. Langford was a confident 23-year-old, Johnson, a super-confident 28-year-old, frustrated that he was still having to box the likes of Jeannette and Black Bill and now Langford, while trying to pin down the new champion Tommy Burns, who had just won the title in a match against Marvin Hart in the February of that year. Jack was in the tenth year of his career, Sam in his fifth.

Much romantic nonsense has been written about their fight: how Langford was robbed of the verdict – a fifteen-round points decision – and how Johnson was on the canvas for a nine count and nearly out. Such fairy tales were largely the work of an imaginative and loyal manager, Woodman, and over the years they were given some credibility. Back then, communications could be sketchy, and a bright manager often painted his own picture of the drama.

But more reliable versions from eye-witnesses relate that Sam was down for several counts and finished quite banged about, suffering a broken nose and a burst mouth. Big Jack won comfortably enough, but he'd had a huge weight advantage of at least 35lb, and over the 45 minutes, he had sampled the power of Langford's punches, enough to become convinced that he did not need the aggravation of an encore.

Do not, however, shed too many tears for The Tar Baby. Financially, he was doing all right; much, much better than all right compared to the average black or white worker of his time. So much so that, in those flush years, he could afford to carry a crisp $1,000 bill in his pocket, just in case he might come face-to-face with Johnson and be able to brandish the grand as a serious stake for a challenge. Sam tried to stalk Johnson just as Jack had dogged Burns, but the champion was very fast on his feet when it came to avoiding officers of the law, creditors, or just persistent and pesky challengers.

Finding opponents who would draw a good gate and fetch an attractive purse was always going to be a problem for Langford, who was now resigned to conceding vast amounts of weight in most of his fights. On the promise of a series of lucrative bouts, in 1907 he sailed for England, but after dispensing with heavyweight Tiger Smith at London's National Sporting Club, thanks to a display of ferocious punching, nobody else would take him on. The following year, back in the States, he produced another electrifying performance when putting away a white heavyweight, Fireman Jim Flynn, within one round in San Francisco. Flynn had already survived into the eleventh against Johnson, and in 1912 would be even granted a return with the title at stake. Crafty Jack!

In England, however, the National Sporting Club promoter A.F. (Peggy) Bettison had unearthed a fighter who he thought might prove too big and rough for the Canadian, and so in 1909, Langford again crossed the Atlantic, this time to face the reigning British heavyweight champion, William Iron Hague, for the biggest purse he would ever receive in his career – $10,000, or £2,500 in Bettison's readies.

Britain in the year 1909. That January, the first old-age pensions were paid out to the over-seventies, a very well-received five shillings a week. In London in March, the most expensive aeroplane at the first Exhibition of Aircraft cost £1,440. And throughout the year, on the Thames Embankment, there was becoming an increasing problem of the homeless and destitute sleeping rough. The Salvation Army fed as many as 650 poor souls every day and provided some welcome shelter during the long, night hours. Langford's £2,500 would have purchased a lot of Sally Army dinners. The one-time teenage stray from Nova Scotia was, in comparison to many Londoners, living the life of a sultan.

Iron Hague would never be rated in the top flight of British heavyweight champions and finished up with a career record of eleven defeats in 37 contests, but he did carry the genuine dig on which promoter Bettison was pinning his hopes. Many of the Club members patriotically thought The Ironman in with a sporting shout, and so the betting odds were quite tight, attractive enough to persuade both Langford and Woodman that there was an easy bonus awaiting them. They decided to punt the entire purse on Sam.

Stories differ whether it was Woodman or trainer John Davis who actually transacted the business; whoever it was momentarily forgot where he was! He struck the bet for 10,000 (thinking dollars) and was accepted by a bookmaker (thinking pounds) – the visitors were horror-struck when they examined the betting receipt; suddenly Langford faced liabilities of $40,000, which he did not have, if Iron Hague got lucky.

When he entered the ring, Sam, understandably, was not in the best mental shape, a trifle preoccupied, and early on, he boxed in a trance, until towards the end of the third, the 38lb heavier Hague scored a heavy knockdown. A bad move for the Englishman. Coming out for the fourth, a now focused and angry Langford immediately feinted the British champion on to the end of a crushing right hand, and the fight was all over, the huge bet won.

Sam had made a fortune in London, but like the majority of his contemporary pugilists, he was a relentless and carefree spender, though a more reliable settler of debts and never as flamboyant or foolishly reckless in his romantic life as champion Johnson. Sam was partial to a drink and, as we have seen, not averse to a gamble. He also regularly associated with prostitutes, but that should neither shock nor scandalise, given his vocation of itinerant prizefighter. Langford was forever on the hop: Europe and Australia, Central and South America; remote outposts throughout the States. Sam would breeze into a city or hamlet with money to burn, and the ladies of the night queued up to put the fires out. Ships that pass . . . and no harm done.

London had been good to him, and Bettison and his N.S.C. patrons were eager to see more of this fighter with the dynamite punch. The promoter had pipe-dreamed that Hague might somehow win and go on to challenge Johnson, but Sam had at least been born a citizen of the Empire, and appealed to the members as a worthy contender, and so an approach was made for a title showdown. In 1907, the Sporting Club had half-heartedly tried to secure Johnson's fight with the other Canadian, Burns, but their bid was laughable, and now, two years later, they were again miserly in their efforts to tempt Johnson.

Bettison's offer of £3,000 – only £500 more than he had paid Langford against Hague – rightly offended the champ, who pointed out that Burns had been guaranteed twice that sum for his defence in

Sydney. He was not going to risk his championship for anything less than six grand in British, and though the words were never spoken, not against a fighter of Langford's calibre. Had the offer been attractive enough, who knows? But that was to be the closest that Sam would ever come to snaring the champion.

Through lack of career-boosting opportunities, he was about to join an exclusive group of black boxers who were destined to fight one another over and over again, simply because so few outside their circle would chance tackling them. Sometimes the matches were grimly serious, but all too often they could turn out sedate waltzes that had the audience baying for a refund. Much depended on the promised wages and the humour of the day.

Langford would wind up fighting McVey as often as fifteen times, and Jeannette became an opponent fourteen times. And when he was not swapping punches with that pair, he would be renewing acquaintances with Jeff Clark or Jim Barry or Bill Tate. He was a 31-year-old when he first started an extraordinary series with a young Harry Wills, a marathon that would stretch to eighteen meetings – but more of Black Panther Wills in later pages. The permutations were endless and many of the meetings no better than vaudeville one-night stands, but that was the only way those men could earn regularly.

Consider McVey and Jeannette, two stars of the cast. Born in Oxnard, California, on 17 May 1885, McVey was a raw seventeen-year-old when he had his first recorded contest – against none other than Jack Johnson in Los Angeles on 27 February 1903. Of course there had been many unrecorded battles before then and the teenager was already sporting scar tissue as proof. He was also backed by his supporters to win $15,000, but the fight, billed for the negro heavyweight title, went to Johnson after twenty entertaining rounds. In the next fourteen months they would fight twice again in California and, on both occasions, Jack was the master. But it must be emphasised that McVey was not yet twenty; Johnson had got to him at the right time.

Joe Jeannette hailed from Hoboken, New Jersey, and did not start boxing until the advanced age of 24. Jeannette, more urbane than most of his contemporaries, possessed great all-round talent, and he was ably managed throughout his career by Dan McKettrick; managed well enough to earn a very good living, particularly in Paris, where many black boxers found a second home, and where Jeannette, in particular, was a great favourite.

The promoter calling the shots there was a busy-busy Australian called Hugh D. McIntosh, an imaginative and successful impressario, who had staged the Burns–Johnson fight at Rushcutters Bay, and who had his ten fingers and ten toes in many, many pies; promoting black boxers in Paris was his current pet earner. McIntosh made money out of promoting Jeannette to beat the white American Sandy Ferguson and also the local idol Georges Carpentier. The Frenchman knocked down Jeannette in the opening round, but was then heavily punished, and at the end of fifteen rounds, the man from Hoboken was a clear winner. Seven years later, Carpentier would get his shot at the heavyweight title against Jack Dempsey. Typical!

But it was two of Jeannette's matches against McVey that best underline the totally unpredictable nature of those black permutations. In early 1909, Joe and Sam had performed a twenty-round tango in Paris, so boring that it could have been their last, and they had sent many spectators home before McVey's hand was raised as a points winner. Yet three months later, they staged another performance in the French capital that historians still regard as one of the most savagely punishing battles of all time.

Because of their pathetic earlier encounter, the 2,000 crowd was considered surprisingly good, and the fighters were under no illusions that they had better deliver something a deal more energetic this time. Their reputations were on the line and the terms dictated a fight to the finish.

That finish did not materialise until the end of round 49, over three hours after the first bell, and not before both fighters had suffered extreme damage. Nobody left before the end this time, and statisticians recall 38 knockdowns, but both McVey and Jeannette were up and down so often that it was nearly impossible to keep score. After a desperate, see-saw struggle for over thirty rounds, Jeannette gradually got on top, and finally McVey, exhausted and with both eyes swollen shut, was unable to rise from his stool when the bell rang for round fifty.

Why this time did Sam and Joe decide to fight away beyond normal endurance, risking not only their careers but their lives? That was a secret that was to remain within the group; they were all masters at carrying an opponent, making an easy fight appear close, often staging a performance rather than a full-blooded fight. No fighter was more expert than Langford, who could shrug, shuffle and feint his way through round after meaningless round, or suddenly erupt with breathtaking fury.

There was the story about when Sam was in London and Bettison asked him if Eugene Corri would prove acceptable as a referee. There was consternation when Langford replied that he had brought along his own ref – until he beamed and made a fist out of his right hand. And the tale about the time that he offered a handshake to an opponent at the start of the sixth. The bemused fighter told him that this wasn't the final round, but Langford explained that it was going to be the last for him – and promptly knocked the poor guy spark out.

Had the two Sams ever shared a room and the alarm gone off, then they would have immediately started throwing leads and counters; in fact, in some of their meetings, they sleepwalked through the rounds. But then again, inexplicably, they could just as easily turn their full artillery on each other. Between 1911 through to 1913, they boxed a remarkable seven-bout series in Australia and every fight was for real; the hard-to-fool Aussies had never seen anything like those ferociously skilful scraps, and the outcome was four to one in Langford's favour with two draws. But by 1916, their double act was too tired and uninspired to fool a cynical gathering at the St Nicholas Arena in New York, and following the jeers in the hall came the newspaper headlines warning them that they were played out in The Big Apple. There was always South America, but then they wore out their welcome there also, and the curtain finally rang down on 14 August 1920 in East Chicago, Illinois, when they fumbled and stumbled their way through a ten-round no-decision affair that was described 'a travesty'.

Although two years later Langford still carried enough firepower to knock out the fledgeling Tiger Flowers, he was now a ring ancient, plagued by cataracts in both eyes. Somehow, he managed to box on until 1926, scuffling through the motions, until on 2 August, somebody called Brad Simmons scored a first-round technical knockout in a place called Drumright, Oklahoma. His money and his talent spent, Sam had opted to bow out at the bottom.

Sam McVey had arrived at an even sadder end. The year following his last ring encounter with Langford, the 36-year-old Californian tough guy died penniless in a New York hospital on 21 December 1921, after failing to beat off a bout of pneumonia. There is a story that Jack Johnson, short of the readies himself, rounded up the cash to ensure that McVey would have a fitting burial and a suitable headstone. Nice if true. Johnson always maintained that McVey had been his toughest opponent and 'the second best heavyweight of my generation'. Jack, however, always had a hidden agenda, and this one was as much to denigrate Langford's ability as to praise the other Sam's.

Joe Jeannette finished his career with enough loot tucked away to open a successful gym in his home town, Hoboken. Among the many useful fighters to work out there would be a young Jimmy Braddock, who went on to become the heavyweight champion that Jeannette and McVey and Sam Langford had never been.

Rough years were ahead for Sam, whose big-spending days were now just a dim memory. He existed, blind and broke in a room in Harlem, until, in 1944, a writer called Al Laney tracked him down for an interview. The blind man still had his fighter's pride and his tremendous spirit, and he told Laney: 'I fought maybe three, four hundred fights and every one was a pleasure.' No whingeing, no self-pity, no bitterness directed towards Jack Johnson. Marvellous!

Laney's subsequent story sparked off a considerable public reaction, and Langford received gifts and donations that soared to $10,000. A trust was organised and the fighter they once called The Boston Tar Baby was able to live out his final years with dignity and in relative comfort − far more comfort than those homeless sleeping on the Thames Embankment away back in 1909.

On one Christmas Eve visit, Laney was told by the old fighter: 'I got my guitar, and a bottle of gin, and money in my pocket to buy my Christmas dinner. No millionaire in the world got more than that, or anyhow, they can't use more.' Don't shed any tears for Sam.

Langford died, aged 72, on 12 January 1956, in Cambridge,

Massachusetts. The most exhaustive records credit him with a total of 293 bouts, but, as the man said, there must have been many more that went unrecorded. Given the chance, he would surely have won a middleweight or a light heavyweight title, but despite all the myths that have been nourished down through the years, the odds against his ever taking the heavyweight title from Jack Johnson would have been great. Over four inches taller and considerably heavier, a peak Johnson should always have been able to beat a peak Langford.

Sam, however, was entitled to find out the hard way, but crafty Jack ensured that that would never be.

14

Harry Wills:
'A False Alarm Smoke'

HARRY WILLS at least twice signed contracts to box for the heavyweight championship of the world, the passport to fortunes. When the photographers snapped him watching Jack Dempsey pen the papers clinching the dream deal, big Harry had all the appearance of a contented man . . . but the fight never happened. And the tickets were actually printed for another eagerly awaited showdown between The Mauler and The Panther, but again, there were never any punches thrown. Wills did pocket a $50,000 non-returnable advance during all the interminable aggro with the Dempsey team, and even today, let alone in the twenties, that is serious money for doing nothing, but he was never to get that longed-for shot at the champion.

And so, the one-time longshoreman from Louisiana, just like Peter Jackson and Sam Langford before him, came to know the gnawing frustration of being the logical challenger doomed to be denied his rights. Sullivan did not face Jackson because the princely Peter was the wrong colour; Johnson blanked Langford because of an intense personal dislike, coupled with a petty jealousy; but Dempsey was neither racist nor spiteful and was never particularly choosy about who occupied the opposite corner. In fact, in the complex tale of Harry Wills's championship crusade, the legendary Jack also became a victim.

How Jack Dempsey would have fared against such future greats as Louis and Marciano and Liston and Ali and Frazier and Foreman through to Holmes and Tyson and the other Lewis is a subject best left to well-heeled pensioners lucky enough to enjoy a healthy pub slate. But, no question, Jack was a genuine tough guy. His punches broke both bones and hearts; he walked scared of no man; and though he could turn vicious even in the training ring, off duty, he was a pleasant, carefree character, always eager to do a favour, ever anxious to please. Yet, when Harry Wills arrived on the scene to haunt him, the champ was anything but a national hero. In fact, he was barely zero-plus in the popularity stakes, and his saga with Wills would further dent an image that was desperately in need of some high-charged P.R.

The Manassa Mauler's career officially got under way on 17 August 1914 in Ramona, Colorado, but the nineteen-year-old was less than sensational in boxing a six-round draw against someone called Young Herman. Before that, however, Dempsey had proved himself to be a tough scrapper in bootleg battles in mining camps and saloons and at country fairs – anywhere that a good fight would earn the price of a meal. By the time he stepped into the ring to face champion Jess Willard on Independence Day 1919, he had fought 69 official bouts and was a hungry, hardened pro with a mean streak. The six-inches-taller Willard never stood a chance from the opening bell, and though heroically brave, was fortunate to escape without lasting damage after the three-round massacre.

Dempsey was the champ, a white champ, and a far more exciting white champ than the dull, cumbersome Willard, who had somehow managed to wrest the title from the detested Johnson. But within 24 hours, he was to discover that being champion could incur some heavy baggage.

Dempsey had not fought in the war: his draft had been deferred, ostensibly because he provided his mother with her sole means of support; because he had contributed to the war effort when working in the Tacoma shipyards; and because he had also raised substantial sums for the Red Cross and the Navy Relief Fund. Most likely, his cunning manager Jack Kearns, viewing the overseas altercation as an impediment to their title drive, handled the army problem with his usual expertise. Who can really tell?

The bottom line was that Jack never joined the boys fighting in France, and on the morning after he had wrecked Willard, he received a hammer blow when a story was splashed to remind the world of his non-participation. Not surprisingly, the newspapers were lavish in their praise of his Toledo demolition job, but in the *New York Tribune*, one of America's leading writers, Grantland Rice, took time out to launch a fierce attack in which he wrote: 'It would be an insult to every young American who sleeps today from Flanders to Lorraine, from the Somme to the Argonne, to crown Dempsey with any laurels of fighting courage.' There was more of the same, and throughout the country there followed an immediate reaction to Rice's article. The new champion was branded 'a slacker' – a reviled term of the time for those who had ducked joining up.

Jack was booed into the ring for his first two title defences against Billy Miske and Bill Brennan; and when he took part in boxing's first million-dollar gate at Boyle's Thirty Acres in Jersey City on 2 July 1921, against the popular Frenchman, Georges Carpentier – dubbed a war hero – many of his countrymen were cheering for the foreigner. Dempsey sported the American flag around his waist that afternoon, and several ringsiders in the 80,000 crowd tried to rip it from him: that's how high temperatures had soared. Once the bell sounded, however, the champion took Carpentier apart in four rounds, but he received little acclaim for beating a lighter man, and by the following year, he was still few people's idea of a pin-up. And so, when Harry Wills began to beat the drums for a crack at the title, he found himself in the unique position, for a black, of having considerable support from both the media and from the public at large.

Harry Wills was born in New Orleans on 15 May 1889. He sprouted into a 6ft 4in 220-pounder, unremarkable by today's heavyweight standards, but a monster back then when Jack Johnson, about three inches shorter, was called The Galveston Giant. Wills worked for a time on the docks, but his size and immense strength led him to believe there was better money to be made in the ring, and in 1910 he had his first recorded contest when Kid Ravarro failed to see out the first round. In those early years, Wills did not appear to be anything special, aside from his tremendous physique, but fight by fight, he sharpened his skills and his speed, and although his punching power was never exceptional, when he hit, he hurt.

By 1914, he felt capable of taking care of himself against just about anyone in the ring and so embarked on a bizarre joust with old Sam

Langford that was to extend over nine years. Wills would face the other usual suspects such as McVey and Jeannette and Clark, but it was those meetings with Langford that moulded him into the polished pro who so fancied his chances against Dempsey.

Not even the most dedicated historians have unearthed conclusively just how many times they fought: the most popular count today would appear to be eighteen times, but there are those who claim that Harry and Sam did the business on three, four, or perhaps even five more dates. Beyond dispute are the facts that they first fought on 1 May 1914 on Wills's home canvas of New Orleans, and the local boy appeared to get the better of a ten-round no-decision match, and they last met professionally on 17 January 1922 in Portland, Oregon, where The Black Panther convincingly outpointed the ageing Tar Baby.

Wills was only days away from his 25th birthday when they first fought; Langford was a well-used 31; Harry was still learning, Sam only earning, but in those early encounters, the veteran still had enough in the tank to stop the younger man twice. Four years on, however, it was Wills who twice won inside the distance, and when their show finally closed, Harry was the undisputed master. They had appeared down south in New Orleans and up north in Boston; and in Syracuse and Tulsa and Los Angeles, and twice down in Panama. They were the fight game's Little and Large – their eight-inch difference in height producing an odd spectacle – and they both made some money. But more importantly for Wills, the countless rounds with a ring marvel convinced his manager, the formidable Paddy Mullins, that challenging for the championship had ceased to be a dream and was fast becoming a possibility.

Victories over the black troupers were all very well, but outside the tight boxing circle, they had no great impact. Mullins knew that only after beating a few name white heavies would Harry be taken seriously as a challenger, and in 1920, his dogged perseverance paid off when he secured a match against Fred Fulton in Newark, New Jersey. Two years earlier, Fulton had failed to last a round against Dempsey, yet such was the paucity of the white heavyweights that he was still widely considered better than useful. But not after Wills destroyed him in three rounds. And then, after crushing the once tough but now tired old White Hope Gunboat Smith in one round in Havana, the heat was turned up for a fight with Dempsey.

Politics inside boxing and in more august offices were about to decide the destiny of Harry Wills. New York's governor, Al Smith, may have played his part, and New York State Athletic Commissioners William Muldoon, James A. Farley and George Brower were certainly involved; but the prime players were promoter Tex Rickard, the ubiquitous Jack Kearns, and Dempsey himself. We will start with the champion.

Dempsey never had a colour bias. As a roughneck youngster he had fought hardcases like The Boston Bearcat (who had a reputation until he faced Jack) and a genuine tough guy in John Lester Johnson; really talented black sparring partners found work at the Dempsey camp; and Bill Tate, once a very good fighter, was part of his corner team for the Willard fight.

Nor was he wary of bigger men: Willard had been just a round or two away from the ultimate disaster, and another giant, Carl Morris, had been felled within a round. But he was a pawn in a very tricky game, and he did himself few favours when, after beating the Argentinian Luis Firpo in an astonishing two-round brawl in September 1923, he stashed the title in the freezer for three long years. And during those years, the demand intensified for Wills to get his chance.

Dempsey took himself off to Hollywood, where he had to learn to pull his punches playing Daredevil Jack in a string of adventure movies, and he even forked out for a nose job to right the damage done in the ring. He had married an iron-willed movie star named Estelle Taylor, and right off, she began grilling Kearns about the champ's earnings and just where they were going (ring any bells with Tyson and Robin Givens?) and within weeks, the two Jacks had a fall-out which quickly developed into a bitter feud that would endure until they were both much older and wiser. For years, the devious Kearns would plague Dempsey with lawsuits, and at one stage, he would try to boost Wills's chances of securing a title fight. But back in 1922, when Mullins started to press his fighter's claims, the good Doctor did not want to know about Harry. At that stage, Kearns did not believe Wills would be a draw; the only colour that interested Doc Kearns was the colour of money. Ironically, it was Dempsey who had awarded him the sobriquet 'Doc' from the times when he believed implicitly in his manager, of whom he often said, 'Always knew best. You're the doctor.'

Kearns was a high-rolling genius, both at making money and spending it twice as fast. Born in 1882, he was only fourteen when he left home to try his luck in the Yukon gold rush, and though he did not make his fortune, he learned valuable lessons there. Kearns was forever on the hustle: running taverns, promoting fights, fighting himself; he was even involved in a scam importing illegal workers from China into the States. Where a buck could be made, there was the Doc. But when he teamed up with Dempsey in 1917, he finally found the gold that had eluded him in Alaska. Kearns, as Dempsey would discover, was a wonderful man to have on your side, but a viper if he ever crossed over.

He would be a livewire in the fight business right up until his death in July 1963, and he made fortunes thanks to a great dual champion Mickey Walker and the tough light heavyweight champ Joey Maxim, and finally with the marvellous Archie Moore, who discovered that having the Doc on the staff was part of the price for getting his chance at Maxim. But it was for his love-hate affair with Dempsey that Kearns will always be best remembered.

Tex Rickard was much more of a straight shooter who, by the time he had hooked up with Kearns and Dempsey, had established a solid reputation as a man adventurous enough to stage huge and successful boxing extravaganzas, and reliable enough to ensure that everyone involved got their agreed money.

George Rickard was born in Missouri in 1871 and, like Kearns, left home early. He worked on cattle drives from Texas to Montana; sampled life as a town marshal; took himself off to Brazil for a stint at cattle ranching; made a pile in Alaska, running a famous hotel in booming Dawson City; went bust, then followed the miners to Nevada, where he opened another hotel.

Tex was a born-again gambler, and he emerged a big winner after paying out an enormous sum to stage the lightweight title fight between Joe Gans and Battling Nelson in the aptly named Goldfield,

Nevada, in 1906. The gate receipts broke records and boxing was now his business. Rickard's reputation was such that he could now raise the money to promote Johnson against Jeffries in Reno in 1910; stage Willard and Dempsey in Toledo; and then, shifting base to New York, mastermind the first million-dollar gate with Dempsey and Carpentier in Jersey City. He was now the undisputed main man, and yet he never professed to be an expert on the finer points of boxing, frequently worried about making mismatches and fretted about the welfare of the fighters he hired.

Rickard was as fair as they will ever come in the world of boxing, but he wanted no part of Harry Wills. The heavyweight they were now calling The Black Panther brought back the nightmares of the aftermath of Johnson's humiliation of Jeffries, which sparked off race riots in many cities throughout the States. Tex had come in for much unwarranted abuse for ever staging the contest and he dreaded a repeat.

In New York, he had quickly forged valuable contacts with the city's leading politicians, and he convinced himself that they too wanted no part of a mixed-race heavyweight title fight; on several occasions, he hinted that no less a big wheel than the state governor Al Smith had told him that he did not want the fight to take place. But Paddy Mullins, becoming even more of a pest, posted a $2,500 forfeit on Wills's behalf with the New York State Athletic Commission, and the Commissioners, rather surprisingly, came out in favour of Harry getting his chance.

Rickard was in a bind and Kearns did nothing to improve his mood when, in the July of 1923, he whisked Dempsey off to a hick town in Montana called Shelby, for a freelance defence against Tommy Gibbons. Dempsey won a lacklustre decision, but the promotion was a financial disaster for the town and its citizens, who had been conned by Kearns into putting up a $300,000 guarantee. When the two Jacks left town, they did so with most of the money in Shelby. The local bank went bust.

The Doctor quickly made his peace with Rickard, and despite the Commission backing Wills's claims, that September, Tex was somehow allowed to promote Dempsey's historic defence against Firpo in New York's Polo Grounds. Firpo was floored nine times and reporters had to assist Dempsey back into the ring after The Wild Bull of the Pampas had sent him flying in the first. Sensational stuff, but that would be the last time Jack would win a title bout. For the next three years, his public would see him only in tame exhibition bouts and acting the hero on the screen, or read about his warring with Kearns and the endless press speculation about when he was going to get around to fighting Wills. Today it seems incredible that a champion could be allowed to take a three-year sabbatical without any sanctions, but with the exception of Wills, and another fine black heavyweight, George Godfrey, there was a dearth of worthwhile challengers.

Godfrey was another huge heavyweight, but surprisingly fast for his 230lb, a good puncher, and very durable. He was born Feab Williams in Mobile, Alabama, in January 1901, but took his ring name after hearing about the exploits of the original G.G. – Old Chocolate from the days of Sullivan and Jackson. The two Godfreys would enjoy similar luck with their title aspirations.

Unlike the focused Wills, who always had manager Mullins battling his corner, big George was an amiable sort, content to fight anyone who would face him. But from 1924, he featured high in the rankings, and in 1928, after champion Gene Tunney had retired and the heavyweight title was vacant, Godfrey and Young Stribling were rated as the two leading heavyweights in the world. Yet he never came close to clinching a title shot . . . the same old story. He fought over one hundred bouts and boasted 75 knockouts from his 89 wins, but such was his lack of ambition that, rather than pursue Dempsey's title, he was more than happy to put his career on hold, and take on the job as the champion's sparring partner. The Mauler was notoriously rough on the hired help, but the much heavier Godfrey never came to too much harm, and the pair became good friends – Dempsey footed the funeral expenses when George died young in 1945.

Rickard would often claim that Godfrey was a better fighter than Wills, but he was only trying to muddy the water; anything that made Harry appear less of a championship threat was okay by Tex, and Wills and Mullins continued to be given the classic runaround.

When the squabble was in its infancy, the wily Kearns, strictly for public relations purposes, had put together a contract for a defence against the man from New Orleans. Trusting him, Mullins had Harry sign, despite the fact that all the vital conditions were either extremely vague or non-existent. The paper was no more than a cosmetic con, one of the Doc's specialities, and of course, was never honoured.

Next up came a genuine bid from a rival promoter, Floyd Fitzsimmons, who rashly paid Wills a $50,000 advance to box the champion at Benton Harbor, Michigan, and although Fitzsimmons did succeed in getting Dempsey and Wills to sit at the same table for the signing ceremony, he never managed to see them occupy opposing ring stools, and by the terms of his agreement, Harry held on to the fifty grand. Rickard had to be favourite to have sabotaged Fitzsimmons's efforts, and then Tex produced another smokescreen, actually having tickets printed for the great fight! Venue: Jersey City. Date: 6 September 1924. Ringside price: $27.50. Just another snow job.

The pantomime continued when the now estranged Kearns resurfaced claiming that he was still Dempsey's official manager, and that a match with Wills now met with his approval! The Doc was ever a trier, always searching out more work for Dempsey's legal team. For good measure, in *The Ring*'s annual ratings, Wills was listed as the number one heavyweight challenger. The compiler of those ratings? None other than Tex Rickard! Crazy, crazy days in those Roaring Twenties.

Throughout the entire sorry story, Wills behaved with admirable dignity and restraint. Not once did he publicly badmouth the champion, and even long after his fighting days were over, he never bought any cheap publicity by alleging that Dempsey had been scared to fight him. But time was running out for him and the years were starting to play catch-up.

He was 35 when he boxed a twelve-round no-decision against Angel Firpo in Jersey City in September 1924. The huge attendance agreed that The Panther definitely had the better of the exchanges and he had scored a knockdown, but still, he had been less than sensational. And now there was a new white kid on the block, who had taken Rickard's fancy as a prospective challenger and who just might eliminate Wills once and for all. He was Gene Tunney, a former Marine, and now a fully fledged heavyweight after holding the U.S. light heavyweight belt. Rickard tried to match him with Wills, and the cautious Tunney took some persuading but finally agreed. According to Rickard, however, Wills priced himself out of the fight with an exorbitant purse demand. Maybe.

Wills could not be blamed for protecting his rating and for what it was worth, he still had the backing of the New York Commission. They could not force Dempsey to fight him, but they could ensure that the champ did not defend against any other challenger in the state of New York. In 1925, they took away Jack's licence, and though Rickard lobbied for months, the Commission stood firm. And so Tex had to switch Dempsey's defence against Tunney to Philadelphia, and on 23 September 1926, before a crowd of 120,757, a new champion was crowned. The years of inactivity and soft living had taken their toll, though the smart boxing of Tunney also played a big part.

For Wills, 1926 was equally disastrous. A month after Dempsey lost the title, Harry accepted a risky but good earner, against the erratic but very capable Jack Sharkey. In so doing, he played right into Rickard's hands.

Sharkey, a former sailor based in Boston, was only in his third year as a pro but he had already beaten a number of good fighters, including George Godfrey, and he was considered a live prospect. The match was attractive enough to lure 42,000 to Ebbets Field in Brooklyn, and the 24-year-old had too much of everything for the now 37-year-old Wills, who was trailing badly when he was disqualified in round thirteen.

Rickard was naturally ecstatic. For some time, in private conversations, he had been referring to Wills as 'The False Alarm Smoke' – a cruel jibe, unjustified and not really typical of Tex. But the big man from Louisiana had cost him many sleepless nights and now he was out of the picture: permanently. There would be no road back for Harry.

Sharkey was rewarded the following year with a final eliminator against Dempsey, now trying to whip himself into shape for a rematch with Tunney, and The Mauler scored a controversial seventh-round knockout. But on 22 September 1927, before 102,000 in Soldier Field, Chicago, he was well outpointed by the champion in the famous 'Battle of the Long Count' when Tunney was on the floor for fourteen seconds in the seventh, Dempsey forgetting to go to a neutral corner. Strangely, it was only after the two Tunney defeats that the fans finally warmed to Jack, and at last he became a public hero.

In contrast the inexorable slide of the once 'Uncrowned Champion' Wills was very low key. The hardy Basque Paulino Uzcudun stopped him in four rounds in Brooklyn in 1927, and though he would remain active for another five years, he was boxing from memory. On 4 August 1932 in Brooklyn, after beating a no-hoper called Vinko Jankassa in one round, he called it a day.

Wills had been no wild-spending fool and he had invested shrewdly in properties in New York. When he quit the ring, his business interests prospered and he was able to live very comfortably until his death on 21 December 1958. A welcome change from the usual fate of the Black Hopes.

But just how great was Harry Wills? He finished up with a career record of 65 wins, eight losses and two draws; there were also 25 no-decision fights and three no contests in his 103-bout total. He had won and lost to the old timers McVey and Langford when he was on a learning curve, but the much smaller Langford had twice stopped him; his most notable victories against white fighters came via the scarcely intimidating Fred Fulton and old Gunboat Smith. He had been made to travel the full trip against Firpo, who had failed to last out two rounds with Dempsey; and he was easily beaten by Sharkey, who a year later was knocked out by Jack.

In a fair world, Wills should have been granted his chance against the champ, but for once, Tex Rickard did not play fair. However, the Dempsey who ripped into Willard and bludgeoned Firpo would have been a terror for any fighter to face, including The Black Panther. And even when Jack was growing soft and vulnerable, Harry was also beginning to show his years.

In some strange way, never getting that title fight may have been one of the best things that ever happened to Harry Wills. He has his place of honour in boxing's Hall of Fame alongside the champions, and will forever be remembered as the man that Jack Dempsey would never face. A unique title, if not quite a championship.

15

Jimmy Bivins:
'The "Duration" Champ'

JIMMY BIVINS, for a brief but heady few months in 1943, could call himself a champion, indeed a champion at two different weights! The Cleveland maestro had won something called the duration light heavyweight title, then in his very next fight became the duration heavyweight champ, and before a hectic year was out, he had even squeezed in a defence of his lighter prize. Do not, however, search for the name of James Louis Bivins in any Roll of Champions because he was never lucky enough to box for a real title.

Bivins peaked at a time when much championship action had been suspended because of the war, and the 'duration' tag was merely a ploy to stimulate interest and boost business at the ticket office. But even if his titles were phoney, the same could not be said about the fighter himself. Bivins was the genuine article.

In Jimmy's boom year of 1943, the Germans were stopped at Stalingrad, the Japanese knocked out at Guadalcanal, but in the States, the black fighters still were battling desperately in the trenches. Joe Louis remained boxing's supreme champion, but in other divisions, discrimination lingered on as a way of business.

At middleweight, right through the reigns of Zale, Graziano, Cerdan and La Motta, not one black fought for the title until Ray Robinson beat Jake the Bull in 1951. And throughout the forties in the light heavies, only Billy Fox, thanks to his powerful connections, was given a championship shot. Because he was with the guys who could make things happen, Fox actually got two tries at champion Gus Lesnevich but flopped both times, and it was unanimous that there were other blacks far more deserving.

No coincidence that at those two weights, there had formed a band of black boxers, all superb talents, and all considered off limits when the talk turned to titles. Leading the pack were Charley Burley and Archie Moore and Holman Williams and Lloyd Marshall and Ezzard Charles and Jimmy Bivins, and the managers of the white champs cynically sat around and watched them knock lumps out of one another. Burley has long been considered the ultimate in artistry, but Bivins, in his first year as a pro, outpointed him in Charley's home town of Pittsburgh; Moore coupled brilliance with unquenchable ambition, but had to overcome a knockout defeat against Jimmy; and Charles, who made it all the way to the heavyweight title, was yet another victim of the Cleveland virtuoso.

A harder-to-please public would no longer stand for the vaudeville exhibitions that the old timers had so often perpetrated and there were no punches pulled when the new breed got it on. Every fight was for real, the rivalry was intense, and sometimes the blood boiled over. After he retired, Moore recounted to writer Peter Heller how fierce and bitter the competition could become.

Archie had been a ringside spectator on the night that Lloyd Marshall stopped Harvey Massey in the final round; later in the dressing room, Moore remonstrated with Marshall for scoring a last-round knockout against a man who was already a beaten fighter; and Marshall told him to mind his own business. But Moore had a good memory, and when the time came for him to meet Marshall, he finished him off in the final round when he was well on top and could have settled for a decision. Only minutes later, into his dressing room burst Marshall's longtime friend, Jimmy Bivins, furious – just as Moore had been furious – at what he figured had been a liberty. Moore explained that he had only done to Marshall what Marshall had done to Harvey Massey. And it was none of Bivins's business. But Jimmy thought otherwise, and Moore told Heller:

'So Bivins didn't like me. We fought in Cleveland. Bivins hooked me and I went down to one knee, and Bivins, mad at me, stood up over me and hit me when I was on my knees and hit me with an uppercut on the left side of my face right underneath the cheekbone, knocked me head over heels, knocked me out. He had struck a nerve and all across my front gum, all the way across my mouth, was numb for two years. I despised Bivins. They gave me ten minutes' rest, and they made me continue the fight, and Bivins eventually knocked me out again.'

Archie would gain ample revenge in four subsequent battles, but there was no disgrace in losing to The Mongoose. Moore may not have been the greatest boxer ever to grace a ring, but he was right up there with the élite, and he put together a record that, by today's standards, can only be described as unbelievable.

Born Archibald Lee Wright in Mississippi, but reared in St Louis, the incredible Moore tangled with all the tough guys over four decades. *The Ring* Record Book credits him with 234 fights and an all-time record 145 knockouts; he was denied a title shot throughout the forties and when he finally did get his chance at champion Joey Maxim, he was paid a pittance and had to cut Maxim's manager Jack Kearns in for a piece of his future earnings. And those earnings were considerable, for Moore would go on to fight twice for the heavyweight championship at an age when he should have been mulling over pension plans.

In September 1955, he came within seconds of knocking out the iron-chinned Rocky Marciano, but was eventually battered into submission in nine rounds; one eye completely shut tight, Moore later that evening was pictured, a huge grin across his swollen face, twanging on a double bass, and having a ball in a New York nightclub. Nothing could keep Archie on the floor. His second bid for boxing's richest prize, however, was one of the few occasions in his marathon career when Moore failed to deliver.

Facing Floyd Patterson for the vacant crown, he was ponderous and predictable and an easy target for the fast-punching youngster, who needed only five rounds. Age appeared to have caught up with Archie that night, but there would be four more successful light heavy defences when making the weight was no little problem, and six years on from the Patterson débâcle, he was still nimble enough to box a draw with future champion Willie Pastrano, and then, fat and ancient, have the nerve to survive into the fourth against the budding Cassius Clay.

If one fight epitomised the extraordinary life and career of Archie Moore, it was his dramatic defence against the French-Canadian strongman, Yvon Durelle, at the Montreal Forum on 10 December 1958. A hot favourite to win, The Mongoose was caught cold in the first, knocked down three times, and it was a miracle that he was able to answer the bell for the second. Fighting on automatic, he was on the canvas again in the fifth, but then his head cleared and he started to take control. The flagging Durelle was dropped in the seventh and clinically finished off in the eleventh. That night, Archie showed all the superhuman perseverance that had carried him through all those long, heartbreaking years when the Madison Square Garden offices were locked fast whenever he came calling.

Compared to Moore, one might be persuaded to judge that Jimmy Bivins enjoyed no more than a mild flirtation with the business. His career spanned a mere fifteen years, and he could manage just a meagre 112 bouts, which was by no means exceptional for the era, but unheard of today among the top fighters who have raked in their millions long before they might approach the magic ton.

Bivins was born on 6 December 1919 in a hamlet called Dry Branch in the state of Georgia and, soon after, his family joined the black exodus north, settling in Cleveland, where Jimmy developed into a chunky 5ft 9in, always a trifle tight at middleweight, short but deadly at light heavy, and conceding all the physical advantages against the full-blown heavies.

Back then, Cleveland was a bustling fight centre, and after having proved himself better than average in amateur competitions, Bivins decided to make some money out of the game and signed up with Wilfred Carter – 'Whizzbang' to the characters who hung out at the gym, and a gentleman who lived right up to his name. Carter booked Bivins for no fewer than twenty fights in his debut year of 1940, and that was truly a whizzbang introduction to the Science for any kid.

Emory Morgan may have been a cosy first-round victim on his début on 15 January of that year, but there were few more easy pay nights. To get the work, The Whizzbang and the novice had to take who they could get.

Today, a likely lad can look forward to a relatively stress-free introduction; perhaps a year or even two years of meeting very carefully monitored opponents: non-punchers and boys with iffy chins and worn-out 'names' and often fighters who have forgotten their reason for fighting. On the plus side, this can build a youngster's confidence, fatten his record, attract television interest, and leave him in pristine nick for the inevitable title shot. The downside is that he may never have experienced even a dozen competitive rounds or a serious whack on the chin when that golden chance comes along, and he is unable to cope.

Bivins, like many of his contemporaries, had to learn to cope early. In only his sixth outing, he was paired with the equally tough and ambitious Nate Bolden; Jimmy was the winner after eight hard-fought rounds in Chicago, yet the following year, Bolden was rugged enough to outpoint Jake La Motta. That gives an inkling of the ferocity of the competition.

By September, Bivins was undefeated in fourteen starts, and his management decided that a match against Charley Burley was no kamikaze mission – Burley, who was already being treated like a fellow with a contagious disease by all the welters and most of the middleweights in the country! Charley had the advantage of experience and a loyal home support in Pittsburgh, Bivins had a useful pull in the weights; but to come away with the ten-round decision was a fantastic achievement for the still twenty-year-old – one of only eleven career defeats for the fabulous Charley.

The year was to finish with Jimmy's first loss. In November in Cleveland, he had outpointed Anton Christoforidis. A former European middleweight champion, the Greek won seven straight in his American campaign before Bivins beat him, but the fight was entertaining enough to warrant a rematch the following month, and this time Christoforidis was awarded the vote. No excuses, but Bivins, just four days short of coming of age, must have been feeling some effects of an extremely strenuous first year. And Christoforidis? In his very next bout, he was rewarded with a chance at the N.B.A. version of the light heavyweight championship, and he outpointed Melio Bettina, again in Cleveland.

At that time, the light heavyweight league was in some disarray –

not the dreadful mess that is the norm in most divisions today, but confused enough, following the retirement of the fine black champion John Henry Lewis in 1939, five months after an abortive try for Louis's heavyweight crown.

There was the usual mad scramble. New York recognised Bettina following his victory over Tiger Jack Fox; in Britain, Len Harvey was hailed the champ after beating Jock McAvoy; Billy Conn earned acceptance throughout the States after taking care of Bettina, but in 1941, he relinquished the title to pursue Louis. Cue for further bedlam. Next Christoforidis bested Bettina to gain New York recognition, but he was quickly deposed by Gus Lesnevich, who in August 1941, gained unanimous American approval by beating Tami Mauriello. Meanwhile in Britain, Harvey was still recognised until Freddie Mills knocked him out in 1942. Still with us?

Bettina . . . Christoforidis . . . Harvey . . . Conn . . . Lesnevich . . . Mills . . . Italian-Americans . . . Greeks . . . Brits . . . Irish-Americans . . . Russian-Yanks. But no black champions, no black contenders, no change in policy.

The excuse could not be offered that the black band was not box-office. In Pittsburgh, Burley was a guaranteed sell-out; Bivins was hot in Cleveland; and Moore could sell tickets in just about any city from San Diego to St Louis to Baltimore to Buenos Aires, Melbourne and Sydney. But Archie was not wanted in New York; nor were the rest welcome.

Moore was a pro nine years before he first showed in the boxing capital – a ten-round win against Nate Bolden in 1944 – and until he won the title, he would appear there only twice more. Burley boxed a grand total of one round in New York; Charles fought only twice there before he became a champ; and in his 112 contests, Jimmy Bivins was invited for just six recitals in The Apple.

There just had to be a conspiracy to exclude so many fine fighters from the Garden, but in the post-war years, all the conspiracy theories were to be spotlighted on Hollywood and a communist witch-hunt; nobody bothered to take a hard look at boxing until the late fifties, when a federal court disbanded the International Boxing Club, the monopolistic machine run by multi-millionaire Jim Norris, with the considerable assistance of the Mafia's representative, Frank Carbo. Norris provided an impressively respectable front, but Carbo had been playing puppeteer long before the I.B.C. was formed, and its inception only provided him with convenient cover. He did not care about a fighter's colour, though whites would always be shown a strong preference; Carbo was more interested in who managed the fighters, if they were represented by a friendly face. Bivins was never able to break into the clique.

In *Ring Magazine*, month after month, publisher Nat Fleischer continued to give the black band the ratings they were due, but few paid any attention. In 1942, Fleischer simultaneously ranked Bivins as the leading challenger to Louis and the number one light heavyweight behind Lesnevich, but as both champions were in the forces, his lists had become hypothetical; the 1943 duration title idea failed to take off, and that was more rough luck on Jimmy, because around about then, he was all but unbeatable, and would certainly have won the real 175lb title given the chance. After all, he had already beaten Lesnevich in a ten-rounder.

On 22 June 1942, when he outpointed another Cleveland favourite, Joey Maxim, Bivins set out on an incredible unbeaten run that would last until 25 February 1946, when he dropped a decision to the future heavyweight champion Jersey Joe Walcott – 27 fights (almost a full career today) against past champions, future champions, future contenders and some feared heavyweight punchers such as Curtis Sheppard and Lee Q. Murray who were considered a no-go area by many their own size.

He even managed two visits to New York. In November 1942, he outpointed Lee Savold, who eight years later would win the British-only-recognised version of the heavyweight title against Bruce Woodcock; he also scored his second success over Tami Mauriello to add the duration heavyweight title to the light heavy bauble he had won from Anton Christoforidis in their third meeting. Mauriello had been a sensational teenage middleweight, somewhat lacking in dedication, but he would never go short of title opportunities. He failed twice but earned well against Lesnevich, and three years after Bivins had proved his master, was rewarded with a spectacularly short but lucrative challenge against Joe Louis. Even when his career was long over, Tami still had the right connections and he featured prominently as one of Johnny Friendly's goon squad in *On the Waterfront*. Ironic?

More champions and nearly champions came out second best to Jimmy during the red-hot spell: there was Bob Pastor (twice a Louis opponent) and Charles (destined to be heavyweight king) and Pat Valentino (challenged Charles) and of course Archie Moore, plus a revenge victory against the former light heavy holder Bettina.

And there was a thirteen-round knockout over his friend Lloyd Marshall in his only defence of the duration 175lb title. Lloyd Marshall . . . just another fantastic performer. He and Bivins met only once in the ring, but their careers intertwined; they suffered similar frustrations and injustices, and their friendship lasted long after their ring exploits were just a memory. Their Cleveland encounter on 8 June 1943 was a thriller, typical of the brand of action the black band produced, and the five-years-younger Bivins had to haul himself off the canvas before eventually wearing down Marshall, whose stamina was never a strong suit.

Cleveland-born, but brought up in California, Marshall would today fit neatly into the super-middleweight category, but for most of his career, he had to concede the advantages at light heavy. A relaxed, brainy boxer and a fearsome puncher, he was blessed with a tremendous reach, and after a lengthy amateur career which included winning a National Golden Gloves middleweight title, he turned professional in Sacramento. Soon, however, he was city-hopping and, like Bivins, he quickly fashioned a living fighting past champions and future champions, but never defending champions.

In 1938, he defeated Ken Overlin, who two years later would win the middleweight belt; the rugged Filippino Ceferino Garcia would prove a bogy, but Marshall was far too good for other middleweight claimants such as Lou Brouillard and Babe Risko and Teddy Yarosz. There were other big wins against Christoforidis, La Motta, Holman Williams, Maxim and Mills, and in 1942 in Los Angeles, he became the only fighter to floor the great Burley. He also bounced Charles all over the ring before stopping him in eight, but Archie Moore always had his number.

For a span of ten years, however, Lloyd was a fixture in Fleischer's ratings, and at one time, was ranked the number one light heavy, when his pal Bivins filled a similar spot at heavyweight. As we have seen, that meant nothing, and one Marshall fight sums up all the iniquity for the black boxers of the forties. Curiously, it was to take place in London and provide Lloyd with his largest-ever purse.

Bournemouth's tough Freddie Mills held a tenuous claim to the 175lb title throughout the war years, thanks to his victory over Harvey, but Lesnevich had set matters straight, stopping Mills in the tenth of a gruelling battle in London in May 1946. Before the end of that year, Mills would suffer two more punishing defeats against Woodcock and Joe Baksi, and now in 1947, after three easy wins, the ever-optimistic Jack Solomons was again promoting Freddie's claims for a rematch with Lesnevich. The 32-year-old Marshall was selected as a suitable stepping stone, but just as he had been wrong in importing Baksi the year before, Solomons was sold a dummy when he booked Lloyd for Harringay on 3 June.

Solomons may never have dealt with Carbo head-to-head, but he certainly did business with his henchmen, and they should have put him wise to the dangers of hiring Marshall. True, Charles had scored a rematch sixth-round knockout over Lloyd the previous year, but losing to Ezzard did not signal the end of a career. Charles and Mills were leagues apart in ability.

Marshall had never been treated so handsomely as he was in London: Solomons paid him a very generous $27,000, and in the promoter's gym, his smooth, relaxed style had the regulars agog; he was even made guest of honour at a reception held in Mills's new Chinese restaurant. Such hospitality just did not happen to black fighters back home, certainly not to the likes of Marshall or Bivins. There were few welcome mats laid out for them as they journeyed around the States.

Trainer Ray Arcel recalled accompanying Bivins to a fight in Washington D.C. The room allotted to Jimmy in a 'coloureds-only' hotel was a disgrace, so Arcel took the fighter to his own segregated hotel where he knew the manager. Straight-faced, he introduced Bivins as his valet, and the manager, aware that this was a boxer, played

along. He agreed that Jimmy could share a two-bed room with the
trainer – but with strict conditions. Bivins had to take his meals in their
room and when the service arrived, he must disappear into the bath-
room; with only one meal being delivered, Arcel also ate alone, but
downstairs. That's how they lived for five days, Jimmy playing The
Invisible Man until the fight, and he did not create a fuss. But other
boxers, like Ezzard Charles, bitterly resented the treatment, and rightly
so.

Lloyd Marshall did not allow the surprise cordiality to sidetrack him
from the principal business in London. Come fight time at Harringay,
he repaid his hosts by completely outclassing Mills, knocking him
down three times in the third and finishing him off in the fifth. An easy
job, but one that did Marshall little good, apart from the cash he took
home.

Such a shattering loss should have eliminated Mills from title
contention, but he still had the backing of Solomons, and Jack could
still get the job done. By the following year, the promoter had wangled
for Mills another shot at Lesnevich, and this time Freddie won a
lacklustre points decision. And Marshall? He was back in the States,
back on the circuit, and still high in the ratings, but with absolutely no
chance of ever getting a rematch with the new champion.

Like Bivins in the Washington hotel, Lloyd had been made invisible.
The rank injustice barely caused a ripple because, in those days, a
champion could not be stripped of his title for failing to defend against
an outstanding contender. Nat Fleischer always declared that a
champion should only lose his title in the ring, and for once, the wise
guys paid him heed, because it suited them. Forget about Lloyd
Marshall.

The sheer hopelessness of their position must have affected the
fighters' performances some nights. The war was over, the holders
back in action, but Louis was defending against Mauriello and Conn,
and Lesnevich was making up for lost money with his two easy
defences against Billy Fox, well-paid non-title appearances (beating
Mauriello for a third and a fourth time) and the always high-income
jaunts to Britain for meetings with Woodcock and Mills. His manager
Joe Vella was doing the right thing by his fighter, but it was all bad

news for Bivins as Vella showed no interest in a re-run of their 1942 ten-rounder in Cleveland, where Jimmy was clearly the boss.

Things were starting to turn sour for Bivins. That 1946 Walcott defeat, which snapped his marvellous winning streak, was followed by further losses to previous victims Lee Q. Murray and Charles. On the day before his 27th birthday, he scored a welcome victory against Colion Chaney in Akron, but there was little doubt that the magic was on the wane. He still retained more than enough ringcraft and power to take care of the good fighters, but no longer the great ones; the likes of Booker Beckwith and Omelio Agramonte were no problem, but Charles and Moore would exact painful revenge over a period of years. Lesnevich and Mills, however, would have been a different matter.

He still had his moments: in 1949, on a quick trip to California, he outpointed the highly regarded Leonard Morrow in Oakland, and a week later, knocked out a Jack Dempsey protégé Clarence Henry in Los Angeles. *The Ring* made him its Fighter of the Month for those exploits, but there was no question that he was slowing down – slowing down sufficiently to qualify for what would be the biggest pay night of his career!

On 15 August 1951, he was matched to face Joe Louis in Baltimore; the wages an all-time high $40,000, the risks not too great, for this would not be the same Louis who had ruled so majestically for so long. The Bomber was now performing for the taxman's benefit and on his comeback, had run up a string of wins against average opponents such as Bivins's victims Agramonte and Savold. If he was somehow going to get another shot at his old title, he would have to beat Bivins, and so he trained down to his lightest weight in years. At 203lb, however, he still had a 23lb pull over Bivins, who scaled only 5lb over the light-heavy limit. Louis's sheer bulk gave him the edge over ten honestly fought but scarcely enthralling rounds, and two months later, he would bow out like a warrior against Rocky Marciano.

Jimmy's final act was far less dramatic and much less publicised. In the last three years of his career, he fought only five times, losing to Tommy Harrison, then finishing off with a grand flourish, winning four straight. On his last appearance, on 28 October 1955, he said goodbye to his loyal Cleveland support when outpointing big Mike De

John, who would go on to be a regular in the heavyweight rankings for years to come. Right to the end, Jimmy could remember a trick or two.

He settled comfortably into civilian life, working for eighteen years as a driver-salesman for a bakery firm, part-owning the Old Angle gym on Cleveland's West Side, and becoming a ringside judge for the local boxing commission. Every once in a while, his old friend Lloyd Marshall would fly in from California for a visit and they would chat over old times. A tape of these conversations would have told us a lot.

Bivins and Marshall were black (strike one!) and their best years came during the war (strike two!) and they were never given a fair shake from the guys in the Garden (strike three and out!). But, between them, they beat a platoon of world champions, earned a fearsome reputation and the respect of their fellow professionals, and Jimmy, at least, won those two duration title belts. A far cry from justice, but, remember, we are talking boxing here.

PART SIX

When the Fates Gang Up

The fans howled when McCarty went down because no punch had landed. Then they stilled, as Luther lay prone.

Les Darcy skipped his native Australia to seek his fortune in the States. But the middleweight curse struck yet again.

Some dubbed Gypsy Joe Harris a ring genius, but even a genius needs two good eyes.

Champs and chumps alike . . . there is no
defence to the fickle finger

16

Luther McCarty:
'The Boy from Driftwood Creek'

BILLY McCARNEY, like all able boxing managers, never believed in letting the facts sabotage a good story, and that gift endeared him to the pack of journalists (a much more relaxed breed back in those free-wheeling days before World War One) who filled their columns with his malarkey. McCarney was an earner, a silver-tongued opportunist, always on the lookout for a fresh enterprise, a new idea, and for Billy, the era of The Great White Hope appeared as a gift from heaven. At least for a time.

McCarney did not object to being called The Professor, a title bestowed upon him by the hacks, because he had once been a college boy in his native Philadelphia. Some friendly stories suggested that he had gained a degree; and he supposedly thought about the priesthood, then considered law, and finally wound up working on a newspaper; more cynical tales hint that his stay on campus was no more than fleeting. Nobody could ever be quite sure about The Prof and what he got up to, and that was exactly as planned – keep them guessing. Billy kidded and conned, bluffed and blustered, and weaved a spell that entranced a compliant press corps, and often fooled a gullible public.

Unlike many of his contemporaries, however, he did not regard his boxers as mere pieces of meat, and when the leather-necked fight boss discovered his heavyweight protégé, Luther McCarty, he quickly formed a bond, unlike any he had experienced with his other fighters; and understandably, he was totally distraught when the big 21-year-old came to grief in such bizarre circumstances in a cavernous Calgary barn. The manager was guiltless for the freak events of that strange and tragic May afternoon in 1913, but he had been a prime mover in the White Hope concept, and in the weeks, months and years following the youngster's death, he just might have taken time to soul-search over his role in what was nothing better than a scandalous, racist scam.

The White Hopes . . . the hotchpotch collection of saddle-sore cowboys and slack-jawed farm boys and steely eyed miners and tough guys from the railyards who all responded to America's trumpet call to wipe out that black devil Jack Johnson. And if no white boy could be found with the ability actually to beat Jack, or for that matter, at least half a dozen other brilliant blacks, then so what? A whites-only tourney would soon put matters right, and to hell with the rightful champ. Billy McCarney could smell the money and his scruples did not keep him awake nights.

The furore that would envelop the States – but nowhere else in the world – first erupted after Johnson had outclassed Tommy Burns in Australia in 1908. But the movement really picked up speed after the champion had humbled the old favourite Jim Jeffries in 1910. Jeffries had answered writer Jack London's call to win back the title for the white race. Now came Billy McCarney's turn to appeal to the nation.

Using the type of language one would expect to read in a Klan handbook, Billy loudly proclaimed: 'Somewhere in this great Republic is a white giant who will respond to the call of the Caucasian world.' The hunt was on for a white hero.

McCarney had no shame, nor had the writers who happily printed his tosh. Today, promoters, managers and journalists alike would all have been hauled off to court, but in 1911, they masqueraded as crusaders, righteous campaigners, who at the same time were not averse to earning a good buck. Oddly, all those would-be saviours became obsessed not only by colour but also by size; they were searching for monsters, buying by the pound, and a total ignorance of boxing's basics was not regarded as a drawback to any candidate's prospects. Billy was right in the midst of the scrum, fly-hopping from one white superman to the next. He was a man in a hurry and he made mistakes; in fact, he made his biggest blunder ever when he severed an early connection with Jess Willard, the cumbersome 6ft 6in Kansan who, surprisingly, would eventually put an end to the long-running farce, when he somehow contrived to beat a poorly conditioned Johnson in Havana in 1915. The fast-talking McCarney and the slow-drawling Jess just could not get on, and their parting was acrimonious in the extreme.

But there were truckloads of other big fellows who thought they could fight. There was Fireman Jim Flynn, who was better than the average, which, of course, was not too high; there was Fred Fulton, who at least knew how to throw a tasty left hook; and there was a South African, George 'Boer' Rodel, and an Irish aspirant, Jim Coffey.

There was Carl Morris, who hooked up with McCarney, though again there was a personality clash and the partnership was short-lived. Morris was another incredible hulk, billed as the Sapulpa Giant, and a former railroad engineer who downed tools one day to enlist in the noble cause. He was not much of a fighter, but he was 6ft 4in, could talk a fierce battle, and looked the part, at least until the bell rang. There was England's lean Bombardier Billy Wells, tall enough, talented, but none too robust; there were Frank Moran and Gunboat Smith, who were both reasonably handy; and among a host of others, there was Luther McCarty, McCarney's million-dollar dream heavy, who, even allowing for all the ballyhoo that surrounded him, just might have developed into the best of them all had he been dealt different cards.

Luther McCarty stood 6ft 3in, weighed over 200lb and therefore measured up before he had ever tossed a jab; he was also movie-star handsome, looked brilliant in his many publicity shots, and thanks to McCarney's beaverish industry, he quickly captured the public's fancy. If not a star of the silent screen, big Lute could have been a comic book hero: a crazy cocktail, with a dash of Li'l Abner, a touch of Joe Palooka, a strong shot of Tom Mix, and even a hint of Bart Simpson, if we were to credit just some of his adventures from his very early years. The youngster was extremely marketable, and in McCarney, he had the super salesman. Making money would be a breeze.

Luther was born on St Patrick's Day 1892, in an outpost called Driftwood Creek, which was situated in Wild Horse Canyon, Hitchcock County, Nebraska – a champion address on any package.

His father, Anton, was an enormous chap, even by white heavy requirements; his mother, also impressively large, died when he was two; and his sister worked the vaudeville circuit, billed as 'The World's Champion Woman Bag Puncher'. Any sparring sessions between her and Luther went unrecorded.

Now, before he had reached his teens, Lute had proved himself a whizzkid on the range, roping steers and riding broncs, and a dead-shot with his pistol – relax, just a typical McCarney P.R. release. The big guy ran away from home aged twelve, hitch-hiked across the country, went off to sea, then worked as a lumberjack and a farmhand – more data from The Professor's files. A more credible account of Luther's early days tells of his accompanying his father on his travels: the huge Anton earned his money as an itinerant medicine drummer, hawking his cure-all potions to the innocents he met along the way, and most likely, that was when the youngster discovered his ability to spiel, and sell himself, and talk the fast talk that would become so familiar in his short life with McCarney.

The pair met in 1911, but McCarty probably had fought two or three times before he signed with The Professor. From the outset, McCarney deluged the country's newspaper offices with stories and pictures of his cowboy giant who could lick any man on the planet.

He kitted out Lute in the traditional cowpuncher's garb – stetson, gaudy neckerchief, chaps, boots and, of course, a six-gun. He stuck Luther on a horse, the prospective pug twirled his lariat for the cameras, and the sports editors could not get enough. Nor could the public, not to mention the amiable teenager, who was proving such a natural when it came to acting out his manager's latest brainwave. But still there remained the relatively important question of whether he actually could perform in the ring. The editors knew he could rope a steer, but could he drop one with a right hand?

McCarney maintained that he had kept Lute under wraps for an entire year, tutoring him on the rudiments, but it was most unlikely that The Professor could have shown such commendable patience and restraint when so much dough was out there for the taking.

When he finally did unleash his desperado, however, there was little doubt that the lad, though naturally raw, knew how to take care of himself. There was a victory over the much smaller Joe Grim, an oddball who loved to boast about how much punishment he could soak up; then he knocked out Joe Cox, which was deemed a minor achievement; but when he exposed the glaring limitations of Carl Morris, stopping the Oklahoman in six rounds on 3 May 1912, Luther was hailed as a genuine Hope. McCarney had lassoed a true western hero! But in reality, the Nebraskan was still a novice, a kid learning his trade.

On his highly publicised New York début on 19 August 1912, he came off second best in a ten-round no-decision with none other than Willard, who was still three years away from the title. There was another disappointing outing against Jim Stewart, but McCarty got back on track with eye-catching performances against Al Kaufman and Fireman Jim Flynn; and with McCarney now beating the drums louder than ever, he was a popular choice when Californian promoter Tom McCarey (McCarty, McCarney, McCarey – sounds like an old Dublin law firm!) booked him to box for the 'white' heavyweight championship of the world in Los Angeles on New Year's Day 1913. His opponent? A rugged, but very limited puncher called Al Palzer.

Palzer was yet another country boy, this time a farm worker from Ossien, Iowa, and like McCarty, he owed much of his rapid rise to his manager, an astute character named Tom O'Rourke, who had done the business for two fine black champions, welterweight Joe Walcott and the great bantam and featherweight George Dixon. Three years older than McCarty, Palzer was no Einstein in the ring, and fought strictly to instructions, bellowed at from the corner by O'Rourke – sometimes through a megaphone! Since the fighter and his manager were forever feuding, the repartee was often more entertaining than the action in the ring. Big Al, however, did possess extraordinary stamina and grit, and when he did manage to land a punch, he could inflict damage. But he was typical of the time: a big, game, white boy who would have been taken apart by a Langford or a Jeannette.

O'Rourke first came across Palzer when he promoted a White Hope tournament in New York's National Sporting Club in May 1911, and the best he could come up with was the boy from Iowa. There had been 23 entrants of every shape and size, and at ringside was an amused Jack Johnson, checking out the competition. He saw nobody who could cause him concern; in fact, there was not one fighter in the club who could be passed off as a credible challenger. Following a marathon session, Palzer reached the final, outpointed Sailor White over four rounds, and was proclaimed 'The White Hope Heavyweight Champion Of The World?' When it came to the hype, O'Rourke needed no lessons from Billy McCarney; and by the terms of his tournament, he was now Palzer's manager, the farm boy tied up fast in a watertight contract. O'Rourke had his White Hope and Palzer had his problems, for they could never agree on the accounting come pay-out time.

In fairness to Palzer, he had not been offered his chance against McCarty in Los Angeles solely on his exploits in O'Rourke's two-bit tournament. He had caused a few raised eyebrows by stopping Kaufman and, in June 1912, he had survived a hectic brawl against Billy Wells in Madison Square Garden. The much lighter Englishman had looked an assured early winner, knocking down Palzer in the first and bursting his nose and mouth. But in the third, a bloodied Al came pounding back to knock out the Bombardier. Those were all the credentials O'Rourke required to clinch big Al's claim to be included in any championship decider. Any *white* championship decider.

Jack Johnson might have been in excellent humour when he viewed what passed as Hopes in New York, but now as 1912 drew to a close, he was in big trouble. In 1910, Congress had passed the Mann Act, in a bid to crack down on the interstate promotion of commercialised vice; and in November 1912, the champ was made a fall guy, being indicted for transporting his companion, one Belle Schreiber, over several state lines. Out in California, the news was greeted with glee by promoter McCarey. He immediately announced that Johnson could no longer be recognised as the champion, and that the Los Angeles showdown between McCarty and Palzer must now be approved as for the real championship. In the mood of the times, McCarey found plenty of support in the newspapers, but not even the presentation of a diamond-studded belt to the winner could turn this into a pukka title bout. There were too many black boxers with far superior claims.

Johnson had other pressing matters on his mind. Come his trial, he was found guilty and Judge George Carpenter sentenced him to one year and a day in the grim prison facility at Joliet, Illinois, plus a fine of $1,000. But Jack was given bail pending an appeal, and proceeded to move faster than he had ever done in the ring, first hopping a train over the border to Canada, then sailing off to France and exile. The true champ was on the lam!

A focused Johnson would have been fancied to beat both Palzer and McCarty on the same evening: Luther was still just learning, and Al could never learn, he simply lacked natural talent.

The farmer boxed like a robot throughout his New Year's Day moment of truth in L.A., as a frantic O'Rourke bawled advice from the corner. But to no avail. Round after round, Palzer presented a wide-open target, and he absorbed a terrific beating from McCarty, who at first could not believe his good luck, but who, as the one-sided battering continued, called several times for the referee to put an end to the slaughter. Finally, in round eighteen, everyone had seen enough blood, and Luther was crowned the new heavyweight champion – but only through white eyes.

Lute had his short speech prepared and he certainly was not going to rock the boat; McCarney probably drafted the lines. 'I will not meet any negro,' announced the cowboy, 'but will draw the colour line absolutely.' There was country-wide media support for the young, so-called champ and his sentiments, but Lute quickly discovered that being bathed in the spotlight could have a serious downside, and that his newspaper pals could turn bothersome when they laid down their glasses on the bar and started snooping around.

For over a year, McCarty had been living out his wildest fantasies. He had basked in the hype in New York and revelled in the adulation in L.A.; he never tired of seeing his pictures in the papers or cutting out the stories that the busy McCarney had planted; and the ten grand he had collected (before managerial deductions, of course!) was the sort of dough that a real cowpuncher could only draw by robbing the stage. Yet everything was happening so fast, he was having such a grand old time, that somehow big Lute had completely forgotten to tell anyone about his young wife Rhoda and their baby daughter Cornelia, tucked away in Moorhead, Minnesota.

When the story broke, the twenty-year-old fighter was at first embarrassed, then indignant, protesting that he had not actually deserted his wife, but was always on the move, and had sent money home when he was able; now that he was in the big money, he planned to open a bank account to take care of baby Cornelia's education. Rhoda had nothing really bad to say about her husband – nobody had an unkind word for Luther – other than that his injections of cash could be more regular. But the bald facts were that Rhoda was slaving in a saloon while Luther was having the time of his life all over the country. The press pack would not have given Jack Johnson such an easy ride over his domestics, but thanks to the expertise of McCarney, Lute remained unscathed, still the All American boy.

The Professor was keeping him busy, not just with so-so ring appearances against Fireman Flynn and Frank Moran, but also on the stage, where Luther performed some nifty tricks with his lariat that apparently went down well with the city folks. Boxing, however, took precedence, and from a bundle of offers, McCarney chose to accept an invitation to take a trip up to Canada for a defence against Arthur Pelkey in Calgary, home of the famous rodeo and eager to play host to the punching cowboy.

The offer came from the former champion Tommy Burns, at 5ft 7in, the shortest ever heavyweight holder. Though no match for Johnson, the man born Noah Brusso in Chesley, Ontario, has often been given a bum rap by the ring historians, remembering only his humiliation in Sydney.

Yet Burns had been a skilled technician and a fast and heavy puncher; he was also a shrewd, hard-headed businessman, well able to counter the tricks of the wiliest promoter or manager. He held out for a record purse to face Johnson, made exceptional money in London, and learned how to promote successfully while still an active pro. Now he looked after Arthur Pelkey.

A French-Canadian, Pelkey was no prize, certainly no Tommy Burns, not even a Carl Morris. But he was big and he was white and he was Canadian, and so he qualified, although few of his countrymen gave him a squeak. The date was 24 May 1913, and an estimated 10,000 packed into the makeshift stadium in Calgary. Once again, Burns had got his figures right.

The boxers entered the ring at one on the Saturday afternoon, McCarty, to all observers, apparently relaxed and in his usual high spirits. But before the action could get under way, there was a curious prelude when a local minister ducked through the ropes and addressed the crowd. For some reason, The Reverend felt it his duty to remind the fans that the preliminary bouts had been contested in a sportsman-like fashion with an absence of brutality. He told his biggest ever congregation that what they were about to see would be no different from 'the honourable struggle engaged in every day of their lives'. Bad vibes! And the good man could not have been further out in his tipping.

The opening bell . . . the last bell big Lute would ever hear, and he advanced confidently to the centre of the ring. Pelkey fell short with a couple of jabs, then McCarty tried with both hands but also failed to land. The boxers clinched but as they obeyed instructions to break, McCarty sagged, then slowly sank to the canvas. A confused referee, Ed Smith, started to count although he had not seen any knockdown punch, and as he ticked off the seconds, a brilliant shaft of light beamed through the rafters of the arena and down on the stricken fighter. This was to provide boxing with one of its most poignant pictures ever.

The hall was in uproar, the crowd convinced that they had just witnessed the most blatant fix of all time. There was a surge towards the ring, quickly broken up by a squad of Mounties, then an eerie silence fell as it became obvious to all that there was something seriously wrong with the fighter. No paramedics back in 1913, no ambulance on hand to speed Luther to a hospital where a team of surgeons would be waiting. As gently as possible, McCarty – all 6ft 3in and 200lb of him – was lifted out of the ring and stretched out on the uncovered grass, where the doctors started to work frantically. They toiled for eight minutes before pronouncing him dead, and another famous photograph shows Billy McCarney, standing legs apart, his head clutched in his hands. Total despair.

What had gone wrong? The good Reverend could sleep easy for Luther might have died in the ring, but his tragedy had nothing to do with boxing. The autopsy revealed that he had died from a cerebral haemorrhage, caused by a broken vertebra. The injury most likely occurred when the boxer had been tossed off a horse just a week earlier.

Such a freak calamity, but one that just might have been avoided had McCarty been the type to create a fuss, and had he gone for a precautionary examination after the fall. Perhaps, but Lute was a happy-go-lucky youngster, seldom heard to moan, and a tumble from a horse would have been more a cue for laughter than a cause for concern. And yet years later, there emerged evidence that McCarty was feeling the effects of the fall before he even stepped into the ring. In a letter written to *The Ring*'s Dan Daniel in 1948, promoter Burns recalled the events of that sad day in Calgary. He wrote:

'I had a talk with McCarty that morning of the fight. He turned towards me and could not pivot his head. He had to move his entire body.

'I asked Luther what was wrong and he replied, "Tommy, I was sleeping near an open window last night and got a stiff neck. It is nothing serious."

'Well, poor Luther didn't realise how serious it was. McCarney loved the big kid and Luther's death really broke him up. Aside from that, McCarty was a fine looking heavyweight and would have made a fortune for Billy and himself.

'I thought a great deal of Luther and his death hit me rather hard. However, that's the way of life.'

Indeed. Burns's protégé Pelkey did not encounter much joy in his new role as pseudo champ. He lost his White Hope title on New Year's Day 1914, when Gunboat Smith knocked him out in fifteen rounds in San Francisco, and thereafter really hit the skids. He was flattened by just about everybody from Joe Jeannette to Jack Dempsey; even Carl Morris got lucky. And then in 1915, Willard was fortunate to get his big chance against Johnson in Cuba, and the era of the White Hopes was at an end.

Yet Billy McCarney kept soldiering on, kept getting within a fingertip of the great fighters and the great fights, but for some strange reason, he always finished one ball short of the jackpot. He had rowed spectacularly with Willard before Jess became the champ, and another expensive bust-up, on this occasion with an equally vociferous and imaginative manager, Joe Jacobs, blew his percentage in a trio of champions, Mike McTigue and Frankie Genaro, and, most costly of all, Max Schmeling, yet another heavyweight holder. Before he linked up with McCarty, The Prof had sampled just about every facet of the business, and once worked as an advance publicity agent on a Jim Jeffries tour. And in 1947 – the year before he died aged 76 – he was still on the road, still beating the tomtoms, this time for Joe Louis, during The Bomber's tour of Mexico and South America. A hustler to the end.

McCarney was never a stickler for accuracy, always had an eye for a headline, but in his autumn years, he might have been speaking from his heart and not his head when he declared that, of all the fighters he had been associated with, McCarty was the greatest. For an all too brief spell, Billy and Lute had formed a wonderful double act, and who can tell just how high they might have climbed? Back in the forties, he told *Ring* writer Daniel:

'I never got over the death of McCarty. I liked the kid as if he were my own son . . . You remember Pelkey. Big and strong, but a mediocre heavyweight. McCarty would have disposed of him in no time at all. Luther could not have missed. He would have become the champion. Certainly he was a far greater fighter than Willard.'

We could never expect McCarney to be objective: he had loathed big Jess and loved Luther, and like most of us, was inclined to extol the virtues of any unfortunate, cut off before or during the prime of life. When he died, McCarty still had so much to prove in the ring, but there is little doubt that he possessed the basic equipment and the temperament, the goodwill of both the press and the public, and, not least, the powerhouse backing of The Professor. With a further two years' experience, he might well have been ready for a Johnson, drained both physically and mentally, but a fall from a horse denied him those years.

Old opponent Al Palzer survived Lute by just over four years. Al never learned to duck and he was shot dead by his drunken father on 25 July 1917, aged 28. And Arthur Pelkey was just 36 when he died on 18 February 1921. Like all the other White Hopes, they had loved their brief moment in the sun . . . but sadly for Luther McCarty, the most popular of them all, the sun did not choose to come out until he was already lying dead in the Calgary ring.

17

Les Darcy:
'A Less Than Artful Dodger'

LES DARCY and Dave Sands, in their respective eras, totally dominated Australian boxing, sent shock waves around the world, and today are still revered as two of the nation's outstanding fighters of all time. In the land of Oz, Darcy was actually recognised for a spell as the middleweight champion of the world, and over thirty years later, the New South Wales aficionados were unanimous that nothing could stop Sands doing equally well, if not better. But those old timers should have paused for a moment and recalled the cruel fate that befell young Les, and realised that Sands might turn out to be just another chapter in the extraordinary hoodoo that has plagued the 160lb class, its champions and near champions, for the best part of a century. And sure enough, Dave Sands, too, would become a victim of the jinx.

Darcy . . . Sands . . . McCoy . . . Papke . . . Ketchel . . . Greb . . . Flowers . . . Cerdan . . . Turpin . . . Monzon. All outstanding middleweights and all doomed to a premature death – by murder and suicide; in plane crashes and car smashes; and there was even the eerie coincidence of two great championship rivals dying on the operating table within thirteen months of each other, having just undergone similar eye surgery.

Darcy still had to gain universal recognition as a champ when he died; Sands was just on the brink of a title shot. But the rest all had the satisfaction of being crowned, before the finger pointed in their direction.

Norman Selby, who boxed as Charles (Kid) McCoy and who first inspired the phrase 'The Real McCoy', was one middleweight holder who opted for suicide, but not before he had lived more lives than a family of cats. The Kid won his title in 1897, beating an Australian named Dan Creedon in New York, embarked on a flamboyant venture that would take him round the world, and saw him try his luck in the early movies, own a tavern and a gym, become a socialite, and beat a jewel theft rap in London in 1912. McCoy's luck finally ran out twelve years later, when he was sentenced to 24 years in San Quentin, having been convicted of the murder of Theresa Moers, who had lived with him after leaving her art dealer husband. Given parole after serving eight years, he spent his remaining days struggling over his memoirs, but the task must have wakened old ghosts, because on 17 April 1940 in Detroit, he overdosed on sleeping pills.

The Kid had lived a long and self-indulgent life, and signed off with a note explaining that he 'could not endure this world's madness' – which was fair enough . . .

Randolph Turpin's farewell, pinned to an upstairs bedroom door in his café in Leamington, was a much more sad and bitter reminder to all of those who he was convinced had robbed and cheated him out of his substantial ring earnings.

Turpin was one of Britain's greatest ever champions, peaking on that heady July evening in 1951 when he outpointed Sugar Ray Robinson at London's Earl's Court. He was a champion for only 64 days until Robinson regained the title in New York's Polo Grounds, but he remained a huge attraction for years after. Randy, however, was a sucker for women and a soft touch for any hard luck story, and both cost him fortunes. When he retired, not only had all the money gone, but the bills for back tax started to haunt him. The pressure proved too much, and on the afternoon of 17 May 1966, he went to his bedroom, shot himself twice, and also wounded his two-year-old daughter Carmen. Randolph was just 37.

Stanley Ketchel and Billy Papke engaged in four brutal title brawls between 1908 and 1909, and then both wound up dying violently. Ketchel, who was the three-to-one winner of their series, was still the reigning champion when he was shot dead by a jealousy-crazed Walter Dipley on a farm in Conway, Missouri, on 15 October 1910. Papke was fifty, and comfortably fixed financially, when on 26 November

1936, he went haywire, driving to the home of his estranged wife in Newport, California, where he shot her dead, then killed himself. No explanations.

Harry Greb, one of the most exciting champions at any weight, fought his last battle when Tiger Flowers, who had won the title from him, again outpointed Harry in the rematch on 19 August 1926.

For a long time, Greb had had been troubled by failing sight, and that October, he entered hospital for treatment, but died while undergoing surgery. He was 32, had been one of the original swingers; his conqueror, Flowers, was a Bible-preaching southpaw. Opposites. But just over a year after beating Greb, The Tiger was also admitted into hospital for an operation to remove scar tissue around his eyes, and just like Greb, he never woke up after the anaesthetic.

The wonderful French hero, Marcel Cerdan, was killed when his plane crashed in the Azores on 27 October 1949. Cerdan was flying back to the States for his title return against Jake La Motta, and his death was mourned by the entire nation. Another tremendous champion, though a far less stable character, the Argentinian Carlos Monzon died in a car crash on 8 January 1995. Serving an eleven-year term following the death of his girlfriend Alicia Muniz, the 53-year-old Monzon was on day release pending parole, when he smashed up, also killing one of his passengers.

None of those fighters, neither the dashing, desperate nor depressed, died so young as Les Darcy, who was still just 21 when he checked out, far away from home in Memphis, Tennessee. Yet despite his youth, Darcy had crammed in 49 pro battles and was widely regarded as one of the finest middleweights ever. He became first a national hero, then a social outcast; and when the more extravagant of the publications that had once relentlessly hounded the Aussie now declared that he must surely have died of a broken heart, there was an enormous outpouring of public grief when the youngster's body was shipped home to Sydney.

The last known picture of Darcy, however, was taken just a week before his death, and shows a cheerful, good-looking boy, smiling out from under a large cap; this snap torpedoes the romantic broken-heart notion, and the most probable cause of death was blood poisoning, brought about by an infected tooth. Tragic none the less.

James Leslie Darcy was born into a large family in Maitland, New South Wales, on 31 October 1895, was apprenticed briefly to a blacksmith, but a natural aptitude for fighting ensured that, after a fleeting amateur career, he was soon earning his keep from the ring. Short at 5ft 6in, but powerfully built, the boy had a terrific reach, punched hard with both hands, and was extremely tough. When he was still only fifteen, his home town professional début against Sid Pasco lasted less than two rounds, and then he proceeded to run up a sequence of sixteen wins before Bob Whitelaw got the vote over him after a twenty-round endurance test for the Australian welterweight championship in November 1913. Four months later, Les knocked out Whitelaw in a rematch, but the teenager had outgrown the welters, and was now being lined up against a collection of good-class American imports who were proving popular in Sydney.

The linear middleweight champion of the world was Al McCoy, certainly not The Real McCoy, and actually born Al Rudolph in New Jersey. An awkward, spoiling southpaw, McCoy caused a major upset when he knocked out George Chip in one round in Brooklyn in April 1914 to win the title, but this was the era when no-decision bouts were the vogue in New York, and the slippery McCoy, almost impossible to knock out, survived as champion until 1917, when Mike O'Dowd finally got rid of him in six rounds.

McCoy lacked charisma, and in Australia, the flourishing Stadiums Ltd, based in Sydney and spearheaded by Harry Keesing, decided to create its own version of the world middleweight title, and granted recognition to American Eddie McGoorty, after he had knocked out the local hope, Dave Smith, in one round on New Year's Day 1914. The Aussie splinter group smacked of today's pirate sanctioning bodies, but in fairness, a number of leading American middleweights did give it their support. Yet when Keesing overturned referee Arthur Scott's decision after McGoorty's defence against fellow Yank Jeff Smith, and informed interested parties around the world that Smith was now the champion, his autocratic manner might not have helped him get wider recognition for his version of the title.

Stadiums Ltd, however, continued to prosper. For the remainder of

1914, Smith was kept busy with defences against Pat Bradley and American Jimmy Clabby, then he lost and regained the title against the Sydney puncher Mick King. But by now, the fight all Australia wanted to see was Smith defending against the sensational nineteen-year-old Darcy, and on 23 January 1915, the youngster finally got his opportunity.

The bout proved a terrible anticlimax, and Darcy blew his chance in the fifth, when he complained about a low blow; the referee, believing the Australian wanted to quit, stopped the fight and gave the verdict to Smith. That was to be the last time Les Darcy was to lose in the ring, and four months later he gained his revenge when Smith was disqualified in the second round. Young Les was the champion, at least in Australia, and in the next two busy years, he outshone all-comers.

McCoy was still the champion by right, but even in the States, Darcy was now being recognised as the world's outstanding middleweight as he beat the pick of the American visitors such as McGoorty, Clabby and Chip, and George K.O. Brown, Buck Crouse and Frank Loughrey. He scored 22 wins, successfully defended his title eight times, and even stepped up to win the Australian heavyweight title against Harold Hardwick. The boy looked unbeatable.

One of Darcy's 1915 victims had been yet another American, Billy Murray, who had lasted the title distance in Sydney, but who was stopped in six rounds in Melbourne. In Murray's corner for both fights was our old friend Jack Kearns, still to discover his Dempsey, but already sharp enough to recognise immediately Darcy's earning potential in the States. He put one of his propositions to Darcy and his manager Tim O'Sullivan, guaranteeing them top dollar in America, a grand tour, and a certain shot at the real title. For once, the Doc's timing was off by miles.

America had not yet entered the war, but Australia was very heavily involved. The ill-fated Gallipoli expedition had come to an inglorious conclusion in December 1915, with the battle-weary British, Australian and New Zealand troops being withdrawn after a savage ten-month campaign. Losses had been heavy, and back home in Australia, feelings were running high against men – men like Les – who had still to enlist. There was also a law which banned males between the ages of eighteen and forty leaving the country, which, of course, effectively scuppered Kearns's plan. But the seeds had been planted.

Darcy maintained his hectic pace throughout 1916, boxing ten times, but the pressure was mounting on him to join up; the newspapers were on his case, and his once adoring fan base was now fast crumbling. His team circulated stories telling how he was the sole support for his parents and their large brood; how his father was an invalid and how one brother was a cripple. But his fellow Australians remained unimpressed: Darcy was seen as a dodger, putting his career before his country.

Nobody could have guessed at the time, but the veteran George Chip would prove to be Darcy's final opponent when they met on 30 September 1916 in Sydney Stadium. Les won easily in nine rounds, but winning had never posed much of a problem; if only he could have handled his outside pressures half as well! But as the year drew to a close, and as the newspapers stepped up their personal attacks, the prospect of America, and all that was promised there, grew ever more appealing. Unthinkable, but Les Darcy was about to make the craziest decision of his young life: he stowed away on a tanker bound for the U.S., and turned his back on his country at war.

The repercussions were devastating. He was vilified in his homeland, but his reception in the States was equally hostile, and the fighter and his advisers were taken totally by surprise. Advisers? Darcy just might be excused his folly on the count of his youth, but what about his manager O'Sullivan? And what part did Doc Kearns play in the flight to the States? Whose interests were they looking out for, and how had they so misread the mood in America?

The United States entered the war in April 1917, and the country was awash with patriotic fervour; if anything, Darcy the Australian draft dodger, was in for an even rougher ride in the States than he had experienced back home. The first scoring punches were landed by New York's governor, Charles Whitman, who announced that any contest involving Darcy would be banned in his state; other governors quickly followed suit; promoter Tex Rickard, no doubt working closely with Kearns, had mapped out an extensive tour for the youngster, but this was quickly scrapped. A distraught Darcy claimed he was only in the country for six months to earn enough money to send home to his family, then he planned to join the Canadian army. Nobody listened.

The 21-year-old was desperate: a theatrical venture had flopped, and crowds only turned out for his boxing exhibitions to hurl abuse. In fact, he was so desperate that the notion of enlisting in the army – any army! – no longer seemed such a bad idea. He had received a rather cautious welcome from the governor of Tennessee, and a Memphis promoter was encouraged to open negotiations for Les to box Len Rowlands. Part of the package involved Darcy signing an oath of allegiance to the U.S. and also enlisting in the American forces, although he would be given ample time to pursue his career. In the circumstances, it looked as if the youngster was about to pull off the great escape, but fate took a hand. Darcy suddenly fell ill in Memphis, and within a matter of days, he died on 24 May 1917.

The shock waves travelled from the States to Australia; some reports said he died of pneumonia, others that he caught a fever; the best bet is that he died of blood poisoning, and the big outsider is the broken-heart theory. Certainly, the stress of his traumatic last two years might have sapped his constitution, but forget all those sob stories about Darcy throwing in the towel and dying a broken man. True, he had turned out a sorry excuse for an artful draft dodger, but he had been in the process of reinventing himself and kick-starting his career when the hoodoo struck.

The hoodoo . . . that same hex that, 35 years later, would shatter the title dreams of the other great New South Wales middleweight, the quiet man, Dave Sands.

Whereas the controversial Darcy had appeared on the scene like a brilliant shooting star, and had achieved so much fame and notoriety so quickly, Sands was more of a slow burn, for whom everything finally looked to be slotting into place when tragedy struck. The date was 11 August 1952, the Helsinki Olympics were dominating the sports pages, and Aussie golds Marjorie Jackson and Shirley Strickland had the country in high good humour.

Sands was driving his truck back to his training headquarters near Newcastle, a traditional fight town where Darcy had earlier thrilled the locals; suddenly the vehicle left the road, overturned down an embankment, and Dave died in hospital from his injuries. Simple as that. He was 26, and but for the jinx, he could well have been world middleweight champion within a year.

Boxing can boast some fabulous fighting clans: the Toweels from South Africa, the Famechons in first France, then Australia, the Zivic boys from Pittsburgh, and the Turpin and Buxton brothers from England. Starting in the early forties, and for over a decade, the name of Sands became synonymous with the fight game in Australia. Alfie and Clem and Richie and George were all tough competitors, all good-value headliners. But no question, Dave was the stand-out, a one-off.

The son of a Puerto Rican father and an Aboriginal mother, he was born David Richie on 4 February 1926 in Burnt Ridge, New South Wales. Compared to Darcy, Dave was a late starter in the business, not turning pro until he was seventeen, but in his debut year of 1943, he lost only once in eighteen appearances, a points defeat against Billy Myers. Right from the off, he was a naturally gifted boxer and a hard and correct puncher, and by the end of 1945, he had compiled a solid record of only five losses in 44 bouts. The time was right for him to be unleashed against the domestic champions and foreign imports of a reasonable standard.

In the next three years, he fought 29 times and lost only once – a later-avenged points defeat against Emery Jackson. He knocked out Jack Kirkham to win the Australian middleweight title; performed a similar number on Jack Johnson to become the boss at light heavy; beat future British champion Alex Buxton and visiting Americans such as O'Neill Bell and The Alabama Kid; settled old scores with Billy Myers and Doug Brown; and in a three-month sojourn in New Zealand, mopped up all opposition.

The shy 22-year-old, homesick during his stay in New Zealand, was now an international name, attracting offers from all over the world. He was ranked just one spot behind Archie Moore in *The Ring*'s light heavyweight list, but curiously, the magazine ignored his obvious claims in the 160lb division. Middle or light heavy, it was all the same to Jack Solomons, and brandishing his cheque book and a contract granting him exclusive rights to Sands's services in Europe, the London promoter invited the Australians over to England for an extended stay and a promised crack at a world title. But after only one fight, Sands was being labelled a false alarm, out of his league when taken away from his own territory.

Not for the first time, Solomons had been careless in his choice of opposition. The American light heavy, Tommy Yarosz, was brought over for Dave's London introduction on 4 April 1949, and he was indeed a shock selection. Managed by Ray Arcel, Yarosz was a brainy boxer, adept at making an opponent look bad, and very hard to catch cleanly. Most U.S. managers turned a deaf ear when he was mentioned, but Solomons was happy enough – until the fight got under way. Yarosz produced his usual sharp, shifty boxing; Sands showed very little.

The Aussie's preparation had not been ideal. Though he had trained diligently at Solomons's gym, the cold and damp had caused him problems, once again he was homesick, and after Yarosz was declared a clear points winner, he must have felt like jumping on the next plane home. The criticism was harsh, and did not ease up a fortnight later, when Dave plodded to a decision against a modest and much lighter Frenchman, Lucien Caboche, at the Albert Hall.

But Sands had not become a bad fighter overnight, and Solomons, to give him his due, neither panicked nor despaired. The ever imaginative promoter sent Dave north for his next bout – to Newcastle, namesake of the town on the other side of the world where both Darcy and Dave had been such favourites. Again the opposition was not great, but at last the Australian showed some spite and more power when stopping Bolton's outclassed Jackie Jones in just eighty seconds; and less than three weeks later, he made a return Tyneside visit to convincingly outpoint the Dutchman, Jan De Bruin. Confidence boosters for both fighter and promoter.

His faith restored, Solomons looked around for a tough guy, and there were few harder nuts around than the chunky Frenchman, Robert Villemain. Two years older than Sands, he was a fierce competitor, and earlier in the year, had survived twelve rough rounds with Jake La Motta. After fighting Sands, he would beat La Motta in a return, also outpoint Kid Gavilan, last out fifteen rounds against a peak Ray Robinson for the Pennsylvania version of the world title, and go the full ten with Bobo Olson. Not bad.

Solomons had set a severe examination, but Villemain's style was perfect for Dave, who gave the Olympia crowd an exhibition of smart boxing and fast, accurate hitting. The Frenchman took counts of six and nine in the second, and did well to survive the three minutes; indeed, he performed heroics still to be punching back at the final bell. But Sands was a wide-margin winner and had looked terrific.

He had weighed just one pound above the middleweight limit for the fight, and so Solomons reckoned that a challenge against Empire champion Dick Turpin – the elder brother of Randolph – was well in order. Dick was no mug, had done as well as could have been expected when lasting into the seventh against Marcel Cerdan five months earlier, and was forecast to make life difficult. But the action lasted only two minutes and 45 seconds, including two counts, as a super-charged Sands treated the Harringay fans to a stunning demonstration of controlled fury.

All doubt about his real ability had been erased, and finally back in Australia, Sands got 1950 off to a flier when he outpointed the future world champion Carl (Bobo) Olson over twelve rounds in Sydney. Two years Sands's junior, the rugged Hawaiian Islander had lost only twice in 35 fights, but he was no match for the Aussie. Another notable success came when he stopped Henry Brimm (who had boxed a draw against Robinson the previous year) in two rounds, then he took a jump to heavyweight to outpoint Alf Gallagher for the national title. He appeared to be unbeatable.

But the big money lay with the middles. In London, Solomons visualised a Sands–Randolph Turpin showdown as his summer spectacular for 1951; Dave's Empire title would be on the line, and the fight could be billed legitimately as a final eliminator, the winner earning a shot at new champion Robinson. Then Solomons got word about the Sugarman's planned European tour and his willingness to defend the title in London. After a few trans-Atlantic calls and cablegrams, Turpin got his chance and won the title. And Sands? He got the elbow and a consolation shift on the Earl's Court undercard against Mel Brown.

Dave was learning to survive away from home, and a trip to the States underlined his title prospects. Renewing acquaintance with two former victims, he comfortably outpointed Olson in Chicago, and again stopped Brimm, this time in Buffalo. He was marking time, awaiting the inevitable title shot, when Solomons called him back to London to face Trinidad light heavy Yolande Pompey on 13 November at Harringay.

Pompey was tough and could punch hard, but with only 22 bouts, he was inexperienced and crude in comparison to the smooth-boxing Sands. This shaped as a handy earner to cover the Christmas expenses, and for five rounds the Australian was in total command and dealing out heavy punishment. Pompey's lip was badly gashed, and he had to be coaxed off his stool for the sixth, but suddenly his luck changed; he opened a bad cut over Sands's left eye, and this spurred him into a ferocious assault that continued into the seventh. Battered and bleeding, Dave refused to go down, but he was reeling drunkenly when the referee rightly stepped in.

A huge upset, almost of Turpin–Robinson proportions, and a sickening body blow to the Aussie's world dreams, but by no means the end of a career. Sands was only 25 and he could come again. The rehabilitation got under way at home with successful defences of his Australian light heavyweight title, then his Empire middleweight crown, and also his national heavyweight championship. Comfortable fights to boost his confidence, and he was in camp, training for another such contest, against New Zealander Don Mullett, when he turned over the truck.

At the time of his death, however, Dave was still a major player on the international middleweight scene – a scene that was about to experience a gigantic upheaval.

Having unluckily failed to take the light heavyweight title from Joey Maxim in June 1952, the 160lb champion Robinson was talking retirement. Sugar Ray would not make the announcement official until December – by then Sands was dead – but in July, everybody in the know knew, and plans were being made. Again Solomons wanted a Turpin–Sands eliminator, the winner to face the best from the States. But when the Australian was killed, France's Charles Humez was brought in against Turpin, who won on points before flopping badly in the decider against the American champion. And that American champion? None other than Carl Olson – the same Bobo who twice had been a loser against Sands!

We are now getting deep into hypotheticals, but allow us to say that Sands would have had an outstanding chance against a Turpin who had started to slide, and an Olson who would have required magic to make sufficient improvement. As it was, in a career that spanned ten years, around one hundred fights, and only eight defeats, Dave Sands was long overdue his big chance when that truck went off the road.

Les Darcy had been able to call himself champion – if not *the* champion – when he hung out in Australia, but had he lived, would he have been as big a hit fighting in the States? And would Dave Sands have sorted out Turpin and Olson, and maybe even Robinson, Basilio and Fullmer? Who knows?

The hobgoblins know . . . and they never tire of playing their fiendish tricks on the middleweights. But do not expect any public statements.

18

Gypsy Joe Harris:
'Just One Bloodshot Eye'

GYPSY JOE HARRIS did not look anything like a fighter: short, and shaven-headed, often with a little pot belly popping over the waistband of his bright red trunks, tiny bells jingling on his red ring boots, The Gypsy shaped up more as a jester than a jolting jabber. And yet, for an all too brief but electrifying period in the mid-sixties, he cast his spell over American boxing, dazzling his opponents, enchanting the fans, and sending the sports writers scrambling for superlatives.

That his career lasted a mere 25 professional fights has to be described as a tragedy; that he fought those 25 contests when totally blind in his right eye is almost beyond belief. But there was really nothing about the little man from north Philadelphia that fitted in with the stereotype pug: he did things his way, which was an eccentric brew of brilliance and buffoonery, and he was a forerunner to the likes of Jorge Paez, who brought a whiff of the circus sawdust into the ring, and even Prince Naseem, who would have been his number one fan had he been around back then.

Gypsy Joe was extra special, good enough to outclass totally the reigning welterweight champion of his era, but never dedicated enough ever to fight for a championship. Even with the crippling eye handicap, Harris was a laugh-a-second hustler; a free spirit and a trainer's nightmare, but a promoter's dream.

He was also a huge embarrassment to boxing's officialdom, or at least, he should have been. How The Gypsy passed his ring medical on 25 different occasions may be a tribute to his trickery, but it is a sad indictment of the health checks in place back then. Back then? Even after Gypsy Joe was finally stood down, there were occasions when big-name boxers were allowed into the ring half blind – or even worse. As we shall see, a former Olympian, Ray Seales, was regularly given the okay even though his sight was in a shocking state, and a great champion, Aaron Pryor, could still appear in Wisconsin and Oklahoma as late as 1990 when cataracts were causing him dire problems.

In far too many instances, there has existed an attitude whereby, if the boxer is prepared to take a chance with his eyesight (and the other parts of his body where the blows land because he cannot see them coming) then fair enough. The problem is all his. But that is criminal nonsense, because fighters, through misplaced macho or desperation for a dollar, so often need protection from themselves.

In most European countries and in the major fight centres in America, the medical examinations are supposed to be responsible and rigorous; but do not always bet on it. And in certain outposts where still anything goes, there is often an ambivalence that can be quite breathtaking. More than one doctor has yawned his way through the eye test as the fighter rattles off the letters on the chart (sometimes a truer test of memory than sight), yet, come the fight, the same doc can be seen making a big deal, claiming blood from a cut is impairing vision. There is a contradiction somewhere, but the bottom line is that too many boxers are prepared to gamble with their sight, and this is one bet that must be denied them.

Sam Langford finished up totally blind. Harry Greb was blind in one eye and died undergoing surgery to repair the other one. Back in 1946, an outstanding lightweight prospect, Wesley Mouzon, injured his right eye training for a title challenge against Bob Montgomery, whom he had already knocked out. His doctor diagnosed a detached retina and offered him a choice: he could either cancel the fight, or – because the eye could not get any worse than it already was! – he could try to pass the commission's eye test. Mouzon sailed through his exam, thanks to being familiar with the chart, but his title hopes ended in the eighth when Montgomery scored a knockout. Wisely, he decided not to box again.

But Gypsy Joe Harris was unique in that he started out with only one good peeper. And when a doctor finally bothered to give him a thorough examination and discovered that he was blind in the right eye, the outed Gypsy at last confessed that the eye had been damaged, not in the ring, but after he had been struck with a brick during a street battle when he was an eleven-year-old tearaway.

Unlike Langford, Seales, Pryor and so many others, he had never boxed any way other than one-eyed, and having won 24 of his 25 professional fights, he could not understand why all the sudden fuss. In retrospect, many of the unorthodox moves that stamped him as a one-off in the ring might have been explained by Joe amending his style so that no opponent could catch him on the blind side. With only that one defeat, his ring trickery obviously worked a treat, but that is not intended as an endorsement for any aspiring one-eyed fighters.

Ray Seales had two good eyes when he became the U.S.A.'s only boxing gold at the Munich Olympics of 1972. In the light welter final, he beat the Bulgarian Angel Angelov, but back home, there were no mouth-watering offers awaiting him to turn pro. This was partly because every event at those Games had been overshadowed by the bloodbath in the Olympic village when Palestinians from the Black September movement raided the Israeli headquarters. The world was stunned and, for once, gold medals seemed unimportant. But possibly a more pragmatic reason for the lukewarm interest in Seales stemmed from his style, which was more cagey, clever southpaw than dynamic, box-office sensation.

Born in the Virgin Islands on 9 April 1952, but reared in Tacoma, Washington, Seales did manage to get himself labelled another 'Sugar Ray' and his early career promised much. It was bad luck, however, that he was on a collision course with another hungry and ambitious youngster, a tough guy from Brockton called Marvin Hagler. They were first matched in Hagler's backyard of Boston in August 1974, and the decision went to Marvin after ten hard rounds. The November rematch in Seattle was as bitterly contested and both fighters considered themselves unlucky when a draw was announced. A third meeting should have been a natural, but somehow, it did not materialise for five long years, and this time, Hagler, on the verge of winning the world championship, overwhelmed Seales in one round.

That was a shattering defeat and effectively eliminated Ray as a challenger.

The following year, his eye troubles started in earnest when, in a winning fight against Jamie Thomas in Baton Rouge, he was accidentally thumbed and was later found to have a torn retina, which required an operation. At first, the surgery was voted a success, and he returned to the ring with a convincing win against James Williams in Tacoma, but then his vision began to deteriorate steadily. Incredibly, however, not only did he continue to pass his pre-fight medicals, but he kept winning most of his fights.

In a 1983 interview with Bart Wright for *The Ring*, he explained: 'I know the eye charts pretty well so I could fake it sometimes, and other times, when you couldn't read a line, they'd go up a line to bigger letters, and up again until you could read one and then they'd pass you. There were other times when they wouldn't use the eye charts at all, they'd just hold up fingers in front of your face and say, "How many?"'

That explained away the examinations, but what about the actual fights?

Ed Garner had taken over as his manager in 1979, but Seales did not confide in him about how bad things were becoming, and in the circumstances, some of his performances must be rated as remarkable, and possibly might have reassured his manager. In 1981, he knocked out Juan Rivas in one round in Bakersfield, California, and in March the following year, he outpointed a fair fighter in Johnny Locicero in New York, before being outpointed over twelve by James Schuler for the North American Boxing Federation title in October in Macafee, New Jersey.

California . . . New York . . . New Jersey. All high-profile boxing states with apparently vigilant commissions, but all failing to spot anything amiss with Seales.

There were, however, signs of his deterioration for those who were watching closely. For an accomplished, experienced boxer, he was now being caught with alarming frequency, even by raw novices in the gym. Suspicions were first aroused and then fears confirmed when, in a sparring session one day, Seales stopped boxing and complained that the ring lights were too low, and asked for them to be turned up to full power. His handlers, at last realising that something was drastically wrong, took him to a specialist who soon confirmed their worst fears: the boxer had been totally blind in his left eye for approximately two years, and vision in his right eye had been seriously impaired for more than a year. Seales had been boxing blurs, and boxing them very well, but for this Sugar Ray, America's lone Olympic hero in 1972, the desperate game was over.

Seales insisted that nobody closely connected to him ever knew the true extent of his problems and that the commissions never took the trouble to find out, which, first off, seems extraordinary, but then no more bizarre than Gypsy Joe keeping his secret throughout a successful amateur career and 25 fights in the pros. Like Seales, Harris boxed in states that supposedly had a solid reputation, such as Pennsylvania and New York, and yet he had escaped the notice of everyone, even his top corner team of manager Yank Durham and trainer Willie Reddish – two of the most respected practitioners in Philadelphia.

Aside from The Gypsy, Durham was moving along nicely with his young heavyweight Joe Frazier, and Reddish, at one time a good heavyweight who had gone the distance with Jersey Joe Walcott, had been the man in charge of Sonny Liston's corner when he beat Floyd Patterson for the title. Could the likes of Durham and Reddish have been fooled by the madcap antics of Gypsy during his sporadic training sessions at Champ's Gym in the north side of the city? Anything is possible, and it was something of a feat even to get Harris into the gym, but one might have expected such sharp cornermen to have noticed something odd.

Durham, Reddish and Seales's Ed Garner are entitled to the benefit of the doubt, because Harris and Seales, out of necessity, had kept things quiet, and both could be streetwise and inventive. But the same cannot be said for the characters who circled around Aaron Pryor and tried to make a final few bucks out of an ailing ring legend. They were left in no doubt about the former champion's condition, and yet they wanted to press on regardless, and saddest of all, Pryor wanted them to press on.

Aaron Pryor has rightly earned his place in boxing's Hall of Fame as a magnificent light welterweight champion who won thirty-five of his forty pro bouts inside the distance; who was beaten only once, and that when he was experiencing all sorts of physical and mental trauma; and who, in his finest two performances, stopped another magic fighter in Alexis Arguello. Born in Cincinnati on 20 October 1955, Pryor became known as The Hawk, but his once sharp eyes let him down, and a powerful addiction to cocaine meant that his last five years in the ring – years that should have been his best – were a sad, stop–start trip to oblivion, which is the toughest ghetto in Palookaville.

There were some misguideds who wished to help The Hawk because they genuinely cared. Men like hardcore boxing veteran Don Elbaum, who wanted to feature Pryor on a 'Night of Legends' show at the Rochester War Memorial on 26 January 1989. On the comeback trail, George Foreman would share top billing against Mark Young, and a former lightweight champion, Harry Arroyo, would also feature on the card. The cynics redubbed the promotion 'Night of the Living Dead.'

Pryor's $5,000 purse for facing the modest Rick Kaiser would be handy money, but more important, according to the fighter's second wife Jeannie, and also the Reverend H.L. Harvey, who was helping Pryor during his drug rehabilitation, boxing was the only hope left, and both expressed fears about what might happen if he was denied a licence to fight. Emotional blackmail.

But Rochester doctors who had thoroughly examined The Hawk found that he had a cataract on his left eye and there might be a detached retina under the cataract. New York State commissioner Randy Gordon, under pressure from all sides to allow the fight, stood firm, and on the weight of medical evidence, refused Pryor his licence. Elbaum and the Reverend had been trying to help the fighter in their way, but they had been wrong and Gordon had been right.

The boxer took the news reasonably well and told the commissioner: 'I know you're only looking out for my best interests. After the surgery, I've got to be better than I was. At least I'll be able to see the punches coming.'

Aaron was in denial. Even after surgery, the commissions in California, Nevada, New York and New Jersey all turned down his applications for a licence, and now there was evidence that there was a cataract developing on his right eye.

Yet Wisconsin was still a possibility because Wisconsin did not have a boxing commission. What Wisconsin did have was a most compliant Department of Licensing and Regulation, whose lady secretary maintained: 'Handicapped people should not be penalised for their handicaps. They should be allowed to do the same things non-handicapped people do.'

Clearly she had not been to too many boxing matches, but equally unnerving was the considered opinion of the prospective promoter, who just happened to be the girlfriend of Pryor's latest manager. She insisted that even if Pryor was blind in one eye, then he still had the use of the other eye. Unbelievable! Somehow the fight went ahead in the unlikely setting of the Masonic Temple, Madison, on 16 May 1990, and The Hawk knocked out Daryl Taylor in the third of a scheduled eight-rounder. It's worth noting that Taylor was a former Pryor sparring partner and had not fought for seven years. There would be another masquerade six months later in Norman, Oklahoma, when somebody called Roger Choate lasted into the seventh, but by now, even the 36-year-old Aaron knew the jig was up.

Like so many fighters blessed with a special talent, The Hawk did not appreciate how much boxing meant to him until it was far too late and he was too far gone to perform. Many years before, Gypsy Joe also had crashed head-on with reality, and had come off a poor second best. He had never been a great champion such as Pryor, would never be voted into any Hall of Fame, but from his earliest days as a professional, on the streets of Philadelphia, the little man was fêted as a champ. And no other city appreciates its boxing and its boxers quite like the City of Brotherly Love.

Long before Sylvester Stallone pounded its streets as Rocky, the boxing bum who made good, Philadelphia was paying homage to its fighting sons: its champions and its contenders, its club fighters, and even the honest triers who could not win the championship of their own gym.

The diminutive Blinky Palermo, chief lieutenant to Frankie Carbo, walked tall in Philadelphia; Herman Taylor's promotions at the Convention Hall or outdoors at Shibe Park and the Municipal Stadium were both artistic and financial triumphs; and J. Russell Peltz maintained the tradition with his shows at the atmospheric Blue Horizon club and the more upmarket Spectrum Arena. Often the action in the local gyms was as fierce as a main event elsewhere.

And the boxers! Champions such as Bob Montgomery and Harold Johnson; the Philadelphia-raised Joey Giardello, and Sonny Liston, a Philly resident for three years; Joe Frazier and Matthew Saad Muhammad and Jeff Chandler, and many, many more. And almost as good, the nearly champions like welter Gil Turner, a brave loser to Kid Gavilan before 39,025 fans in the Municipal Stadium, and featherweight Percy Bassett and Sugar Hart and Lennie Matthews and Von Clay, just a light heavy, but who stoically accepted his daily gym sessions with Liston.

The Philadelphia devotees were impossible to fool, and almost straight off they latched on to Gypsy Joe, and not because he was the only game in town. The sixties also saw the rise of Frazier from Olympic gold in Tokyo to heavyweight champ; and there was another fine heavy, Leotis Martin, who would knock out Liston; the rock-hard Bennie Briscoe had a loyal following, and there was another terrific welter prospect, Stan Hayward, nicknamed The Kitten, but no pussycat. Those guys were all headliners, but nobody sold more tickets than the little man with the wide smile and the crazy style.

In 1964, the year that Harris turned professional after losing only three of his seventy-odd amateur bouts, Muhammad Ali had shocked the world by beating Liston, but he had still to impress the traditionalists. The old-timers bitched about his ignorance of the fundamentals: how he was forever dropping his hands and offering his chin; how he swayed back from a hook, rather than move inside. They refused to see that Ali was in the process of rewriting the textbook, but already he had gathered many disciples. Gypsy Joe was the most flamboyant.

Anyway, he never could have been successful boxing by the book: he was too short and there was that one eye. At 5ft 5in, he would not have stood out as a flyweight, but he possessed blinding speed, brilliantly improvised footwork, and very fast hands which delivered a swarm of stinging punches from the most unlikely angles. The Gypsy was never a concussive puncher, simply because he was always on the move, always switching direction, feinting, fooling, and seldom set to deliver a really heavy shot.

Harris borrowed from Ali and old Jersey Joe Walcott and Willie Pep and invented some tricks of his own, like standing with his hands at his side, inviting his opponent to hit him. Old hat now, perhaps, with Hamed and Herol Graham having mastered the knack in Brendan Ingle's Sheffield gym, but back in the sixties, little Joe brought the crowd to its feet. He might have refined that party piece in the gym, but Harris seldom spent much time at rehearsal, and trainer Reddish, accustomed even to hard cases like Liston taking instruction, often despaired.

The Gypsy skipped sessions, was frequently fined for being overweight, sometimes even missed the official weigh-in, but for a time, at least, everyone was prepared to dance to his tune because he was so special and such a draw. He was a street person, happiest in a poolroom, a game of craps, or at a bar, sipping Scotch; life was one mad merry-go-round of personal appearances and parties and handshakes and backslaps, and sometimes he had to earn some money and turn up for a fight and that was never a problem.

In 1966, having been a pro for two years and having built up an incredible following, The Gypsy was ready for the big money. Kitten Hayward had defeated Bennie Briscoe in a battle for Philadelphia pride, and he was now being tipped as a good bet to win the title. Hayward and Harris was a dream pairing, and The Kitten looked an even better title bet when he floored The Gypsy early with a left hook – a useful punch against an opponent blind on the right. But that was to be Hayward's only success; he was overwhelmed by the little man's speed and the sheer volume of his punches; and he was bewildered and badly banged about facially when the referee called a halt in the seventh.

Gypsy Joe was top monkey in Philadelphia and the number one challenger to champion Curtis Cokes, and he confirmed his rating by comfortably beating the Cuban José Stable. The pressure was on Cokes to defend his title, but the Texan, showing a good head for business, opted first for a non-title meeting in Madison Square Garden. The money would be attractive, and if Harris turned out all that they claimed, then he would be made to travel to Dallas to get his title shot.

On the night of 31 March 1967, Gypsy Joe was a revelation in the Garden. Cokes was a skilled and worthy champion, had gone unbeaten in his last nine starts, including title victories against Luis Rodriguez, Manuel Gonzalez and Jean Josselin, but he could scarcely land a glove on The Gypsy, who ran out a unanimous and wide-margin winner. The media went bananas.

One writer likened him to a combination of Beau Jack, Kid Gavilan, Gil Turner and Henry Armstrong. Another wrote of him as a fighting clown and declared that there had never been anything like him before. The prestigious *Sports Illustrated*, not prone to going off the high dive, splashed him on its cover – until then, only champions or heavyweights had been afforded the honour. *Illustrated*'s Mark Kram depicted Harris as: 'The most exciting and creative fighter since Sugar Ray Robinson . . . his punches pile out from all angles, and they are thrown from any position. He is a machine gun and a jester with a Chaplinesque walk and the brass of a pickpocket.'

Of course, none of those writers ever imagined that The Gypsy had only one good eye, and only a very few of them had a notion about his wayward training habits. But by the time the Cokes celebrations had slowed down to a sprint, the little man from north Philly had turned into a very chubby little man, well over the welter limit, and requiring miracles of discipline ever to scale 147lb again.

In Dallas, however, the promoters could scent serious money, and when Cokes made an already scheduled May defence, stopping Frenchman François Pavilla in ten rounds, Harris was an exciting additional attraction on the card, coming off the canvas to halt Benny Bowser in four rounds.

The crowd loved him, and a Cokes–Harris title match appeared a formality. *But* . . . the promoters had short-changed the champ on his purse for the Pavilla fight, and further investigation exposed them as being somewhat dodgy; meanwhile, back in Philadelphia, Harris decided that he could never again make 147lb. He had allowed himself to outgrow the division, and now, to win a championship, he would have to tackle even bigger guys.

Although his training schedule was still a chaotic shambles, amazingly, he could still produce the goods when it mattered, and continued to draw bumper crowds when finishing off 1967 with two wins over Puerto Rican Miguel Barretto and an easy decision against Bobby Cassidy. The streak stretched into 1968 with a victory over Dick DiVeronica, and that set him up for the biggest fight of his career – a twelve-rounder against the phenomenal Emile Griffith.

Earlier in the year, Griffith had lost his middleweight belt in a decider against Nino Benvenuti, but he was far from punched out, would compete for another nine years, facing the best, including three more unsuccessful challenges for world titles, and was already a legend. But on the night of 6 August 1968, a record 13,875 packed into the Spectrum, confident of seeing The Gypsy produce yet another scintillating exhibition.

The weigh-in should have been a warning for those looking to get rich backing the local boy. First time on the scales, Harris touched a shock 163½lb; the Griffith camp insisted that he make the contracted poundage, and after sweating for two hours, he managed to get down to 160¼lb.

The weight was the tip-off that even preparing to face an opponent of Griffith's stature, Gypsy Joe had not bothered to extend himself in the gym and had not forsaken his social obligations. Big, big mistake: for the entire twelve rounds, Harris was on the receiving end of a painful lesson as the polished former champ outboxed and outpunched him to cop an easy decision. That was the first time that Joe had failed to deliver for his fans – and the last time he would ever appear before them.

Griffith's co-manager Gil Clancy later recalled: 'I think Griffith was just a little too big, a little too strong for Gypsy Joe that night. Harris had the ability to be a champion. It was just the luck of the draw.'

Luck. Invited back to Philadelphia for his very next fight, Griffith was outpointed by Kitten Hayward, who earlier had been so decisively beaten by Gypsy Joe, adding further evidence that the little man had squandered his big chance. But there was no changing his ways. A proposed bout against Manuel Gonzalez was postponed because again he was overweight, and it was when the date was rescheduled that the bombshell exploded at the pre-fight medical, the doctor discovering that Joe was blind in his right eye. Discovering? How many times had Harris taken an eye test in Philadelphia?

But that was the end of the line for The Gypsy. Appeals failed to get his licence returned, and then there was the familiar story of alcohol and drug abuse, and hard times living on hand-outs, and then spells in hospitals and clinics.

He finally did conquer his drug addiction, but his frantic lifestyle, his refusal to conform, had taken a severe toll, and there followed a succession of heart attacks. The little man with the blinding speed in and out of the ring was at last burned out. He died in hospital on 6 March 1990, aged 44.

On one of the few occasions that Gypsy Joe slowed down long enough to offer a brief self-assessment, he declared: 'They say I spend all my time shooting pool, hanging out in bars, dancing all night, and playing with women all day. I must be one helluva man to do all that and still win fights with only one bloodshot eye.'

Says it all, doesn't it?

PART SEVEN

Impossible Dreams

Mickey Rourke could play the tough guy, but there was no director to shout 'cut' when he stepped into the ring.

Cerdan's son and Ali's brother were fair fighters, but 'fair' is no good when you are kin to a legend.

Rex Layne had beaten Walcott, but Jersey Joe was getting the title shot. Guys from Utah never got the breaks.

> There are times when everyone
> would like to be somebody else

19

Mickey Rourke:
'I Fought a Little Dirty'

GEORGE GORDON, better known to the punters as Lord Byron – the sixth baron to be precise – would have made a terrific publicity man for the fight business. When he was not quilling verse that would prove hugely influential to later poets, or ducking his many creditors, or gadding around Europe, George could be found taking instruction in The Noble Art at the school set up by Gentleman John Jackson in his rooms at 13 Old Bond Street, London.

Jackson had impeccable credentials, having won his prize ring championship belt in April 1795 by virtue of grabbing the older, smaller and 42lb lighter champion Daniel Mendoza by his long hair, holding him fast, and bludgeoning him silly with his free hand. After that, however, he cleaned up his act, frequently played host to the nobility, and always insisted on gloves being worn during his tutorials. Byron, despite his club foot, was one of his most enthusiastic and able pupils, and he recorded his gratitude to Gentleman John with a priceless plug:

> 'And men unpractised in exchanging knocks,
> Must go to Jackson ere they dare to box.'

Byron was by no means the first writer to become fascinated by the mechanics of boxing, and he would not be the last. More than 150 years after George had exchanged punches with Gentleman John, Norman Mailer, small, chunky and very competitive, would regularly work out with José Torres, an excellent light heavyweight champion, who, of course, had to be extremely careful when delivering his shots. Mailer, however, absorbed enough knowledge, if not punishment, to be able to delve further than most into a fighter's psyche, and in return, Torres was given the chance to hone his writing skills, which he would put to good use.

George Plimpton took participation a stage further when, among other sports, he wrote about his time as an ice hockey goalminder for the Boston Bruins, and the three rounds he boxed against Archie Moore before a full house one evening in Stillman's gym. Not knowing exactly what was expected of him, old Archie had been a trifle uncomfortable at first, but he behaved himself, and only by accident did Plimpton finish with a bloody nose. But he had learned what it was like to be close up to a ring legend at work; watching his eyes, hearing him grunt, experiencing the apprehension as the champ rolled his shoulders, feinted a hook, or sent out an exploratory, lazy cuff to the side of the head.

Ernest Hemingway always considered himself the heavyweight champion of the literary set and was pugnacious in the extreme. He liked to boast of his sparring sessions with the New Zealander Tom Heeney, who had been Gene Tunney's last championship opponent, and he used to pester a most reluctant Tunney to shape up whenever they met.

Hemingway, relating his experiences, was apt to give the impression that he and the fighters were competing on something like equal terms, but, of course, he was kidding himself. Either Heaney or Tunney would have hospitalised Papa H. if just one blow had been thrown with bad intentions.

Even the much less combative A.J. Liebling, an unlikely shape or mind to leap headlong out of the trenches, could not resist the challenge of squaring off against a good pro, and so he took pride in his sessions with the former light heavyweight champion Philadelphia Jack O'Brien, and Jack, who had a great respect for learning, reciprocated by using only the most choice of his vocabulary. Like the others – Hemingway excepted – Liebling merely wanted to discover more about this mysterious and challenging subject; a subject that might truly be understood only by those who have participated at some level, no matter how humble. A bloody nose, a swollen knuckle.

That those writers were prepared to experience fleeting pain, but much more likely, a humiliation that would require double measures to erase, speaks volumes for their determination to search out a difficult truth.

Yet, at the same time, their efforts make the strange story of Mickey Rourke, and the hostile reaction to him when he decided to box professionally, all the harder to comprehend. Rourke is a film actor, not a writer, but an artist nonetheless, and when in 1991, he made public his intention to box as a professional, he might have expected a warm response. Not the case.

Rourke's P.R. machine had made no outlandish claims: Mickey just wanted to test himself against comparable professionals. If he could improve enough to box eight-rounders, then he would be delighted; title fights were somewhere over the rainbow. This was a personal crusade, but for Rourke, there was to be none of the amused tolerance that greeted Plimpton's exhibition against Moore, or the mild admiration to which his fellow writers grew accustomed as they sparred ever nearer to boxing's Holy Grail.

In hindsight, the Hollywood star could have done worse than read Sir Walter Scott's advice to prospective pugilists. Not only was Sir Walter a most enthusiastic follower of the sport, he was also a self-appointed adviser to young men contemplating a career in the prize ring, and in a letter to an aspiring fighter, he underlined the pitfalls, writing:

'I do not find fault with your ambition to try to stand in the London P.R. [prize ring] but mind you are not made foolish in the experiment. The accepted men of every class in the great metropolis of England have all been put to the test of severe trials before they were enabled to obtain anything like popularity or eminence. So beware of the ridiculous.'

In other words, do not be made a mug.

Because of his world fame, and because so few people troubled to understand his motives, Mickey Rourke's adventure into pro boxing was doomed from the outset, and he ended up, looking . . . well, looking rather ridiculous, a bit of a mug.

Had he been just plain old Joe Schmoe from Idaho, nobody would have bothered much that the veteran débutant went into the ring looking nervous and a wee bit apprehensive; most would have made allowances when he mauled and missed and then ran out of puff before the final bell; they might even have given him a clap, and gone home sure that he would be a far better fighter the next time. But this was Mickey Rourke, a marquee name, a Los Angeles outlaw, a publicity-hyped tough guy with more money than sense, and fair game for the freakshow nuts who could afford a ticket, and the fast-lane media who queued up to take their best shot.

Everyone was intrigued. The chic Beverly Hills clique, the fight mob in L.A. and Miami, the columnists, the camera hounds, his fans, his friends, his many foes. They all wanted to know why this major movie star was prepared to risk getting his brains scrambled. What was the hidden agenda? Was his career on the skids? Had tough Irish Mickey suddenly gone nuts?

His film record suggested the opposite. In the eighties, his work would have satisfied even the most hungry of agents, might even have brought a grin to the face of Doc Kearns. Among his credits were *The Pope of Greenwich Village* (1984), *Nine and a Half Weeks* (1986), *Angel Heart* and *Barfly* (both 1987) and Homeboy (1988). No Oscars, but not the C.V. of a guy in trouble. He had been topping the bills alongside the likes of Robert de Niro and Christopher Walken and Eric Roberts and Kim Bassinger and Faye Dunaway; working in the best of company and for championship wages.

And yet, here he was, in his mid-thirties – an age when most fighters would trade their best punch for just a few good lines – prepared to gamble on a whim. Actors and other artistic sorts did not overnight transform into fighters; the process had always worked the other way around.

Craggy-faced Victor McLaglen went the distance with champion Jack Johnson back in 1909, but rightly copped an Oscar for Best Actor in John Ford's 1935 classic *The Informer;* Jack Palance's flattened features and Robert Ryan's cool menace backed up their claims to pro experience; many more actors have hinted at a past boxing life, but most have come up sketchy on detail; and the most ludicrous tale of all was the story that Frank Sinatra, whose father had boxed as Marty O'Brien, had done a bit as an amateur. Just imagine!

Then there are the fighters who never quite achieved leading actor status, but who earned a steady income from the screen, the box, the radio and the stage. Top professionals like the brothers Baer, who both did all right when they switched over to acting. Heavyweight champion Max was a thirties knockout thanks to several long-running radio serials; he also had a smash Hollywood nightclub act with his pal, light heavyweight champ Maxie Rosenbloom; had some good lines in *The Harder They Fall*; and enjoyed a packed social and business diary until the day he died – 21 November 1959 – just 24 hours after refereeing a Zora Folley fight.

Brother Buddy tangled twice with Joe Louis, but was just as well known as the mild-mannered giant who killed the bull when Deborah Kerr was looking a goner in *Quo Vadis*. And big Bud had another beefy role when he teamed up with Kirk Douglas in *The Big Sky*.

Fact and fantasy, however, got into a muddle when Max co-starred with Myrna Loy in the 1933 production *The Prizefighter and the Lady*. Heavyweight champion at the time was the huge Italian Primo Carnera, whose crew arranged for him to play a supporting role in the movie. But there were problems . . . the script called for Baer to chin big Primo and win the fight and the lady, but the Italian's team demanded a different finale. Not even in the world of make-believe could the reigning champion be seen to lose.

Pride was at stake, more importantly the knowledge that Carnera and Baer would soon be fighting for real, and with the world championship, rather than Myrna Loy, the big incentive.

There was much table-thumping, but director William van Dyke always knew what was required, and eventually the Carneras compromised; the movie climax would see referee Jack Dempsey giving the fight as a draw – honour satisfied, and Myrna, Max and Primo all living happily ever after. But before the film had been long out on general release, Carnera and Baer signed to get it on for real; no directorial coaching from van Dyke this time. And so, on 14 June 1934, Max made a few alterations to the original screenplay, bounced the hapless Italian all over the ring in New York's Long Island Bowl, and duly became the new heavyweight champion of the world. What Myrna Loy made of the result can only be imagined.

Baer, Carnera, and on through Louis and Walcott and Johansson and Ali, all offered their chins before the cameras. Graziano and Marciano, and Archie Moore (he keeps cropping up and he was at his crafty best as Jim in the 1960 version of *Huckleberry Finn*), Mark Breland, Tommy Morrison, Vito Antuofermo . . . there is an endless cast of star fighters who have more than earned their Equity cards.

In many ways, the professions complement one another: both require tremendous discipline, dedication, and a determination to overcome inner fears – fears that can never be allowed to show themselves in the ring or on the set. The fighter and the actor may be cosseted by trainers and seconds and dressers and coaches and managers and agents, but there are many times when they are all alone, and that is when they have to dig deep. Boxing even four-rounders, Mickey Rourke quickly discovered that he must dig very deep.

By movie standards, the young Rourke really was a hard piece of work, and he had the tattoos to prove it. He was raised in Miami – according to the publicity handouts in the tough projects of Liberty City where they took no prisoners – but that is standard P.R. for any budding screen hard case. Mickey, however, really did box as an amateur, and his claimed record of nineteen wins from 25 contests suggests an honest trier, nothing sensational, but good enough to make him believe that he could always do better. And that thought lived on, even after he struck gold in Hollywood.

Rourke did not follow the easy route, and become a celebrity fan like many of the stars who flock to the ringside on big-fight night in Vegas or the Garden or Atlantic City, allowing their egos to be massaged by the grateful promoters. He preferred to hang out around the gyms, befriend the fighters, and if he really got lucky, work out with the superstars. His experiences with Thomas Hearns in L.A. and Roberto Duran in Miami may have been only slightly more serious than Plimpton's joust with Archie Moore, but Mickey felt he was competing and learning.

And if those legends took things very leisurely, then there were other guys in the gym, for whom a film star was too good a target to be true, and he often left the place, the bells still jangling in his ears. Mickey had a legion of female fans, but when it came to the fight business, he was as much a groupie as any of them.

About his time in the ring with Hearns, he told writer Graham Houston for *Boxing Monthly*: 'He hit me with a left hook in the first round and I went down on one knee. I got up and finished the three rounds, but I was out to lunch [in a mental fog] for the whole day . . . a scary guy. He looks at you with those cold eyes like he wants to kill you.'

Rourke had taken the grand tour of boxing's gyms. In Los Angeles, he regularly went through his paces at the establishment run by Bill Slayton, who had once trained Ken Norton; on his trips home to Florida, he would never pass Miami's famous 5th Street gym, where he completed some rounds with Duran; in London, he had been a visitor to the historic Thomas à Becket in the Old Kent Road; and in Paris, he had knocked around with the former W.B.A. super middleweight champion Christophe Tiozzo.

Nigel Benn, then training in Miami under Londoner Vic Andreetti, became a mate, though not a spar-mate. At times Mickey's training would be supervised by Adolph Pruitt, a one-time good welter; and for his fights, the experienced Freddie Roach would assist from the corner. For regular sparring, he relied on Tony Montgomery, who had been good enough to box Don Curry and Terry Norris. Rourke was surrounding himself with the best of help and hoping some of the magic might rub off; and Montgomery did not take liberties when the novice made mistakes.

Rourke never tried to conceal the fact that he was a novice, nothing more than a willing learner. How much any thirty-something could learn, and how boxing-fit he could ever become after a hectic number of years, would always be questionable, but he had decided to immerse himself in the sport, and just like Mailer and the rest, he was prepared to go to the limits in his journey of discovery. And for him, that meant going public.

Although his friend Benn maintained that he could comfortably lose another 10lb from around his middle, the 6ft Rourke declared himself satisfied weighing 178lb, and the date for the première was set for 23

May 1991. The selected opponent was called Steve Powell, a motor mechanic, whose ring record was announced as three wins and five losses (boxers with far worse records have been chosen as fodder for débutants), and the venue was the War Memorial Auditorium in Fort Lauderdale, Florida.

If Mickey thought that he might be able to make an unobtrusive introduction – perhaps something akin to a play being first tried out in the sticks before being brought into the big city – then he was back living in film fantasyland. He claimed that, originally, he had asked the promoter if he might box using an assumed name, but of course, that was a no-no. From a promoter's perspective, the whole object of the exercise was to cash in on the star's name; plaster his mug across the tabloids; headline him on all the television and radio newscasts.

The first day in any new job can bring sweat to the brow; in boxing, even an experienced amateur will endure agonies before the first pro bout – more than a few have succumbed to stage fright and failed to make it out of the dressing room; and even a brash character like Rourke would have been suffering first-night nerves.

This was one time when being the Hollywood superdude was a minus rather than a plus. He had been comfortable enough working out in the gyms, and away back when, in his amateur days, he had not been troubled performing in front of crowds of fewer than a hundred. But here he was, making his way to the ring, through a sell-out crowd of 2,300, already jeering, booing, cat-calling and baying for his blood. He had not counted on that.

A knowledgeable fight crowd never looks for too much from the four-rounders. These usually involve raw apprentices or are merely fillers to pad out the programme. But Rourke was not fighting before a typical boxing audience: this was a crowd who had read all about Mickey and his wild life in movieland, and few were in the mood to be charitable.

Not surprising, then, that he came out very nervous for the first, and the crowd roared when Powell caught him flush with a good right early on. But he took it well, and that right-hander turned out to be the limit of the motor mechanic's ambition. For the remainder of the four rounds, he allowed himself to be bullied and bulldozed around the ring, as Mickey scuffled and taunted, and at one stage, wrestled his opponent through the ropes. The decision was unanimous, but this had not been an edifying spectacle, and the film hero had done little to champion his cause, especially in the second round, when he grabbed his genitals in an obscene reaction to the hostile fans.

Fighters should not act like that; actors should not act like that; Hollywood outlaws . . .? But had Mickey Rourke been a play, he would have closed after the opening night.

Instead, he searched for the positives in his performance, and tossed in a few excuses. 'I think the next time I can look better. The ring floor covering was thick and I couldn't move the way I wanted to . . . I couldn't throw my right properly because of my shoulder trouble. And after not fighting for fifteen years, I had kind of burned myself out . . . Sure, I fought a little dirty, but I didn't want to lose.'

Predictably, he had some rough words for the crowd, and his reviews, if he read them, were anything but generous. But what had his critics expected? Despite his boundless enthusiasm, Rourke was never going to be a Sugar Ray, and he had never tried to con anyone that he might be; he was pursuing a personal dream, was not committing fraud or any other crime, and though his performance could be summed up as more freak than fight, he had done nothing to harm boxing's image irrevocably.

Graham Houston has for many years been a serious writer on the sport. A very young editor of *Boxing News*, he now provides an excellent American coverage for *Boxing Monthly*, and spends more time than can be healthy at ringsides all over the States. Houston is conservative in his approach, and frowns on anything or anyone who might harm the business. When Rourke next surfaced publicly in the ring, the writer gave him a fair crit.

Three months had passed since the Fort Lauderdale début, and Mickey had accepted a bit part in a championship promotion in California, where the I.B.F. super middleweight champion Darrin van Horn would knock out his challenger John Jarvis in three rounds. The fight was staged in a Los Angeles suburb called Irvine, an afternoon show in the college gym, and as a bonus, Rourke, sporting a headguard and a singlet, emblazoned 'Shamrock Social Club', boxed three exhibition rounds against former champion Frank Tate.

Houston wrote: 'Rourke appears to have a decent left jab and a fairly good right hand, even though he punches slowly. Tate, a former world champion seen in Britain knocking out Tony Sibson, basically played around with the actor, flicking away with the left hand, putting a few tippy-tappy combinations together, although once or twice he looked semi-serious.

'But Rourke, thick in the midsection at 13st 9lb wasn't overawed. He threw punches and brought a "whoop" from his supporters in the small crowd when he landed a right-hander in the third round.'

Houston had not been particularly impressed, but commended Mickey's courage for sharing the ring with Tate, and concluded he was doing nothing to hurt boxing. That would be as favourable a review as Rourke would get, and when he returned to Florida for his second fight, the press were out for his blood. And on this occasion, they had their reasons.

For his début against Powell, more than two hundred press credentials had been issued and at least fifty photographers from all over the world had been at the ringside. The media attention was equally heavy for this match against Francisco Harris, a local boy, at the Miami Convention Center on 25 April 1992. Realising that Rourke's image could do with a wash and brush following his controversial first performance and the ensuing negative publicity, the promoters this time made Mickey available for interviews and photo opportunities; he was affable and told his stories, and the resultant exposure was brilliant – until the star's agent Jayne Kachmer arrived in town. In a matter of hours, she managed to wreck all the goodwill that had been forged, and soon Rourke and the media were at each other's throats.

Kachmer reviewed the list of press applications and slung out those she deemed undeserving, or whose pre-fight stories had not pleased; there was also a cull of the photographers, some of whom had travelled from Europe; and there was even a half-hearted dodge to persuade the cameramen to sign a release, passing over control of their pictures – of course none of them did. But the media did not appreciate being at the wrong end of the Hollywood powerplay, and the mood had been set for Mickey's second coming.

Aside from the press gang, there was a decent crowd of 1,500 in the Convention Center to see Rourke, trimmed down to 177¼lb and sporting a villainous mandarin moustache, square off against Harris, loser of his two professional contests, but who, in a build-up story, had vowed to 'Kick Mickey's ass'. And while he did not exactly succeed in doing that, Francisco did manage to convince the majority of the crowd and the ringside hacks that he was a clear winner. Two of the judges, however, voted for a draw, and it was their opinions that counted.

Rourke showed few of the moves that he had produced in the Tate exhibition. He just might have shaded the first round, but Harris was the boss in rounds two and three, concentrating on a body assault that had Mickey gasping and spitting out his gumshield to get more air. The fourth was close enough, but all too often, the star posed rather than punched, held too frequently without incurring warnings, and ignored cornerman Freddie Roach's pleas to make more use of his jab.

Harris felt he had been robbed and was less than gracious when discussing his illustrious opponent. 'My sister punches harder than he does. He did some nasty fighting. He tried to push my neck down and stop me from breathing. He was choking me.'

Rourke had nothing to say. He was the only boxer on the six-fight card who did not give a post-fight interview, he and trainer Roach remaining holed up in their dressing room, the obligatory minders guarding the door. The story was that agent Kachmer had decreed the media ban – another bad call. In any event, Mickey would not have been announcing his retirement; his love affair with the game had still to run its course, and there would even be some lighter moments.

Readers with good memories may remember a television actor called Robert Conrad, who cropped up as a tough-guy hero in several successful series, and who liked to think of himself as even tougher off-camera. A fitness nut, he had worked out as a youngster at Johnny Coulon's gym in Chicago, and still loved his boxing and his boxers – he was in fact a much older version of Mickey.

Conrad had been one of the notables on hand at Rourke's début in Fort Lauderdale, had been unimpressed and had claimed he could lick Mickey. Rourke, on the other hand, had been equally unimpressed when Conrad, wishing him luck at the weigh-in, grabbed his hand and squeezed as hard as he could. Clearly the thirty-something and the fifty-something did not get along and – only in America! – an enterprising Houston businessman, Paul Allen, took out an ad in *Variety*, offering to promote a winner-take-all match between the two Hollywood hard men.

Rourke, however, with customary benevolence, stated that the only place he would take on Conrad would be in an alley. Fighting another actor in the ring would not have fitted into his agenda.

Mickey wanted to share his moments in the ring with the likes of Hearns and Duran and Tate; and if the guys in the opposite corner in his real fights never rose above the mediocre, he was still facing genuine professionals. As he said he would, he continued on his strange fact-finding mission with bouts in Japan and Argentina and Spain, and over a four-year span he compiled a record of nine wins, two draws and no losses. And then he was satisfied and returned to Hollywood and what he does best.

Mickey Rourke had never been remotely near shaping up as a contender; in fact, he was not even passably good. He had waited too long to turn pro and his wild lifestyle had already taken its toll. But it required true courage to live out his special dream, and at least he can always tell himself that it never turned into a nightmare.

20

Rahaman Ali:

'I Became Champion Too'

MUHAMMAD ALI . . . . just to hear his name can lift the clouds on the darkest of days. Somehow, twenty years have streaked past since his last fight, but Ali remains a superhero in the eyes of the world; far more loved and admired than any of today's sporting icons; certainly more respected than the majority of heads of state; and in steamy jungles and hot, dry deserts, on tiny, remote islands and in bustling, noisy capital cities, Muhammad, in this new century, can still rightly call himself The Greatest.

When he lit the Olympic flame in Atlanta, there was trembling evidence of just how far he had deteriorated physically from the enchanting days when he floated like a butterfly. But his eyes are still alive with that marvellous twinkle, and his smile still gamely outpoints the now rigid countenance. The Lip may be all but buttoned, but the magic and mischief will never die.

Boxing can never repay its debt to the upstart from Louisville. He was truly a champion of all the nations of the world and paraded his genius in some of the most unlikely venues that ever could be imagined. He could make boxing appear both balletic and then suddenly brutal; he invented a new style in the ring and an equally revolutionary outlook when it came to hype, and the fight business will never see the like.

Forget Sinatra. Muhammad really was the guy who did it his way. He knew the risks to his career when he embraced the religion of Islam and joined up with Elijah Muhammad's Black Muslims, a sect both feared and despised throughout white America at the time.

225

Nobody knew better than he that serious jail time awaited when he held to his beliefs and refused induction into the U.S. forces during the horror story that was Vietnam; and that led to the loss of millions of dollars in earnings when his country barred him from pursuing his livelihood, at a time when he should have been enjoying the sweetest years of his boxing life. Ali took the blows and did it his way.

He had started out as Cassius Marcellus Clay, born in Louisville, Kentucky, on 17 January 1942, had won gold medals and trophies and world championships, and had kept shocking the world, until that world grew to love being shocked by him. Today, he might be compared to some old Sioux medicine man, his great days on the battlefield long gone, his scalps now worn mementoes, but his great deeds remembered, his words forever respected. No fighter will ever stand higher than Ali and he surpasses any ring rating. Thee-ee G-r-e-a-t-e-s-t!

So, pause for a moment, and reflect on what it must be like to be born the baby brother of a living legend; to be Rahaman Ali, who once was Rudy Clay before the press started calling him Rudolph Valentino Clay (although his second given name was Arnette) and before he transformed into Rudolph X, which was a kind of halfway house before he finally became Rahaman Ali. He too liked to box a bit.

No easy gig being the other Clay, X, or Ali, the kid brother to the most brilliant star in the constellation. Rahaman, however, earns full marks for the manner in which he adapted, and even for a ring career was zircon compared to Muhammad's diamond, but nonetheless, painstakingly honest. He did not so much dream the impossible dream, but rather find himself living deep in the heart of one, where his brother would always be the champ.

Rahaman is the younger by two years, having been born in 1944, and has managed to share practically all the definitive moments of life with The Greatest. It cannot have been easy. Neither parent − not the loquacious Cassius Sr or the sweet and serene Odessa − ever made much mention of Rudy in their countless interviews. But this was only because the subject of Cassius deluged all other conversation; even as a very little boy, he hogged the limelight although he was already very protective of his brother. But the younger Clay was no dummy either, nor, as we shall see, was he a slack-jawed sycophant, just along for the ride. And, like his big brother, he loved the competition of boxing.

Nothing too unusual in brothers making the bigtime in boxing. But two world champions from the same family is a rarity. Vince and Joe Dundee, and the Galaxy twins from Thailand turned the trick. There have been others, but the most extraordinary of all were the Spinks boys, Leon and Michael, who not only both won gold medals at the 1976 Montreal Olympics, but who both became heavyweight champions of the world – Leon in meteoric fashion, and the three-years-younger Michael by a more circuitous route.

Leon sprang one of the biggest upsets in heavyweight history when, on 15 February 1978, in only his eighth pro fight, he outpointed none other than a lethargic and ill-trained Ali, who, of course, put matters right in the September rematch, and won the title for a record third time. After that, Spinks proceded to self-destruct in the most spectacular fashion, and brother Michael for a time put his own career on hold in a bid to get Leon back on track, but to no avail. Eventually he pressed on with his own life, won his titles and deservedly made his millions.

A closer resemblance to the Clay brothers would be the Pattersons: Floyd, a brilliant teenage Olympian, then a two-time heavyweight champion; brother Ray, a tough, reliable journeyman, fairly successful on the European circuit, but nowhere near Floyd's class. The comparisons, however, always would be made.

Early on, the young Rudy Clay also had to live with comparisons, and he coped exceptionally well. Cassius was always going to be the superstar, right from that first day when the two youngsters tugged on the gloves at the Columbia gym. The gym was run by a Louisville policeman, Joe Martin, who had first met Cassius when the twelve-year-old reported that his bicycle had been stolen – a lucky day for Cassius, maybe a luckier day for Martin, who would become world renowned as the man who first taught the Clays how to box.

In later years the champ was loath to heap too much credit on any of his trainers, and for sure, nobody ever taught him his unique style. But there were other teachers apart from Martin.

Fred Stoner was a black trainer who produced a number of good prospects from the rival Grace Community Center gym in Louisville, and during a temporary split with Martin, the Clays worked out there. Stoner, who was in charge of Clay's corner for his pro début against Tunney Hunsaker, thought much of Rudy's ability. He maintained that if Rudy had been really pushed along, he could have developed into a really capable heavy; in fact, whenever he discussed the brothers, Rudy emerged the more favourably.

In amateur competition, he was much better than average, and in March 1960, he accompanied his brother to Chicago to compete in a big event, titled the Tournament of Champions, with Cassius boxing at heavyweight so that Rudy could compete in the light heavy class. They both came out winners, but the following month in Louisville, Rudy was beaten in the Eastern Regional Olympic trials, while Cassius won all three of his bouts inside the distance. On 5 September, he would strike Olympic gold in Rome. And Rudy? He would be waiting at the airport in Louisville, a huge smile on his face, when the new local hero descended from the plane, his medal strung round his neck for all to admire. Rudy's role as principal cheerleader had been established.

That did not mean, however, that he was now ready to quit boxing himself; he liked the sport too much, and though he knew he could never hope to match Cassius, there was still an important role for him to play in helping to develop his brother. He would not be content acting the stooge, living on handouts, and basking in the reflected glory.

They did their roadwork together, and when Cassius was preparing for his début against Hunsaker, Rudy provided the main sparring assistance in Stoner's gym. Clay's managerial syndicate did not appoint Angelo Dundee to take charge of strategy until after that points win on 29 October 1960, but even when the base of operations switched to the 5th Street gym in Miami, Rudy still had an important part to play. A young fighter, alone in a strange town, can easily fall into the wrong company, but Cassius always had Rudy at his side; and although there was now a more varied and experienced selection of sparring help, the brothers still thrived on working out together.

Gordon Davidson, attorney for the syndicate of Louisville millionaires who were bankrolling the future champion, remembered that they met with no interference from the Clay family, not even from the sometimes pushy Cassius Sr Davidson also recalled how close the two brothers were, how Rudy was put on the payroll as recognition of his worth, and how they arranged some preliminary bouts for him. If that sounds somewhat condescending, then it is probably unintentional, but Davidson's recollection is misleading.

It was not until 1964 that Rudy made his professional début, and by that time, his big brother had gone undefeated in nineteen contests, and had made himself headline material throughout the States and even Europe, thanks to his outrageous utterances, his cornball poetry, and his eerie knack of calling the exact round that he would finish off an opponent. The writers loved him, but they were also unanimous that his big mouth would be badly bloodied when he finally caught up with the fearsome champion, Sonny Liston.

The match was set for 25 February in the Miami Convention Center, and this was also the night selected for the nineteen-year-old Rudy to have his professional introduction against another young fighter called Chip Johnson. Even now, it seems incredible that the younger Clay would agree to making his pro bow – always a very nervy occasion – on the same evening that his big brother was due to face the most intimidating challenge of his life; a fight in which he was an 8/1 outsider who many good judges forecast would finish up in intensive care. The brothers were so close, yet they were prepared to saddle one another with this tremendous, additional pressure on what would be a momentous night for both of them. Only the brothers Clay!

Despite the extravagant hype, the Miami Convention Center was just over half full with an official paid attendance of 8,297. Reasons for the meagre turn-out were not hard to find: Liston was unpopular because of his arrest record and his underworld connections; Clay's boasting irked many whites, and stories about his association with the Muslims were beginning to circulate; and anyway, the majority figured that it would not be much of a fight, indeed a mismatch.

Very few of the customers had turned up when young Rudy Clay came out for the first round against Johnson. The hall was eerily empty, but not silent; Cassius Clay was there, halfway down one aisle, shouting encouragement and instructions. Difficult to believe that this was the same young man who, just hours earlier at the weigh-in, had been described by the commission doctor, Alexander Robbins, as 'scared to death and liable to crack up before he enters the ring'. But Cassius had fooled the doctor and everyone else at the weigh-in, eventually being fined $2,500 for his crazy behaviour.

Rumours had swept Miami in the afternoon that Clay had fled town, but there he was cheering on his brother when he should have been resting up in his dressing room, apparently unconcerned that he was about to go head-to-head with an ogre.

Chip Johnson was no man-eater, but the following year, he was considered able enough to be invited to England, where he was knocked out by Henry Cooper. In Miami, Johnson clearly won the first round and had a very nervous Rudy on the verge of a knockdown. But once the younger Clay found his rhythm, he was never going to get beaten, and he was awarded a unanimous decision, although he had taken some hefty licks. He graphically described to Thomas Hauser, author of the definitive Ali biography, what he felt that night:

'The greatest night of my life was February 25 1964. That night was ecstasy, the epitome of joy. I made my début against a fighter named Chip Johnson, who'd had about eight pro fights. I was nervous, and he shook me up in the first round. He had me in a daze. Then my head cleared in the rest period between rounds, and I won a unanimous decision. But what that night was about for me was my brother winning the heavyweight championship. I've always shared in my brother's joy. My whole life, his goals have been my goals. His happiness has been my happiness. His sorrow has been my sorrow. So when he became heavyweight champion of the world, I became champion too.'

After Liston, claiming an injured shoulder, retired on his stool at the end of the sixth, pandemonium reigned in the ring, and once again – just like at the weigh-in – the supercharged Cassius looked as if he might take off for the moon.

Yet back in his dressing room, amid all the wild jubilation, he found the composure to tell Rudy that he did not want him to box again; that there would be no need now, and that the new champion would always look after him. Rudy did what he was told for a time, but fourteen months later, in April 1965, he reappeared in a Miami ring, outpointing Levi Forte over ten rounds, and the following month in Lewiston, Maine, he stopped Buster Reed in the second on the undercard on the notorious evening when Cassius stopped Liston inside one round in their rematch.

That would be his last fight for five years; five years that saw the brothers announce their belief in Islam, change their names, and live through the darkest days when the champ was barred from boxing for three years, and threatened with a five-year jail stretch. Those days were to prove an enormous test of faith for both Muhammad and Rahaman, and neither was found wanting.

There is a notion still widely held that Rudy only transformed into Rahaman when Cassius became Muhammad, but that is not the way it was. The elder brother indeed was the first to discover the Muslims, but he was initially cautious and kept an uncharacteristically low profile; Rudy, once he was introduced to the movement, immediately became by far the more enthusiastic, and he officially joined the Nation of Islam before his brother. Muhammad correctly feared that he would never get his title shot if his religious beliefs became public; Rahaman had no such worries to deter him.

Their enlistment at first created a huge strain on the relationship with their parents, and not only made them targets of hatred among the majority of white America, but also alienated them from all the conservative black movements. Rahaman, especially, became very cold and hostile in his dealings with whites.

All observers agree that no two brothers have ever enjoyed a closer bond but there are plenty who are convinced that far from being the wide-eyed baby brother, Rahaman, on occasion, could become the puppeteer, instigating many of his brother's moves, planting seeds. *Sports Illustrated*'s Jack Olsen, another biographer, remembers spending an extremely uncomfortable few days with the entourage in Miami, when he was often the only white in the company. He was treated with, at best, a polite coolness, and Rahaman in particular would never acknowledge his presence. Tensions were high back in those days, and grew higher in 1967, when the champ started his battle to stay out of the army. But as the years passed, and Muhammad triumphed in the appeal courts and then resumed his career, the younger Ali tempered his views and life started to be fun again. He also decided to take another fling at the ring.

Muhammad's second coming was to provide some of the most sensational fights of his career, historic events that will forever live on in boxing history; Rahaman's return was not fuelled by any burning ambitions, but more the urge to keep competing, keep testing himself in his own class. He resumed with a ten-round win over Tommy Howard in Miami on 12 August 1970, and then he boxed on the supporting cards for Muhammad's first three comeback bouts.

The cream of black society turned out in Atlanta on 26 October 1970 to witness Muhammad's return against tough guy Jerry Quarry. Sydney Poitier, Bill Cosby, The Temptations, The Supremes, the Reverend Jesse Jackson and Mrs Martin Luther King were just a sprinkling of the celebrities packed at the ringside as Ali stopped Quarry on cuts in round three. Just how many of them had taken their seats in time to see Rahaman beat Hurricane Grant – also in three – is a different tale.

Another star-studded gathering turned out at Madison Square Garden, where Muhammad knocked out Argentinian Oscar Bonavena in the fifteenth, and Rahaman was voted the winner over Howard Darlington in a four-round filler. And then, it was back to the Garden for one of boxing's most memorable nights ever, 8 March 1971, and the battle of the undefeated champions, Muhammad and Joe Frazier – a black night for the brothers, who were both beaten for the first time as professionals. Frazier emerged the stronger, scoring a last-round knockdown in the epic war of the champs, and less dramatically, Rahaman was outpointed by the Irishman Danny McAlinden, who would become British heavyweight champion the following year. There was now no logical reason for him to box on, but he still had an appetite for the business, though never again would he figure on one of his brother's gala promotions.

Rahaman boxed another seven times, finally calling a halt after the huge Jack O'Halloran stopped him in eight rounds in San Diego; he had gone as far as he could go and he was satisfied. Perhaps as a teenage amateur he had nourished dreams of winning titles, but his career had always lacked direction, and, of course, there was no way he could have escaped the giant shadow cast by his brother – not that he had ever harboured such a wish. Even before Muhamnad won his gold in Rome, Rudy-Rahaman had become known as 'the brother' and expectations were never too high, the pressure never overwhelming.

The same could not be said for another young fighter from around the same era who had to carry a famous name into the ring.

In 1960, Cassius's Olympic year, a sixteen-year-old French boy made his amateur début in the Salle Wagram arena in Paris. The bout was not only headlined in every French newspaper, but also earned space in journals as far afield as London and New York, all because the youngster's name was Marcel Cerdan, and he was the son of the finest and most popular fighter France ever produced, and one of the greatest middleweights of all time.

Marcel Cerdan was an extraordinary boxer who was beaten only four times (twice on disqualification) in a career that tragically was cut short after 115 bouts. He was the European welterweight champion, the European middleweight champion, and finally the middleweight champion of the world, but to the French, he was much, much more. Marcel was adored by the fight fans, but also by folk who never went anywhere near a boxing match; the Italians could not help cheering him when he beat their local idol Saverio Turiello in Milan; the Americans took him to their hearts; even the Nazis tried to adopt him for propaganda purposes in occupied Paris, but Cerdan and his manager Lucien Roupp refused to play ball.

Born in Sidi Bel-Abbes, Algeria, on 22 July 1916, Cerdan boxed only once for the Germans, a brief one-round knockout, before he and Roupp got on their toes to Casablanca, travelling with doctored documents, and arriving just in time for the American landings in North Africa. Cerdan was celebrated as a hero for hoodwinking the Nazis, and soon word of his terrific fighting ability filtered back to the States, as he demolished all-comers in Oran and Algiers and Casablanca, then Rome, and finally back in a free Paris. But he had to wait until 1948 to get his title shot and he made no mistake, stopping the rugged Tony Zale in Jersey City.

Cheering from the ringside was his lover, the singer Edith Piaf; crowded around the radio back home in his bar in Casablanca were his wife, Mannette, and his three sons, Marcel Jr, René and Paul. Everybody loved Marcel and somehow convention just did not count where he was concerned.

Even when he lost his title to Jake La Motta in his very first defence, he remained a hero in France. He had injured his shoulder early in that fight and had to retire in the tenth, but confidence was high when a large crowd waved him off at Orly airport for his return to America and the rematch on 27 October 1949. However, the plane crashed in the Azores, and there were no survivors. In Casablanca, the Cerdan family was shattered; in New York, Piaf collapsed and cancelled her shows; the whole of France shuddered to a halt and went into mourning. Marcel Jr, eldest of the sons, was just five.

Junior was born in Casablanca on 4 December 1943, and but for his famous father, who can really tell if he would have decided on a career in the ring? When he was eighteen, he told the French sports paper *L'Équipe* that he had always intended to follow in his father's footsteps, but by that time, he knew the value of a good quote, although he was still an amateur.

The Cerdan name, naturally, was still magic at the turnstiles. The old fight crowd turned out to rekindle golden memories; the younger set stumped up to see what all the fuss was about. Marcel turned professional in 1964 amid a huge fanfare of publicity, but it soon became apparent that few risks were going to be taken with his build-up; *beaucoup* francs were on the line and brave matches against tough guys were off limits.

There is nothing unusual in a young prospect being given a gentle introduction, but Cerdan's learning period just went on and on and on again for an incredible six years and a tally of 47 wins and no defeats. At first glance a marvellous record, and *The Ring* was impressed enough to include him in its ratings, first as a junior welter in 1966, then as a full welterweight. Closer inspection of the calibre of his opponents, however, might suggest that the magazine had been generous. They could not all have been bad fighters, but there were very few big names. In 1966, for example, Marcel won eleven times and boxed a draw, but not one of his contests was staged in Paris. Bizarre. He was performing in Avignon and Toulouse, Chalons and St Brieuc, though he did appear twice in Bordeaux, and once in Marseilles, which was always a thriving fight city. Yet a black-out in Paris seems very strange.

Junior showed a remarkable likeness to his dad in the publicity shots, but all similarities to the wonderful fighting machine ended there. He was a fair enough boxer, both strong and courageous, but he lacked a heavy punch, and an overall assessment by the knowledgeable English agent and cornerman Richard Reekie marked him as 'limited'. Nevertheless, that long unbeaten run looked so attractive on paper that Madison Square Garden, recalling his father's tremendous popularity in the States, came calling. Any guy called Cerdan would be such an easy sell in the boxing capital. The offer was too good to turn down, and although the opponent, a popular young Canadian called Donato Paduano, was considered a prospect, he was not regarded as a dangerous puncher and the risk was worth taking.

This was a big-money fight, at least by the standards of both Paduano and Cerdan, and the takings were boosted with a live satellite transmission to the Palais des Sports in Paris. Time now for Marcel to deliver, but Paduano (he was given a boxing lesson by Ken Buchanan later in the year) was always in control, exposed the Frenchman's limitations, and copped a unanimous decision.

The dream was not quite ruined, but now the management was less picky about the opposition: in 1971, Marcel did well to draw with former W.B.A. light welterweight champion Sandro Lopopolo in Paris, and there were wins over Ricky Porter, Pietro Vargellini and Klaus Klein. But he was beaten by Pietro Gasparri, and the following year, he took several counts when being outpointed by a very sharp Canadian, Clyde Gray, and he was on the canvas again when losing against Robert Gallois in a bid for the French welterweight title.

Marcel was through as a fighter, but he would still box for the world title – though only on the screen. In 1984, he played the part of his father in the movie *Edith and Marcel*, the story of the great romance, directed by Claude Lelouch. More than ever, he looked like the great Marcel, even fought a little bit like him. And just possibly, like Rahaman Ali on the memorable night when Muhammad won the title, Junior briefly felt what it was like to be a champion.

Both Rahaman and Marcel fell far short of ever being contenders, but they competed honourably in a hard business. And most important of all, they never embarrassed two of the most famous names in boxing legend.

21

Rex Layne:
'It Was the Strangest Feeling'

ROCKY MARCIANO was one of the good guys, a cheerful, unassuming individual, though notoriously tight with the dollar; a champion of the blue collars, who broke both records and bones with a disarming modesty that endeared him to his legions of fans, not only in the Italian communities throughout America, but all over the world. Rocky produced proof that hard work and dogged determination can make the wildest dreams come true; that even the most unlikely of contenders can become a champion. In 49 professional fights, nobody ever managed to beat him, and only six rivals were still standing at the final bell.

Rocky not only ruined opponents: he wrecked the sweet dreams of their managers, in particular three, who convinced themselves that they held the contract on a future white heavyweight champion, the first since Jimmy Braddock. Jackie Levine, a well-connected Broadway operator, Marv Jensen, a wealthy mink farmer from West Jordan, Utah, and Jack Hurley, an old-style ballyhoo expert from Fargo, North Dakota, all thought that they knew the score, and they were each prepared to take on Marciano, not least because he was short and clumsy and prone to cuts and missed as often as he landed. But after Rocky, the trio would never sleep so soundly again.

Rocco Marchegiano was born on 1 September 1923 in Brockton, Massachusetts, and from his earliest years, he was crazy about sports, particularly baseball. He did army service in Britain and France, then, encouraged by his boyhood pal, Allie Colombo, took up boxing. Although he was wild and untutored, his punching power was remarkable, and in 1948, he was advanced enough to represent New England in the Golden Gloves All-Eastern championships. His opponent was Coley Wallace, a New York youngster already being tipped as the new Joe Louis, and after their three rounds at the Ridgewood Grove in Brooklyn, Wallace was given a decision that sparked off a small-scale riot and infuriated Marciano for years after. Wallace had been the more cultured boxer, but on sheer aggression and blows landed, Rocky had looked to be the clear winner.

Coley proved a disappointment as a pro, progressing far enough to reach the fringe of the ratings, but Jimmy Bivins, in his twilight years, still knew far too much for him and knocked him out in nine rounds, and Ezzard Charles caught up with him in the tenth. The highlight of his career was when he was picked to play the part of Louis in a movie about The Bomber, and he could always count himself fortunate that he never had to face Marciano again.

Aged 23, Rocky was a late starter in the pros and in response to a letter from Colombo, our old pal Al Weill none too graciously consented to become his manager. At the time, The Vest's principal interest lay in a South American heavy called Arturo Godoy, and his association with Frankie Carbo guaranteed he could make things happen. He also employed a brilliant trainer, Charlie Goldman, who was to prove an inspiration in Rocky's rise to the top.

So, Marciano started to wreak havoc among the professionals, won his first sixteen fights inside the distance, and although he was none too pretty to watch, he could inflict serious damage. He would, of course, go on to win the championship, thanks to a thunderous right hand to the jaw of Jersey Joe Walcott when all seemed lost in the thirteenth round of their bitter battle in Philadelphia on 23 September 1952, and he would defend his title six times before announcing a shock retirement in 1956, largely prompted by his disillusionment with The Vest and his machinations. Sadly, his well-earned life of leisure was brought to an abrupt end in a plane crash in Iowa on 31 August 1969.

Rocky had sacrificed so much of his home life, had worked so relentlessly to reach the top; had been made to dig so deep when everything was on the line to beat guys like Carmine Vingo and Roland LaStarza and Rex Layne. They were all major white heavyweight hopes of the time, and they all fancied their chances when Marciano was marching towards the title.

Vingo was a 6ft 4in puncher who had been fighting for money since he was seventeen. He was managed by Levine, who handled a string of good fighters from his office on Eighth Avenue, and who firmly believed he had a heavy who just might go all the way. Levine had been patient, nursing the Bronx teenager, and in his first eighteen fights, he had been beaten only once – by Joe Lindsay, who was also regarded a reasonable prospect. He had improved since then, and fighting Marciano would be his big chance, his springboard to the serious money.

By the time he signed to meet Rocky, Vingo had lost only three out of thirty fights, and both his manager and his large, enthusiastic Italian following saw him as a sure thing against the much smaller Marciano, who they figured would be outreached and outpunched. The Italian crew from New England and the wise guys from the Bronx wagered heavily on the outcome, and Vingo, who had set his wedding date for February, bet one hundred dollars out of his purse. That was important money to Carmine.

Vingo turned twenty on the day before the fight and planned to combine his birthday celebrations with a victory bash on the night of 30 December 1949. Instead, he would spend those hours and many others battling for his life in the Saint Clare's Hospital.

That evening, the Madison Square Garden crowd witnessed two men fighting to their limits and beyond. There was no preliminary sparring, no cautious sizing up; both fighters started throwing their best shots from the first bell and Vingo was soon on the canvas for a nine-count from a Marciano left hook. Not only did he rise and come roaring back, but before the end of the round, he shook Rocky with a tremendous right hand. More of the same in the second, and again Vingo was dropped for nine, and again he fought back to stagger The Rock.

The Garden was in an uproar and would remain so throughout the next three thrilling but brutal rounds as the heavyweight hopes clashed with a frightening intensity. In the fifth, Marciano was sent reeling across the ring from a terrific right, but by now Carmine was too exhausted to follow up, and the sixth was all Marciano. Vingo was spent, and with blood pouring from his eyes, nose and mouth, he was an easy target; Jackie Levine screamed for the referee to step in, but another Marciano left hook got there first, and Carmine was slammed down, his head hitting the canvas with a sickening thud.

The roar of the crowd quickly stilled when it became clear that Vingo was seriously injured. From the ring, commission doctor Vincent Nardiello called for an ambulance, but disgracefully, none was available, and eventually the stricken fighter was wrapped in blankets and carried out of the Garden, out into the cold December night, and lugged the two blocks to the hospital. That nightmare journey could have topped Marciano's earlier work, but Carmine was a real tough guy and a tremendous battler.

For three days he was on the critical list and the bulletins were not encouraging. But then Vingo, just as he had done in the ring, started to fight back, and in another few days he was sitting up and was able to talk; and a few days later, he began to recognise old friends, although the six rounds with Rocky would always remain a total blank. His fighting days were finished, his purse had been gobbled up by the hospital expenses, and a year would pass before he was fit for any kind of work. His girlfriend Kitty stayed loyal and eventually they married, but all their teenage dreams had been wrecked by The Rock's dynamic punching.

That night in the Garden, Marciano had displayed all the qualities that would make him a champion: his utter refusal to be beaten, his ability to take the other guy's best shots and return them with interest, his total belief in his own invincibility, and, of course, his awesome punch. Rocky was a throwback, not to the barefist days, but right back to the time of the gladiators in the arena.

To many of the boxing critics, however, he was just a crude slugger who would only go so far. They had yet to learn that any Marciano punch that landed caused distress; that even a wild blow to the arm could paralyse. Most writers still regarded him as inferior to Rex Layne, a boy from Utah who was attracting rave notices, and also to Roland LaStarza, a technically gifted heavy, who, like Vingo, hailed from the Bronx. Al Weill wanted no part of either of them. There could be less dangerous routes to the championship, but for once, The Vest outsmarted himself.

Weill's lust for money and power made it impossible for him to turn down the job of matchmaker for the International Boxing Club, the outfit headed by millionaire Jim Norris which back then exerted a stranglehold on bigtime boxing in the States. Because there was now a conflict of interests, Al could no longer be a manager, and so he brazenly signed over Rocky to his son Marty. Everyone knew that Al was still the chief, but he, too, now had a master, and Norris was keen to see Marciano box LaStarza. Weill was cornered.

The fight took place in the Garden, three months after the Vingo drama, and there was much speculation that Rocky might be haunted by memories of the near tragedy, but where business was concerned, nothing could sidetrack The Rock. LaStarza's cool, controlled boxing, however, gave him much grief, and despite Rocky scoring a fourth-round knockdown, there was little between the fighters at the final bell, and Marciano was relieved to get a controversial split decision. LaStarza was not badly bust up and still retained his ambitions, and three years later, Rocky would grant him a title rematch and stop the New Yorker in eleven rounds, but at least Rollie had got his chance, and no fighter can ask for more than that.

The paranoid Weill had survived a close squeak, and for the remainder of 1950 and for the early part of the following year, he confined his star to a series of contests against mostly ordinary opponents back on his home turf of New England. But Layne was looming a larger threat than ever, was rated above Rocky, and – more grim news for The Vest – his boss, Norris, saw a Marciano–Layne clash as a big money-spinner.

Rex Layne was born on 7 June 1928 in Lewiston, Utah, and started to box as an eighteen-year-old while serving in the forces in Japan. He showed a degree of natural talent, and when he returned home, he joined the West Jordan Athletic Club, which was run by the well-heeled mink farmer, Marv Jensen, who had a custom-built gym in the basement of his large ranch house. Jensen had been a fair amateur, and now his dream was to discover, train and manage his own world champion; Layne shaped as if he just could be the one, especially after he won the 1949 National A.A.U. heavyweight title. Marv could hardly wait to turn his tiger loose on the professionals.

Right from the start, Rex was kept busy and he ran up a sequence of sixteen consecutive knockouts against the usual suspects, guys like Young Harry Wills and Bearcat Carter and Bobby Blevins and Sonny Orrock – scarcely household names but good experience for the youngster. In the October of that début year, he also boxed a four-round exhibition against the reigning champion Ezzard Charles in Salt Lake City and had not disgraced himself.

Into 1950, and he avenged the only blot on his record, outpointing rugged Dave Whitlock, and then he caused a few raised eyebrows when he travelled to San Francisco and knocked out a respected black prospect, Bob Dunlap, in nine rounds. Layne had looked really sharp, his power had been impressive, and his manager rewarded him with two quick follow-up jobs, easy wins over Willie Parker and Jack Huber – but three bouts inside thirty days was a testing schedule for any youngster just turned 22. Jensen, however, was convinced that his protégé could beat any heavyweight placed in front of him; unlike the ultra-cautious, suspicious Weill, Marv feared nobody.

For sure, Weill never would have consented to Marciano taking on the crafty veteran Jersey Joe Walcott back in 1950, but in his capacity as matchmaker, he was delighted to book Layne into the Garden for a 24 November date against the old-timer. He probably looked on the fight as an ideal opportunity to remove Layne from the title picture, and most New York managers were in agreement that Jensen must have suffered a rush of blood. True, Jersey Joe was a 36-year-old and already had lost in three challenges for the title, but as later results would prove, he was far from used up. The sprightly Camden grandfather had a very tricky, confusing style, was a fast and hard puncher, and always kept himself in good shape. The mink farmer was asking plenty from his fighter.

Walcott made Layne look like a novice in the opening round, suckering him on to a hard right hand, but the youngster came back well in the second and third, and from then on, every round was very closely contested.

The Utah boy was performing surprisingly well, and in the fifth he scored with an eye-catching combination, but before the end of the round, he was dropped to one knee, though the referee ruled a slip and made no count. Into the ninth, and despite being badly cut over the left eye, Rex finished the round strongly, doing better work than the tiring Walcott. But everything depended on the final three minutes, and Layne never eased up, after hurting Walcott with a hard right; an exhausted Jersey Joe could not match the youngster's strength, and at the final bell, Layne had done enough to earn a narrow decision.

Jensen had proved all the smart guys wrong and Layne had shown the New Yorkers that he was a genuine fighter, but it was old Jersey Joe who had the last laugh. The following year, he somehow secured not just one, but two cracks at the title, and on 18 July 1951, at his fifth attempt, Walcott scored a stunning seventh-round knockout over Ezzard Charles, and he was champion at last.

A month after Layne's big win, Marciano pulverised the unfortunate Bill Wilson in one round in Providence, and followed up with meaningless victories over Keane Simmons, Harold Mitchell and Art Henri; compared to Layne, he was fighting nonentities, and once again the heat was turned up under Weill to arrange a match from which he feared the worst. Perhaps Al was just a born pessimist, but he never seemed to share the bubbling confidence of cornermen Goldman, Colombo and Freddie Brown; and of course, Marciano himself never lost a wink about his next opponent. But Norris appeased the manager somewhat by promising him the larger cut of the purse, and the showdown was arranged for 12 July 1951 in the Garden.

Again questions must be raised about Jensen's gung-ho approach to management. Granted his gamble had paid off against Walcott, but just six days after Marciano–Layne, Jersey Joe would again be the one boxing for the big prize. And granted again that his fighter had survived severe tests against another of Weill's South American, Cesar Brion, and a very dangerous light heavyweight puncher, Bob Satterfield, but should he have been facing such tough opposition at such a crucial stage? Layne may have been rated higher than Marciano, but The Rock was being paid more.

The pride of Brockton went into the Garden undefeated in 35 fights; Layne could also boast 35 wins but the Whitlock loss marred a perfect record. Rex was five years younger, bigger, heavier, and like most of Marciano's opponents enjoyed a considerable reach advantage. For the first time, Rocky had been sent to a training camp, at Greenwood Lake, and he entered the ring looking hard and ready; as in other fights, Layne seemed just a mite fleshy around the middle.

From the opening bell, both fighters determined to turn the battle into a test of strength, Layne trying to make his weight count by leaning on Marciano and banging to the body; Rocky, happy to work inside, shooting for the head. The Brockton corner could not have written a better scenario. A right opened a cut above Layne's left eye in the second; Rocky scored heavily with both hands in the third and stunned Rex, who was forced to hold on. The Utah fighter still tried to stick to his game plan, but Marciano was plainly the boss.

The end came rather unexpectedly in the sixth; Layne was still fighting stubbornly, and then Marciano unleashed one of his specials, a crushing right that landed flush. The blow knocked out all of Rex's front teeth, and yet for a second, it seemed as if he might remain on his feet. But then started the slow collapse and he slumped almost dreamily, first on to his knees, and then down on to his face, and with no chance of rising in time.

Later he said, 'I heard the count from one to ten. I kept telling myself that I had to get up, but I couldn't move. It was the strangest feeling.'

Fighters can have only one career, but the Al Weills and the Marv Jensens can enjoy many, and the mink millionaire finally realised his ambition when another Utah brawler, middleweight Gene Fullmer, won the title. But for big Rex Layne, the dream was over, the romance gone. He would earn some useful money out of a three-fight series with Ezzard Charles, which included one dubious points decision back home in Ogden, Utah. Referee Jack Dempsey was also the sole judge, and the old champion produced a very weird scorecard, awarding two rounds to Layne, one to Charles, and giving seven even. Ezzard would then twice fight Marciano for the title, but Rex would never get the chance.

Layne died of a stroke on his birthday, 7 June 2000. He was 72 and down the years, he often must have speculated on what might have

happened if he had got a title shot after beating Walcott, and also
wondered if his tactics had been wrong against Rocky. Marciano never
had time for such daydreams, and as he grew closer to the championship, he was about to dash possibly the wildest dreamer of them all.

Jack Hurley was a soberly dressed, bespectacled, scholarly
gentleman, who might have passed himself off as a country lawyer or
a doctor, or even a man of the cloth, because in his circle of
acquaintances, he was known as The Deacon. Jack, however,
happened to be one of the most imaginative boxing managers who
ever took a percentage off the top, and he spent a lifetime dreaming
impossible dreams that suddenly did not seem quite so impossible. In
the thirties, he just missed the jackpot with a hard-punching
welterweight named Billy Petrolle; in the forties, he caused a
considerable, if short-lived, stir in New York with another big
puncher, Vince Foster; and now, he had got himself a heavyweight –
at least The Deacon liked to dream that he was a heavyweight!

Harry 'Kid' Matthews was a fair fighter from Seattle, nothing special,
but with a record padded out with wins against no-accounts. He was
no longer a kid, his career was headed nowhere, and in *The Ring*'s 1949
annual classifications, he was listed as a Class 2 middleweight. But after
pleading with Hurley to manage him, things started to buzz for Harry,
and by the summer of 1952, he was just one fight away from
challenging for the heavyweight championship of the world. Now that
really is moving a fighter! Just Matthews's and Hurley's bad luck that
the one fight had to be against Marciano.

The Deacon did not come cheap: he demanded 50 per cent of his
fighter's wages but he would soon prove he was worth every cent to
Matthews. The partnership got off to an inauspicious start in Omaha,
where Baby Joe Walcott turned out so bad that he was suspended
indefinitely. Things could only get better, and The Kid was soon
winning with monotonous regularity.

On the strength of the sequence of West Coast victories, Hurley was
able to land an important slot for his hero in the Garden, against Irish
Bob Murphy, a popular performer and high in the ratings. Matthews
was a comfortable winner, and a title fight against Joey Maxim was
now the goal, but in New York, nobody was too excited about The

Deacon and his fighter . . . for a time. Once Hurley started pressing Harry's claims, his targets never stood a chance – and those targets included the formidable Doc Kearns, who managed Maxim, Al Weill and Mister Big himself, James Norris. Hurley launched a newspaper campaign, alleging that Norris and his monopolistic I.B.C. were denying Matthews his rights; for good measure, he fired a broadside at Weill, deploring his dual role of matchmaker and undercover manager.

He caused enough fuss for a grand jury investigation to be instigated, and a worried Norris overruled the protests of Kearns, who had other plans for Maxim, and offered Hurley his title shot. But by now, Jack reckoned that he had Norris on the run and he got greedy; he was no longer interested in Maxim and was now aiming for Walcott and the heavyweight championship.

Weill was appalled, Marciano incensed, but Norris was only intent on keeping the lid on any scandal. There was no way Matthews could jump the queue past Marciano, but he could be matched in a final eliminator against The Rock. For the third time, Norris put the squeeze on Weill to accept a match he did not want, and for the third time, Weill folded under pressure. With so much at stake a less avaricious individual would have quit the matchmaker's job and gained his freedom from Norris, but every dollar was important to The Vest.

All the more ironic that Al should lose his cherished post simply because of a careless remark that he uttered at the weigh-in. Matthews and Hurley were late for the ceremony, and when asked their whereabouts, Weill shrugged and replied: 'All I know is my fighter's here.' *His* fighter: damned by his own quote. New York commission chairman, Robert Christenberry, annoyed with all the bad publicity, seized his chance, and four days later Weill announced his resignation as I.B.C. matchmaker.

On the evening of 28 July 1952, Harry Matthews entered the ring in the Yankee Stadium for the biggest fight of his life. His record showed only three losses from 87 contests, and at 179lb – only 4lb over the light heavy limit – he gave Marciano a rare weight advantage. Hurley was upbeat and told reporters how he had devised a blueprint to beat Rocky, but how many plans had Marciano already ruined with a right hand or a left hook?

The fight was a non-event. Matthews could claim the first round because Rocky was only moving around, loosening up. But by the second, he considered himself loose enough, and he backed Matthews into a corner, then fired two terrific left hooks. The Kid's mouthpiece flew into the night, his head struck the bottom rope, and there was never any chance of his regaining his feet. Marciano had not even worked up a good sweat! The cantankerous Hurley laid all the blame on his fighter for not following instructions, and even when he was hauling the stunned boxer back to his corner, he seemed to be giving out.

Nobody could deny The Rock his title chance after that, and two months later, he would knock out Walcott in Philadelphia.

The Kid and The Deacon would soldier on, but their dreams were in tatters; they had gambled everything, and they had finished up big losers. After all the hassle he had caused, the IBC was not prepared to do Hurley any favours, and Norris only laughed when he tried to reopen talks about a title fight against Maxim. Jack, however, still had a good nose for a buck.

In 1953, he struck up a profitable arrangement with Londoner Jack Solomons which guaranteed Matthews three excellent paynights against the British heavyweight champion Don Cockell. That Harry lost all three bouts – two in Britain and one in Seattle – was irrelevant. Those were strictly money fights; all his ambition had been strewn on the canvas in Yankee Stadium.

Good young white heavyweights would soon become an endangered species, and although managers like Jackie Levine and Marv Jensen and Deacon Hurley would continue the search, never again, thanks to Marciano, would they reach so close to the stars . . . dreams almost cost Carmine Vingo his life and robbed Rex Layne of his front teeth. All things considered, Harry Matthews had not too much to complain about.

PART EIGHT

Ladas before Rollers

Winning an Olympic heavyweight gold is like being handed the combination to a bank vault. and if the guy happens to own three golds . . .?

Don King and Bob Arum have grown accustomed to getting their own way. But even talking millions, they couldn't reach first base with the Cuban.

Teofilio Stevenson was content with his lot and could not be bought, which makes him rather special.

And not just in the big, bad world of boxing

22

Teofilio Stevenson:
'The Model Revolutionary'

TERRY MALLOY went out of the fight game with nothing to show for all his blood and sweat, apart from the mounds of scar tissue around his eyes, and his one-way ticket to Palookaville. Schulberg's pug never saw much money during his career, never got that shot outdoors in the ballpark, and back then, nobody even kidded about purses of a million-plus. These would not become reality until long after Terry was all washed up and swinging a hook on the docks.

Terry, and all the real-life Terrys back in those tough, grim days before television and technology transformed title wages into funny money, seldom believed what they read in the newspapers – they were familiar with the fairy tales that their managers and their press agents and the promoters could dream up over a few friendly drinks with the hacks; that was all part of the business. And if they had ever heard the one about an amateur, not even a guy who had gone six rounds, turning down a fortune to go pro, then they would have just laughed, and bet that some character had slipped a mickey to the writer.

And even in the 1970s, when a million still went a very long way, the story of Teofilio Stevenson and how he knocked back the hotshot promoters and their guarantees and contracts and options still seemed more fiction than fact.

As this is being written, Audley Harrison, Britain's super heavyweight hero from the Sydney Olympics, is having a ball. He has popped up on all the channels as a guest celeb, put together his professional backup team, decided on his promotional alternatives,

251

picked up his M.B.E., and somehow found the time to make a brief and controversial pro début before an enthusiastic, though not capacity, crowd at Wembley and a decent B.B.C. television audience. But the real graft is yet to come. He has proved himself a champ in the amateurs, a natural for the marketing gurus, and a lad who is easy to like. But that will all count for nothing if he doesn't keep delivering, hopefully, against ever more testing opposition.

The hype that Harrison has generated is no longer considered unusual: we live in the age of the hard sell and the fast buck, and good luck to the former graduate in Sports Science. But back when Teofilio Stevenson was giving the thumbs down to the likes of Don King and Bob Arum, million-dollar offers to amateurs were unknown. The Melbourne Olympic winner, Pete Rademacher, did make history when he challenged Floyd Patterson for the heavyweight title in his very first pro fight, but Rademacher – game and tough, but not exceptionally talented – was paid in thousands, and not such a great number of them that he could retire when Patterson knocked him out in six rounds.

Not counting the former Eastern bloc boxers, most Olympic golds have tried their luck in the pros if the offer was good enough. But Stevenson was not the first amateur star to resist heavy pressure to make the switch. Scotland's Dick McTaggart had already set a precedent after Melbourne in 1956.

The elegant southpaw from Dundee won the lightweight class and also the Val Barker Trophy, awarded to the best stylist at any weight. Cue for huge celebrations in Scotland and a crazy scramble among the professional managers, each with something unique to offer. There were no mega-buck sponsorship packages back then, but still serious money was being discussed – figures that would have altered dramatically McTaggart's lifestyle. He turned them all down flat, added a bronze to his gold in Rome in 1960, and was still sprightly enough to land a European title in Belgrade the following year. Five A.B.A. championships topped off an outstanding career, and he was able to retire happy and healthy with a roomful of trophies and so many marvellous memories. He had made up his mind that the pro game was just not for him and he had the steely character to resist all overtures.

But there must have been many times when he was sorely tempted to put his name to a contract.

Teofilio Stevenson was never tempted. When on New Year's Day 1959, Fidel Castro took control of Cuba, finally ousting General Fulgencio Batista, one of his earliest edicts was to ban professional sports on the island, bringing Cuba into line with his Soviet paymasters and their satellites. Teofilio was brought up under the Castro regime and was a staunch admirer of his leader; to become a professional boxer would have entailed skipping the country. That would not have been an insurmountable problem, but for Stevenson, it was never a consideration.

When Castro first won power, however, many fine Cuban boxers chose to defect in order to continue their careers. José Napoles from Oriente and Sugar Ramos from Mantanzas both split to Mexico; Luis Rodriguez, reared in Camaguey, turned up in Miami; Benny Paret, born in Santa Clara, headed for New York; and another budding star from the Oriente region, José Legra, journeyed all the way to Spain. They all became world champions.

Cuba had enjoyed such a proud history of great fighters, and none was better than the dazzling Kid Chocolate, a featherweight and junior lightweight champion who thrilled the New York crowds throughout the thirties. Eligio Sardinias-Montalbo was beaten only nine times in 146 contests, squandered fortunes on the high life, and spent his final days in poverty back in Havana, where he became a curious cult attraction for journalists and photographers from all over the world. The Kid died on 8 August 1988.

Kid Gavilan became as popular, both in his native country and in all the major fight cities of America. Born Gerardo Gonzalez in Camaguey, this Kid took on all-comers at welter throughout the ultra-competitive forties and fifties; faced all the hard nuts like Ray Robinson and Ike Williams and Beau Jack and Billy Graham and Carmen Basilio and Bobo Olson and dozens more; and held the championship through four action-packed years and seven successful defences, until he was robbed of his title thanks to an extremely dubious decision in favour of Johnny Saxton in Philadelphia. Gavilan was never given the chance of a rematch.

Chocolate, Gavilan, Napoles and the others are still fondly remembered in Cuba, and although Stevenson did not carry on their proud tradition into the paid ranks, he, too, is now part of the country's ring legend. In fact, his reputation overshadows all of them.

Teofilio was born in 1952 in the sugar-producing town of Delicias in the Oriente district. His father, Teofilio Sr, hailed from the English-speaking isle of St Vincent, part of the Windward Islands, and travelled to Cuba in search of work. Prospects turned out not as rosy as he had imagined, and after several false starts, he settled in Delicias, where he humped backbreaking sacks of sugar as a stevedore for the local mill. The pay was a pittance, and when he married Dolores Lawrence in 1948, they had to settle for a rundown house, the property of the mill. Four years later, they were still living there when Teofilio arrived, the first of five children.

The young Teofilio, no wilder than many another youngster, got into schoolyard scraps, and when he was twelve, a friend suggested that he would be better off taking up boxing. His father, who had fought briefly as an amateur, encouraged him, and just a year later, he was considered promising enough to be sent to Havana to study and train at the Orbein Quesada boxing camp, run by the formidable national coach, Alcides Sagarra, who was also an influential member of Castro's party machine. Sport was being given a high priority in the revamping of the nation; the Soviet Union and other communist countries were sending over coaches to speed the development; and the Quesada camp was the headquarters of the boxing élite.

Sagarra led a team of ten trainers, had places for just over fifty fighters, and aged thirteen, Teofilio was by years the youngest. But he was soon to unveil his natural ability and his freakish punching power, all the time growing into the 6ft 4in 225lb giant who would spearhead Cuba's inexorable rise to becoming the masters of amateur boxing.

Competition at the camp was as fierce as anything seen in a Philadelphia gym, but by the time he had turned seventeen, Stevenson was impressing not only Sagarra, but also the top Russian coach, Andrei Chervorenko, who pressed for him to be upgraded to the national squad. In 1970, he was Cuba's heavyweight representative in a prestigious international tournament in Havana, but he was beaten in the final by a more experienced East German, Bernd Andern. Another highly publicised loss came the following year in the Pan-American Games, when the well-regarded American Duane Bobick was given the benefit of a majority verdict. But Teofilio was still growing, still learning, and he would not have to wait too long to gain sweet revenge over the American sailor.

Before the 1972 Munich Olympics, Cuba never had won a boxing gold; in Germany, they would collect three. Bantam Orlando Martinez and welter Emilio Correa struck first, but in reality, Stevenson actually beat them to the magic medal. His scheduled opponent in the final, the Romanian Ion Alexe, had been forced to scratch because of injury, and so Teofilio was already guaranteed gold before the evening's boxing got under way.

He had demolished his first opponent, a Pole named Ludwig Denderys, inside the opening round and had looked awesome. The stage was then set for his showdown with Bobick, and Yankee hopes were high. The clash was billed as 'The Final Before the Final' and for two rounds the exchanges were fairly even, the Cuban winning the first round, Bobick coming back in the second. But the American had suffered considerable facial damage and had expended much more energy. He fell apart in the third, taking three counts before the referee intervened. In comparison, Stevenson's semi-final against Peter Hussing was something of an anticlimax, the German being stopped in round two.

The Cuban contingent was ecstatic. Three golds and an additional accolade with Teofilio being awarded the Val Barker Trophy. The professional pack, once so hot for Bobick, deserted him as if he had suddenly contracted something nasty, and he would never fulfil his early promise; the men with the readies were now shopping for Stevenson. Security was tight, and the Cuban officials always kept a close watch on their athletes, but at least two offers, one allegedly from Bob Arum — at that time the world's most influential promoter — reached Stevenson. For the first time, the magic million figure appeared in print.

The heavyweight, who claimed he had boxed through the tournament with a broken hand, reacted to the offers as if someone had just insulted his mother: 'I will not trade the Cuban people for all the money in the world. What is a million dollars compared to the love of eleven million Cubans?'

A great quote and even greater propaganda for Castro, who made a speech praising Teofilio's fine achievement and branding the professional promoters as 'traffickers of bodies and of souls'. For a beleaguered island nation at economic war with the mighty U.S., the heavyweight had become a symbol of massive achievement against the odds, especially as he had beaten America's best on his way to the championship. There would be more offers as Teofilio steamrollered to another two Olympic golds and three wins in the newly inaugurated world amateur championships, and on every occasion, the fighter responded that his country meant more to him than any amount of money.

But just once, there seemed as if a compromise might be reached and Stevenson could get the opportunity to test his skills against Muhammad Ali! Arum had put together a proposition whereby he would pay $1m for the Cuban to box five three-round exhibition contests against Ali, dates and venues to be agreed. Castro was intrigued by the idea: a test of strength between the two boxing codes and the two nations; he even earmarked Stevenson's purse to help alleviate social problems. But the deal was a non-starter as the U.S. Treasury Department claimed the project violated the terms of America's trade embargo against Cuba. Perhaps the wily Fidel had been aware of the likely outcome all along, and was only scoring points for his team.

The indefatigable Arum would keep persevering, and in 1976, he wanted Stevenson to fight Leon Spinks; again the lure was a million bucks. His arch rival, Don King, tried his luck, using top-level politicians from Panama to mediate on his behalf, but he got nowhere. King, despairing of all the revenue going abegging, said, 'Stevenson would simply have been phenomenal as a pro.'

The Don might have been talking from his pocket, but back in action after Munich, there was little doubt that the Cuban heavy seemed to intimidate the opposition just by stepping into the ring. In fact, he sometimes found it hard to get bouts: opponents would fail to turn up or would discover an injury, and in several internationals, the opposing country would decline to select a heavyweight representative.

Teofilio's first series opponent made no show when Havana played hosts to the first world amateur championships in 1974. In the final, he outpointed an American, Marvin Stinson, and the Cubans wound up with five golds. The next important milestone was the 1976 Olympics in Montreal, and Stevenson's second gold after stopping a game Romanian, Mircea Simon, in the third round. But his most significant win had come in the semis when he poleaxed the American John Tate in round one. Tate would become a world champion in the pros.

Incredibly, around this time, Cuba could also boast the second best amateur heavyweight in the world, one of the few fighters who could provide Teofilio with a true test. He was called Angel Milian, and in a 1975 match, they both took standing counts before Stevenson won a narrow decision. And as a warm-up for Montreal, Milian again gave him trouble in another thriller, fought before 20,000 fans in Havana. Milian, of course, saw few international opportunities, but in 1977, with the champ sidelined, he proved his class when outpointing yet another future world champion, Greg Page, in a U.S.A.–Cuba international at the Houston Astrodome. He eventually drifted out of the game, and in 1987 was stabbed to death in a pub brawl.

There was nobody of Milian's calibre to trouble Stevenson when he travelled to Belgrade for the second world championships in 1978: he easily outpointed the American hope Tony Tubbs on his way to the final, where the local Yugoslav, Dragomir Vujkonic, retired after soaking up more than enough punishment. Once again, the amazing Cubans collected five golds. And when, two years later, the Olympics came round again, Teofilio's task was made even more simple because of the U.S. boycott of the Moscow Games. He completed his golden hat-trick by outpointing the home favourite Pyotr Zaev in the final. Little sweat.

The years from Munich to Moscow were his best in the ring, and off duty, life was also sweet. Stevenson might not have been able to bank the millions promised in the States or motor around in a Rolls, but by Cuban standards, he was doing better than all right. For winning the gold in Munich, the government rewarded him with a two-storey apartment in Havana and a five-bedroom house in Delicias. He was also presented with two Lada cars, one for each home. Those were riches beyond the wildest dreams of most Cubans, but nobody resented Teofilio's new affluence. As far as his countrymen were concerned, he was a champion of the people – and still is.

The party line was that the rewards were not given just for his boxing prowess, but as much for his loyalty to the communist ideal. One member of the national assembly described him as 'the model sportsman and the model revolutionary'; and for ten years (1976–86) Stevenson was a deputy in the assembly. Adored by the masses, wooed by the politicians, life could not have been better.

In 1980, he decided to become the model husband, marrying a dance teacher named Mercedes; four years later, they had a daughter, Helmis, but before long the marriage was in trouble, they eventually divorced, and soon after, he wed again, this time to Anabel, a doctor. There were other upheavals: his father died of cancer, his mother suffered serious heart problems, and his woes spilled over into the ring.

He no longer looked invincible and in the build-up to the 1982 world championships in Munich – scene of his first great triumph – he was outpointed in Cuba by a promising Italian called Francisco Damiani. But he was confidently expected to gain revenge in Germany and for the tournament to be just another showcase for his talents. His team-mates played their part, winning their customary five golds, but there would be no medal for the skipper. He was drawn against Damiani, and again the Italian won a unanimous points verdict. Not just Cuba, but the entire boxing world, was stunned.

There were other defeats, and when Cuba and the rest of the communist countries boycotted the 1984 Olympics in Los Angeles in retaliation for the American boycott of Moscow, he was denied his chance to win a fourth gold. Whether he would have been good enough right at that time is open to question. Stevenson had been boxing for over twenty years, and that is a long, long time for either an amateur or a pro. Training becomes a boring grind; outside interests encroach on what was once an all-consuming pursuit; and in Teofilio's case, even winning his sport's greatest prizes had become like just another day at the office.

There were polite, well-intentioned suggestions that he might consider retiring, especially after losing to a fellow Cuban, Osvaldo Castillo. But great champions have even greater egos. The Castillo embarrassment provided the necessary motivation, and urged on by his career-long mentor, national coach Sagarra, who was convinced there was still plenty of petrol in the tank, he started working with a renewed zest towards honing himself into the proper shape, both physically and mentally, for the 1986 world championships, due to be held in Reno, Nevada. The old fire had returned: in one gym session, he squared accounts with Castillo, knocking him unconscious, and there were also hectic training jousts against a teenager called Felix Savon which were to prove hugely beneficial.

Savon was the latest Cuban hotshot, another giant with incredible potential. He would take over the banner from Stevenson and carry it into the new century, and in 2000 in Sydney, he emulated the feat of his old teammate by winning his third Olympic gold.

Both Savon and Stevenson were Reno-bound, the youngster boxing at heavyweight, the 34-year-old representing at super-heavy. Perhaps, some of Savon's hunger and enthusiasm helped reignite the veteran, but there were to be no surprises this time: Felix and Teofilio won their divisions; Cuba bagged an extraordinary seven titles; and Mr Stevenson had the added satisfaction of being voted the tournament's best boxer, an award that may have irked the ambitious Savon.

With all his old assurance regained, Stevenson began to make plans for the Seoul Olympics of 1988. By then, he would be 36, but he was convinced that he could win a record fourth gold. Politics, however, again intervened, and the Cubans did not send a team to South Korea. Looking back, he is convinced that had he boxed in Los Angeles and Seoul, he would have finished up as a five-times Olympic champion . . . and who is going to give him an argument? But going out on the Top C that was Reno, retiring as the undefeated world champion, was the perfect way to bring down the curtain on a fantastic career. He reached a pinnacle that very few ever attain, and now, like Ali and Pele, he performs his duties as a revered sporting ambassador, shaking hands, patting heads, spreading goodwill and good sense; still representing his country years after he last pulled on a singlet, and still so proud of Castro and Cuba.

Could he have beaten Ali? Had he been born in another land, would he now be a millionaire, or would he be broke and bitching about the robbers who promoted him? Could he have lasted twelve rounds as well as he could fight over three? Just how good was Teofilio Stevenson?

A perfectly proportioned 6ft 4in, he would have attracted any fight manager's interest at first glance. Well schooled in the basics, he was an upright, methodical boxer, always searching for openings to deliver that one big shot that would end matters, and it was his terrific punching, particularly his chilling right, that set him apart. Many opponents were beaten before the first bell and were interested only in survival; even before the biggest events, the question was: who is going to win silver? And winning silver meant getting beat up by the big guy from Cuba.

Over twenty years ago, Laszlo Papp – the first and, aside from Stevenson and Savon, the only boxer to win three Olympic golds – wrote an article for *Boxing Illustrated*, analysing the Cuban and weighing up his prospects for the upcoming Moscow Games. The Hungarian maestro did not exactly go overboard about his pal, who at that time was considered at his peak. Papp did not so much knock Teofilio, but rather, severely slated the opposition he had faced, and by implication, cast doubts on the Cuban's right to be called great. He wrote:

'I have only seen Stevenson fight under pressure once, for about 90 seconds when facing John Tate of the United States in the semi-finals of the Montreal Games, but being a lot more experienced, Teofilio assessed Tate in that time, tagged him and that was that.

'Otherwise, he simply coasted through the Montreal and Munich Olympics, and similarly had no creditable opposition at the Havana and Belgrade world championships either.

'There were some danger signs in Belgrade last year when he fought and was unable to reach Tony Tubbs of the US. Stevenson could not have hit Tubbs more than four or five times all told. The American proved a real mover but he was only a light puncher and didn't make much use of those light punches.'

The old campaigner was obviously hard to please, and he should have added that all fighters can only beat the opposition put before them. On the upside for Teofilio is the fact that he beat Tate and Tubbs and Michael Dokes, all briefly heavyweight champs, and on a line through Milian, he had the beating of Greg Page, another fleeting title holder.

But he beat them all over three rounds. To box eight rounds or over, Stevenson would have required a totally revised training programme; as a pro, he would have had to start from scratch. Even after his first Olympic triumph, a normal build-up might have taken him into 1975 before he was ready for a title shot. And who were then the main men? Only Ali and Frazier and Foreman and Norton . . . monsters all. Even with a few years' pro experience, he would have suffered his lumps against that quartet. And to suggest that he might have held his own straight from the amateurs is lunacy, but there was no shortage of offers. The only feasible proposition was Arum's idea to stage a series of three-round exhibitions against Ali. That would have been enlightening.

The model revolutionary, however, chose to remain in his own country, snubbed the chance of millions and a crack at the champions, and has never regretted his decisions. He made the wise choice.

Yet the great Peter Jackson never would have understood that choice. Over a century ago, he left his homeland and travelled the world in pursuit of a title shot, but never got a fair shake. And fabulous Charley Burley? Forget the millions, Charley would have jumped at a championship fight for expenses only. And many, many of the others who were shunted aside or were the wrong colour or were double-crossed or were plain unlucky would have drooled at the chance Teofilio passed up.

And what about Terry Malloy, whose dearest wish in life was to become a contender? When finally convinced that there really was a fighter who had turned down a million bucks to go pro with a title shot thrown in, Terry most likely would have sat silent for a moment, then sighed. And then called the guy a fruitcake.

Inspiration

Thanks to an extraordinary shaker and mover called Harold Conrad, ringside handshakes were exchanged with Budd Schulberg on the evening that Ali boxed Al Blue Lewis in Dublin in 1972. Mr Budd seemed pleasantly surprised that his *On the Waterfront* was still playing in a Dublin art house, and was all but bashful that before him stood a fan, a groupie. Budd, who has given birth to such wonderful characters as Sammy Glick and Johnny Friendly and Charley The Gent, and, of course, Terry Malloy, must have been at one time a contender. But he grabbed his title shot and now must be recognised as one of the great champions. Thank you.

Bibliography

Anderson, Dave. *Ringmaster*. Robson Books, 1991.

André, Sam, and Fleischer, Nat. *Pictorial History of Boxing*. Hamlyn, 1975.

Atyeo, Don, and Dennis, Felix. *Holy Warrior*. Bunch Books, 1975.

Barrow Jr, Joe Louis, and Munder, Barbara. *Joe Louis*. Arthur Barker, 1988.

Berger, Phil. *Blood Season*. Macdonald Queen Anne Press, 1989.

Birtley, Jack. *Freddie Mills*. New English Library, 1977.

Collins, Nigel. *Boxing Babylon*. Robson Books, 1991.

Duff, Mickey. *Twenty and Out*. Collins Willow, 1999.

Duncan, John. *In the Red Corner*. Yellow Jersey Press, 2000.

Fried, Ronald K. *Cornermen*. Four Walls Eight Windows, 1991.

Graziano, Rocky, and Barber, Rowland. *Somebody Up There Likes Me*. Simon & Schuster, 1954.

Hauser, Thomas. *Muhammad Ali*. Robson Books, 1991.

Heller, Peter. *In This Corner*. Robson Books, 1985.

—— *Tyson*. Robson Books, 1989.

Illingworth, Montieth. *Mike Tyson*. Grafton, 1992.

Isenberg, Michael T. *John L Sullivan*. Robson Books, 1988.

King, David, *I Am King*. Penguin Books, 1975.

Lewis, Morton, *Ted Kid Lewis*. Robson Books, 1990.

Mead, Chris. *Champion Joe Louis*. Robson Books, 1986.

Mee, Bob. *Heroes and Champions*. Colour Library Direct, 1998.

Mills, Freddie. *Twenty Years*. Nichols and Watson, 1950.

Mullally, Frederic. *Primo*. Robson Books, 1991.

Mullan, Harry. *Illustrated History of Boxing*. Hamlyn, 1990.
Newfield, Jack. *Don King*. Virgin, 1996.
Olsen, Jack. *Cassius Clay*. Pelham Books, 1967.
Pep, Willie, and Sacchi, Robert. *Friday's Heroes*. Frederick Fell, 1973.
Remnick, David. *King of the World*. Picador, 1998.
Roberts, Randy. *Papa Jack*. Robson Books, 1986.
Skehan, Everett M. *Rocky Marciano*. Robson Books, 1983.
Torres, José. *Fire and Fear*. W.H. Allen, 1989.

Records Books

Boxing News Annuals, Boxing Register, Nat Fleischer's *Ring Record Books*, Barry Hugman's *Boxing Yearbooks*, Giuseppe Ballarati's *Pugilatos*, Jack Solomons's *Annual* (1948).

Magazines

Boxing Digest, *Boxing Illustrated*, *Boxing Monthly*, *Boxing News*, *Boxing Outlook*, *Boxing Yearbooks* (1958–60), *Fight Game*, *K.O.*, *World Boxing*.

Index